BOBBY FLAY'S
MESA GRILL COOKBOOK

BOBBY FLAY'S
MESA GRILL COOKBOOK
EXPLOSIVE FLAVORS FROM THE
SOUTHWESTERN KITCHEN

BY **BOBBY FLAY** WITH **STEPHANIE BANYAS** AND **SALLY JACKSON**

PHOTOGRAPHS BY **BEN FINK**

CLARKSON POTTER/PUBLISHERS
NEW YORK

ALSO BY BOBBY FLAY

Bobby Flay Cooks American

Bobby Flay's Bold American Food

Bobby Flay's Boy Gets Grill

Bobby Flay's Boy Meets Grill

Bobby Flay's From My Kitchen to Your Table

Bobby Flay's Grilling for Life

Copyright © 2007 by Boy Meets Grill, Inc.

Photographs copyright © 2007 by Ben Fink

All rights reserved.
Published in the United States by Clarkson Potter/
Publishers, an imprint of the Crown Publishing
Group, a division of Random House, Inc, New York.
www.crownpublishing.com
www.clarksonpotter.com

Clarkson N. Potter is a trademark and Potter and
colophon are registered trademarks of Random
House, Inc.

Library of Congress Cataloguing-in-Publication Data
is available upon request

ISBN 978-0-307-35141-8

Printed in Japan

Design by Wayne Wolf

10   9   8   7   6   5   4   3   2   1

First Edition

To Jerry Kretchmer . . . for giving me a chance

ACKNOWLEDGMENTS

OVER THE LAST DECADE AND A HALF, THOUSANDS OF HARDWORKING, DEDICATED EMPLOYEES HAVE BEEN A TREMENDOUS PART OF MESA GRILL'S EXISTENCE. HERE ARE A FEW OF THOSE WHO HELPED SHAPE THE CUISINE AND ENVIRONMENT OF MESA GRILL:

Larry Manheim
Neil Manacle
Christopher Hewitt
Katy Sparks
Patricia Yeo
Christine Sanchez
Wayne Harley Brachman
Vicki Wells
Joe Antonishek
Craig Petroff
Rick Pitcher
Daryl Swetz
Manny Gatdula
Bob Mundell
Alfred Stephens
Nicole Reisman
Stephanie Banyas

Tara Taylor
Sally Jackson
Monique McCall
John Kushner
Brian Ray
Paul Delfavero
Anthony Fusco
Rene Forsberg
Theresa Scala
Mario Sanchez
Billy Steele
Giovanni Bonilla
J. P. Francois
Lucille Jaccarino
Osiris Brito
Fran Bernfeld
Tara Keeler

A special thank-you to my amazing editor, Rica Allannic.

And to the greatest partners in the world, Jerry Kretchmer, Jeff Bliss, and Laurence Kretchmer.

And, of course, to my daughter, Sophie, and to my wife, Stephanie, who endures every menu change, restaurant opening, and manuscript deadline with open arms and a warm heart.

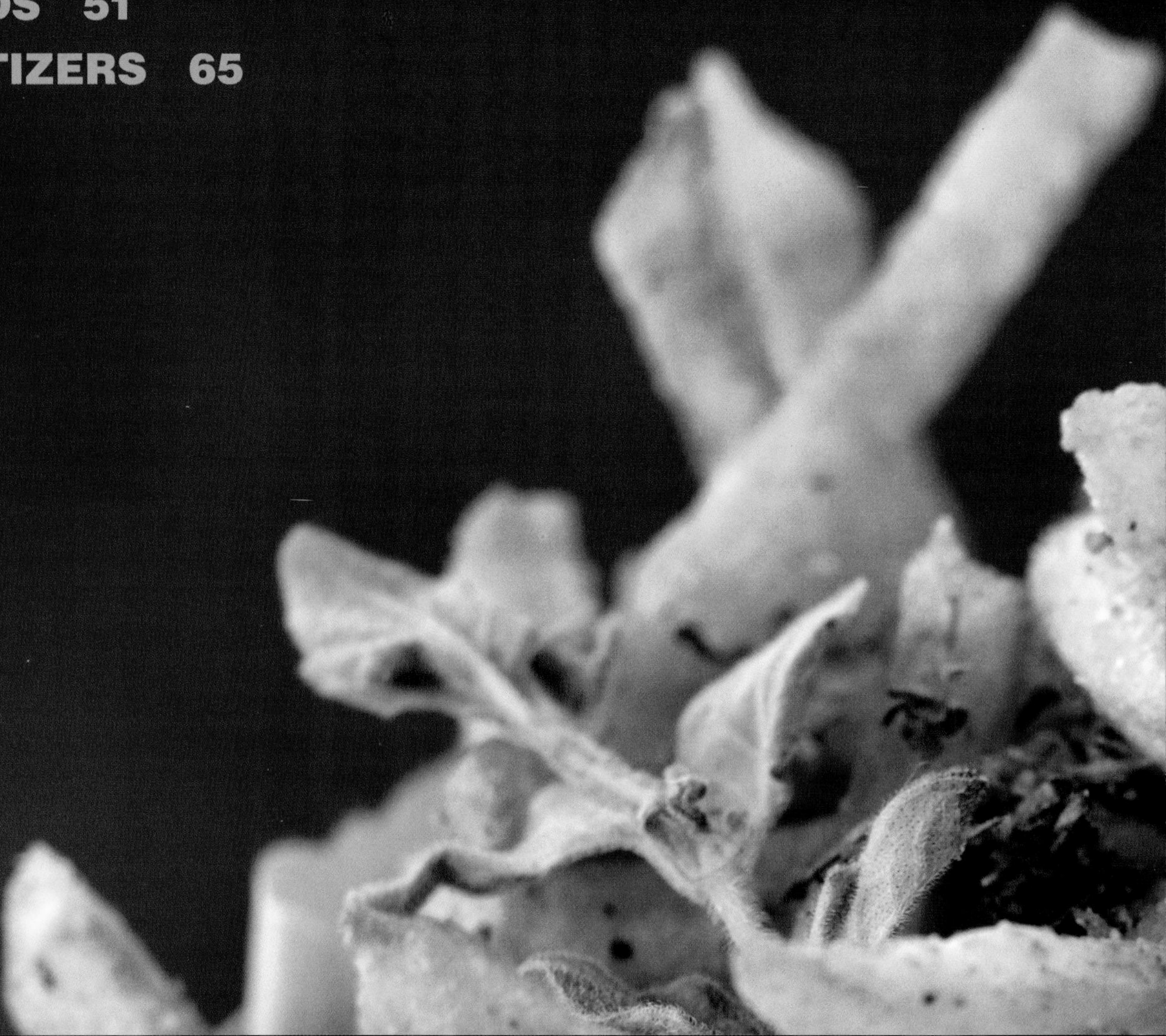

CONTENTS

MESA GRILL WAS THE RESTAURANT I ALWAYS DREAMED OF ONE DAY OPENING WHEN I WAS A YOUNG LINE COOK CRANKING OUT COUNTLESS MEALS AT A RESTAURANT CALLED JOE ALLEN IN NEW YORK'S THEATER DISTRICT. IT DIDN'T TAKE ME LONG TO REALIZE, EVEN IN MY FIRST DAYS AS A DISHWASHER, THAT I HAD FOUND MY PLACE IN LIFE—AND IT WAS IN THE KITCHEN.

As I continued to learn the ins and outs of my chosen craft in other restaurants, my father would always talk to me about setting goals for myself, my future. Little did he know that I had already designed my dream restaurant in my head.

I imagined soaring ceilings, dramatic colors adorning the walls, a large bar on one side of the room but not separate from the dining room. I wanted a sense of energy. I wanted a restaurant that would take you to another place as soon as you walked in the front door. An experience that was unique unto itself. And, of course, my dream restaurant would be in New York City, my birthplace.

But it was early in my career. It was all fine and good to dream big, but I needed the skills first. I had no culinary point of view of my own yet. I was cooking other chefs' food to the best of my ability, but I had yet to formalize my own palette of flavors.

My first experience with Southwestern ingredients was at a restaurant called Bud's, which was located on the Upper West Side of Manhattan. Jonathan Waxman, the chef and owner, would become my culinary mentor. Bud's was one of the most innovative restaurants in the country back in the mid-1980s and I was mesmerized by the ingredients, the presentations, and the combinations of flavors. Most important, it was an unbelievably fun place to go to work. Every day was an adventure.

The food at Bud's was California cuisine with some stops in the Southwest. It was my first head-on collision with blue corn, fresh and dried chiles by the dozen, fresh mesquite wood for grilling. We used ripe fruits to counter the heat of the chiles and roasted corn on the cob to create salsas, relishes, and sauces that were smoky, sweet, tart, and spicy. It was a whole new world for me—and I loved it.

After working for Jonathan for a few years, I made a few pit stops in other New York restaurants before I was offered the head chef job at a modest but fantastically popular East Village restaurant called Miracle Grill. It gave me a chance to experiment on my own, which I did for three years. But I knew I wanted to take the signature contemporary Southwestern cuisine I was developing to another level.

NOW THAT I WAS BEGINNING TO GET MY ARMS AROUND A CUISINE I COULD CALL MY OWN, I WANTED THE RESTAURANT I'D ALWAYS DREAMED OF—I WANTED MESA GRILL!

In the fall of 1990, a man named Jerry Kretchmer walked into Miracle Grill for dinner with his wife, Dorothy. I knew of Jerry; he owned one of the most well thought of restaurants in America, Gotham Bar and Grill. I didn't give his presence a second thought, though I was, of course, happy to cook for him. It didn't cross my mind for a

moment that he might be interested in partnering up with me for a restaurant someday.

I didn't know that Jerry and Dorothy had just come back from an extensive trip through the American Southwest. Jerry is a hard-core native New Yorker, but he had always wanted to be a cowboy. Was it possible that two New Yorkers from different generations—one obsessed with the culture, the beauty, and the people of the Southwest, and the other fully entrenched in its ingredients, techniques, and flavors—could come together to create something that fulfilled both of their dreams?

Mesa Grill was born on lower Fifth Avenue in the Flatiron District of New York on January 16, 1991. Although New York was in a deadly financial recession, opening night of Mesa Grill was raucous . . . until the first bomb was dropped on Iraq, signaling the start of the First Gulf War. Half of the dining room got up from their tables to go home and watch the first-ever televised war. It was not an illustrious start.

Over the next few weeks, customers started coming back to the restaurant, and Mesa Grill was under way. It was far from easy. Food critics were in every corner of the dining room to see if we could deliver what we had promised. But the reviews were upbeat and generous and the restaurant I had dreamed of had become a reality.

AS I WRITE THIS, IT HAS BEEN SIXTEEN YEARS SINCE THE DOORS FIRST OPENED. THERE ARE NOW OUTPOSTS AT CAESARS PALACE IN LAS VEGAS AND AT ATLANTIS, PARADISE ISLAND, BAHAMAS.

The menu has changed and evolved over the years but has always stayed true to its Southwestern roots. In fact, two dishes remain today from that opening menu— Shrimp and Roasted Garlic Corn Tamales and BBQ-Duck-Filled Blue Corn Pancakes with Habanero Sauce. Temptation to integrate the hot and trendy ingredients or cuisines of the moment has been fended off by an allegiance to a cuisine that has helped shape my career.

When people ask me to describe the food of Mesa Grill, I usually answer them in two words: "Contemporary Southwestern." It's a simple description of a cuisine that to me is still as exciting as it was when I first got to know its flavorful ingredients a couple of decades ago: the roasted corn fresh from the cob; the cornmeals in a myriad of colors; the dried red chiles that are earthy, smoky, fruity, and spicy; the fresh chiles that are peppery, herbaceous, and mouthwatering; the ripe, creamy avocados; the sweet fruits like mango and papaya; pineapples hot off the grill, ready to be made into a salsa; the meats, fish, and vegetables that are gently rubbed with spices to accent their flavors and help create a crust that is savory and mouth-tingling; the glazes and barbecue sauces; the marinades and rubs; and don't forget the tequila.

It all makes up the culture of Mesa Grill, which started as a New York City restaurant with colorful walls, energetic patrons, and soaring ceilings high enough for your cowboy hat.

BOBBY FLAY
NEW YORK CITY

THE INGREDIENTS BELOW ARE THE BUILDING BLOCKS OF FLAVOR FOR SOUTHWESTERN COOKING. THESE ARE MY GO-TO INGREDIENTS, THOSE THAT HAVE INSPIRED ME TO CREATE HUNDREDS OF RECIPES OVER THE YEARS, AND I NEVER TIRE OF USING THEM. WHEN I OPENED MESA GRILL IN 1991, MANY OF THE ITEMS LISTED BELOW WERE ALMOST IMPOSSIBLE TO FIND IN LOCAL GROCERY STORES, AND THE INTERNET WAS YEARS AWAY FROM BEING THE POWERFUL TOOL THAT IT IS TODAY. THANKS TO THIS COUNTRY'S EVER-EVOLVING PALATE AND THE POPULARITY OF FOOD NETWORK, YOU CAN GET ANYTHING, ANYWHERE, TODAY.

AVOCADO

Although there are several varieties of avocados, the one that I prefer and use in my cooking is the Hass avocado, which is grown extensively in California and Mexico. It is a medium-sized oval fruit with a thick, pebbly skin. The flesh is very flavorful, with an almost nutty flavor, and because avocados ripen off the tree, not on, if they are properly stored in a cool, dark place, they will keep for several days. A ripe avocado will range in color from dark green to black-brown and should yield to firm, gentle pressure.

CAJETA (KAH-HAY-TAH)

This thick, dark syrup or paste is made from caramelized sugar and milk—traditionally goat's milk, although cow's milk is often used. Cajeta can be found in several flavors (primarily caramel and fruit) in Latin markets. It's used in Mexico and in some South American countries primarily as a dessert by itself or as a topping for ice cream or fruit.

CHAYOTE SQUASH

A member of the gourd family, this vegetable from Mexico is pear shaped and light to dark apple-green in color. Chayote can be roasted, sautéed, or grilled. Its shape and texture are perfect for stuffing.

CHILE PEPPERS

See Guide to Fresh and Dried Chiles, *page 12.*

CHORIZO

Chorizo is coarsely ground dry pork sausage that is heavily seasoned with garlic and paprika. When produced in Mexico, this spicy sausage is uncooked and made from fresh pork. The Spanish product, which is also very spicy, is produced from smoked pork that is dry-cured. However, there is also a fresh uncured Spanish-style chorizo variety, which I prefer to use in my recipes (see Sources, *page 272*).

CILANTRO

Cilantro is definitely my favorite herb and makes an appearance in almost every dish at Mesa Grill because its distinctive, herbaceous flavor lends itself perfectly to South-western cooking. Cilantro is a somewhat fragile herb, so look for bundles with bright green full-grown leaves. I use only the leaves in my cooking, but the stems are full of flavor and can be used to flavor stocks or sauces. It should be washed in cold water when brought home from the grocery store and left to dry before wrapping it in paper towels and storing in a seal-top plastic bag. Stored properly in the refrigerator, fresh cilantro will last for a week.

CINNAMON, MEXICAN (CANELA)

Canela is the Spanish word for "cinnamon." The cinnamon used in Mexican cooking is the softer loose-bark variety grown in Ceylon rather than the more commonly found hard-stick cinnamon. Canela is easily ground in a mortar and pestle (or an electric coffee/spice grinder). It can also be purchased already ground, but I always prefer grinding my own spices.

CITRUS

I love the freshness that citrus brings to dishes and I use it in everything from mari-nades to vinaigrettes at Mesa Grill. Not only do I use the juice of grapefruit, orange, lemon, and lime, but I also utilize the essential-oil-laden zest for its bright flavor and color.

COCONUT MILK, UNSWEETENED

Readily available in cans in the Asian aisle of most supermarkets, coconut milk is not the liquid inside the coconut but rather the result of squeezing and straining fresh coconut meat. Naturally creamy and slightly sweet, it has a mild coconut flavor that is a great counterbalance to the strong flavors of chiles and curries.

CORIANDER

Coriander is the dried ripe fruit of the herb cilantro and is prevalent in Southwestern and Mexican cooking. The light brown seeds have a sweetly aromatic flavor that tastes like a combination of sage and lemon. The spice is available preground, but the flavor is improved infinitely if you buy the seeds whole and toast them in a dry sauté pan over low heat on top of the stove until just fragrant and then grind them yourself in a coffee/spice grinder.

CORN, WHITE AND YELLOW

Fresh corn is one of my favorite ingredients come summer. Sautéed, roasted, grilled, served on the cob or off, nothing beats its sweet flavor. One ear of corn will yield approximately ½ cup of kernels. I am able to get fresh corn year-round at the restaurants, but frozen corn can be substituted in any of my recipes that include corn.

CORN HUSKS, DRIED

Dried corn husks are essential for making tamales. The husks must be soaked in warm water for at least 1 hour to make them pliable before being used for wrapping.

CORNMEAL

Cornmeal is available in white, yellow, and blue varieties as well as in fine, medium, and coarse grinds. Medium and coarse grinds are great for making polenta, muffins, and breads, while fine and medium grinds are used for breading fish and chicken.

Blue corn has a sweeter, nuttier flavor than white or yellow corn and when dried and ground into cornmeal takes on a grayish-purple color.

COTIJA CHEESE

This firm-textured, somewhat crumbly, white Mexican cheese is traditionally made from goat's milk but is also now made from cow's milk. When it is produced, it is a hard ripened cheese with a closed texture, providing a distinctively salty flavor. Cotija cheese is often considered to be similar to Parmesan.

CREMA

Crema is a slightly soured and thickened cream with a tangy taste similar to sour cream but with a smoother finish. If not available in your market, crème fraîche or sour cream can be used as a substitute.

CUMIN

Pungent and smoky, cumin is one of the most prevalent spices in Southwestern and Mexican cooking. The spice is available preground, but the flavor is improved infinitely if you buy the seeds whole and toast them in a dry sauté pan, then grind them yourself in a coffee/spice grinder.

GARLIC

Sharp when raw, sweet when roasted, garlic is without question the king of all of these flavorings! It has an oniony and, well, garlicky taste. It adds aroma and flavor to pretty much every dish imaginable—except, of course, desserts. I can't think of another ingredient that adds so much to whatever it touches.

JICAMA

A sweet, crunchy root vegetable, jicama tastes almost like a cross between an apple and a potato. It can be cooked, but I prefer to use it raw in salads and relishes.

MANGO

I love to use this sweet orange-fleshed tropical fruit in salsas, vinaigrettes, and sauces. A ripe mango should give slightly when pressed, and the color should be yellowish-orange to red. Put mangoes in a paper bag to ripen at room temperature; store ripe mangoes in the refrigerator.

ONION

In my opinion, everything good starts with onions and garlic. That also goes for shallots, members of the onion family that taste almost like a mix between the two. I use white, yellow, and red in my cooking. Grilling onions gives them a sweet, mellow flavor that I love—cooked and raw onions have very different qualities, each with their time and place.

OREGANO, MEXICAN

Mexican oregano has an earthier flavor with less of the mintlike taste and aroma normally present in Greek or Mediterranean oregano. Unlike Mediterranean oregano, Mexican oregano is best if used dried. It's available in flakes or as a powder.

PEPPER

Next to salt, pepper is definitely the most used seasoning in my kitchen. Peppercorns come in green, white, and black varieties and all have different flavors. I prefer the taste of black pepper in my cooking. Whole black peppercorns retain their flavor indefinitely, so pepper should always be bought whole and ground fresh from a pepper mill.

PLANTAIN

Native to India, plantains are grown most widely in tropical climates. Although they look a lot like bananas and are close relatives, plantains are quite different. They are starchier and are used as a vegetable in many cuisines, especially Latin American. As they ripen, plantains change in color from green to black, with green being the least ripe and black being fully ripe. When green, they are very starchy and should only be boiled or fried. Once they completely ripen to black, they become very sweet and are great in desserts and any savory recipe where a sweeter taste is desired. You can speed up the ripening process by storing plantains in a paper bag until they ripen and turn black.

To peel a plantain, use a sharp knife to cut off the top and bottom ends. With the tip of the knife, make one slit in the skin of the plantain from top to bottom. Use your thumb and fingers to work the peel away from the pulp of the fruit beginning at the slit. Less ripe plantains have tougher skins and are best peeled under cold water to avoid bruising.

POSOLE

Posole (also known as hominy) is dried corn kernels that have been soaked in a weak lye bath until softened. The puffy kernels have a somewhat bland corn taste but a fantastic, hearty texture that is perfect in soups and stews. Posole can be purchased canned or dried. If using dried, it must be soaked overnight in cold water before cooking.

SALT, KOSHER

Salt plays the most important role in my cooking. Salt intensifies the taste of whatever you are cooking and allows the true flavors to come through. I personally prefer kosher salt to standard table or sea salt not only because of the taste but also because of the large fluffy grains. The texture makes it easy for me to pick up kosher salt with my fingers and I always have a good feel for how much I am using.

TOMATILLOS

Relatives of the tomato and members of the nightshade family, tomatillos are about the size of a lime and provide a tart flavor when used in sauces and salsas. Remove their papery husks and rinse the pale green-yellow fruits before using. Tomatillos can be used raw, or roasted to bring out some sweetness.

TORTILLAS

Tortillas are Mexican flat bread and are made of either cornmeal (white, yellow, and blue varieties) or wheat flour. Both types can be fried and baked, but only flour tortillas can stand up to grilling; corn tortillas become too brittle. I love the flavor of corn tortillas and the versatility of flour tortillas.

GUIDE TO FRESH AND DRIED CHILES

IT BECOMES QUITE OBVIOUS AS YOU READ THIS BOOK THAT FRESH AND DRIED CHILES PLAY AN IMPORTANT ROLE IN MY COOKING AT MESA GRILL. I SIMPLY LOVE THE RANGE AND DEPTH OF FLAVOR THEY ADD TO MY RECIPES AND I USE THEM IN EVERYTHING FROM VINAIGRETTES AND SAUCES TO SPICE RUBS. CHILES ARE ABOUT MUCH MORE THAN JUST HEAT. THE MORE YOU USE THEM, THE MORE YOU WILL COME TO LEARN ABOUT AND APPRECIATE THE COMPLEXITY OF THEIR FLAVORS.

FRESH CHILES

Most supermarkets today offer a wide range of fresh chiles in their produce department. If your market doesn't, then look at the source section at the end of this book for Internet sites that offer mail order. When purchasing fresh chiles, it's important to buy chiles that have shiny, smooth skin and are heavy for their size. They should be dry and firm to the touch. Chiles should be kept dry and stored in the crisper section of the refrigerator. Never wrap them in plastic, because too much moisture can spoil them.

I recommend wearing rubber gloves or disposable plastic gloves when handling fresh chiles to protect your hands from capsaicin, the volatile chemical in chiles that is responsible for their heat. Most of the capsaicin is located in the internal rib of the chile and removing it will significantly reduce the level of heat. If you choose to forgo the gloves, then just be careful not to touch your eyes or face after handling fresh chiles.

ANAHEIM

Named for the city of Anaheim, California, this chile has a fresh green flavor but very little heat. Anaheims are 6 to 10 inches in length and are most often used when green. They are one of the most common chiles in the United States.

FRESNO

Named after Fresno, California, where it was first grown, the Fresno chile is similar to a jalapeño in flavor and appearance but is often less spicy. It is available in green and red varieties, with the red variety being sweeter. If you can't find Fresno chiles, you can definitely substitute jalapeños.

HABANERO AND SCOTCH BONNET

Fresh or dried, these small bell-shaped chiles are the hottest of all chiles. Both habaneros and Scotch bonnets are green in their unripe stage, but their color at maturity varies, ranging from orange to red. These chiles aren't just about heat; they also have an incredible fruity, almost citruslike flavor and a floral aroma.

JALAPEÑO

Named after the region of Jalapa, Mexico, this is probably the most well-known and available fresh chile in the United States. It comes in both green and red varieties. Jalapeños' heat can be inconsistent due to the soil and climate they are grown in. It's always good to add jalapeño in increments to your recipe or—if you dare—cut off a little piece and taste it before using, to gauge how much heat it will add to the recipe.

POBLANO

This dark green chile tapers down to a point and is normally 4 to 6 inches long. This is the chile that is used to make chiles rellenos. The poblano has an amazing pepper flavor and just the right amount of heat. I call it a starter chile.

SERRANO

Turning from green to red as it matures, the serrano is long and slightly curved and ranges from 1 to 4 inches in length. Serranos are very spicy but also flavorful.

DRIED CHILES

Drying chiles concentrates their natural sugars and intensifies their flavor. I love using dried chiles to deepen the flavor of a sauce, soup, or vinaigrette. Dried chiles add not only an earthy flavor but a spiciness, too. More and more supermarkets are carrying them today, but as with fresh chiles, if you can't find them near you, the source section in the back of this book lists Internet sites for mail order.

When selecting dried chiles, look for those that are clean and not discolored; they should not be faded, dusty, or broken. Freshly dried chiles will be soft and supple, with a distinct earthy aroma. They will keep, stored in an airtight container and out of direct sunlight, for several months. Most dried chiles should be toasted or rehydrated before using.

ANCHO

Anchos are dried poblanos. They are red and have a spicy raisin flavor.

CASCABEL

Cascabel chiles are bright red to dark red in color and round in shape. *Cascabel* means "rattle" and when you shake one of these chiles the seeds make a rattling sound. The chiles are medium to very hot, with a nutty, woodsy flavor.

CHILE DE ÁRBOL

Árbol means "tree" in Spanish and these slender, tapered chiles resemble small trees. Tiny and very hot, these chiles also have an almost herbaceous flavor.

CHIPOTLE

Chipotles, which are dried and smoked jalapeños, are brownish in color, with a fiery, smoky flavor. They are often sold canned in adobo sauce.

GUAJILLO

Guajillos are moderately hot chiles with a distinct flavor reminiscent of pine.

NEW MEXICO RED

These chiles are a brick-red color, with a pointed shape that measures around 6 inches long. They have a deep, roasted flavor but not a lot of heat.

PASILLA

Also known in Spanish as *chile negro, pasilla* means "little raisin" and the skin of these chiles is indeed black and wrinkled. They are used most often in moles and salsas and give moderate heat.

SCOVILLE UNITS: DETERMINING THE PRECISE PUNGENCY OF CHILES

In 1912, Wilbur L. Scoville, a pharmacologist with the drug company Parke-Davis, was using capsaicin in a muscle salve called Heet, when he developed the Scoville Organoleptic Test. This test used a panel of five human heat samplers who tasted and analyzed a solution made from exact weights of chile peppers dissolved in alcohol and diluted with sugar water. The pungency was recorded in multiples of one hundred "Scoville units."

The following are the approximate Scoville units and numerical ratings from the Official Chile Heat Scale for the varieties of chiles used at Mesa Grill. The higher the rating, the hotter the chile. Ten is the highest/hottest possible rating. Keep in mind that these ratings are not foolproof, because chiles can vary in degrees of hotness due to the local conditions where they were grown. To pretest the heat of a chile before you add it to a recipe, cut off a very small piece and taste it raw. To be safe, I recommend that you have a glass of cold milk or a bowl of yogurt on hand because dairy is really the only way to offset the burn of a hot chile.

CHILE	SCOVILLE UNITS	HEAT SCALE RATING
Habanero, Scotch Bonnet	100,000–300,000	10
Cayenne	30,000–50,000	8
Chile de Árbol	15,000–30,000	7
Serrano	5,000–15,000	6
Jalapeño	2,500–5,000	5
Fresno	2,500–5,000	5
Chipotle	2,500–5,000	5
Cascabel	1,500–2,500	4
Guajillo	1,000–1,500	3
New Mexico Red	1,000–1,500	3
Ancho, Pasilla	1,000–1,500	3
Poblano	1,000–1,500	3
Anaheim	500–1,000	2
Bell Peppers	0	0

CAPSAICIN: THE HEAT SOURCE OF CHILE PEPPERS

Capsaicin is produced in chiles by glands at the junction of the rib and the pod wall. It spreads unevenly throughout the inside of the pod and is concentrated mostly in the ribs. The seeds are not sources of heat as commonly believed. However, because of their proximity to the rib, they occasionally absorb capsaicin through the growing process.

Capsaicin is an incredibly powerful and stable compound seemingly unaffected by drying or temperature. It will retain its original potency no matter how long the chile is dried, cooked, or stored in the freezer.

BLANCHING

This technique is normally used to cook vegetables, green vegetables in particular because it helps them to retain their vibrant color; it can also be used to prepare shellfish for a ceviche. Prepare a large bowl of ice water. Bring salted water to a boil, add the vegetables or shellfish, and cook, either until tender or for as long as directed in the recipe. Drain the vegetables and plunge into the ice water to stop the cooking. Drain again.

COLD-SMOKING

Cold-smoking is a technique that imparts a smoky flavor to meat, fish, or vegetables. Since no cooking takes place, the interior texture of the food generally isn't affected and further preparation is required, such as roasting, grilling, curing, or sautéing. I love using smoked tomatoes in salsas and smoked fish or shrimp for tacos.

Prepare a small charcoal or wood fire in a domed grill or on a stove-top cold-smoker. Lay chips of soaked aromatic wood, such as hickory, apple, or mesquite, over the ashes—you just want to get the smoke going, not a very hot fire. (Remember that food isn't cooked by this method, but is infused with a smoky flavor.)

Arrange the food on the grill rack over the chips, open the top vent slightly, and cover the grill so that the smoke stays inside. Smoke for the amount of time indicated below:

Meat—15 minutes

Fish fillets and peeled shrimp—10 minutes

Peppers and chiles (rub with oil first)—20 minutes

Tomatoes (rub with oil first)—10 minutes

ROASTING PEPPERS AND CHILES

Preheat the oven to 375 degrees F. Brush the peppers with olive oil and season with salt and pepper, place in the oven on a rimmed baking sheet, and rotate until charred on all sides, 15 to 17 minutes. Remove from the oven and place the roasted peppers in a bowl, cover with plastic wrap, and let sit for 15 minutes to allow the skin to loosen. Then peel, halve, and seed. Treat chiles exactly the same way as the peppers. Roasted peppers and chiles can be covered and stored for up to 5 days in the refrigerator.

TOASTING DRIED CHILES

Toasting chiles intensifies their flavor. Heat a dry sauté pan over high heat until almost smoking. Add the chiles to the pan and toast for 20 to 30 seconds on each side. Remove and let cool slightly, then remove the stems and the seeds. Toasted dried chiles can be kept stored in a cool, dark place in a container with a tight-fitting lid for up to 6 months.

MAKING CHILE PUREE

Place dried chiles in a bowl, pour boiling water on top, and let soak for about 30 minutes, or until soft. Remove the chiles from the water and remove the stems and seeds, reserving the water. To puree them, place the chiles in a food processor with a little of the soaking liquid and process until smooth. To make chipotle chile puree, empty the contents of a can of chipotles in adobo sauce into a food processor and process until smooth. Chile puree can be covered and stored for up to 5 days in the refrigerator. Chipotle puree will last up to a month because of the vinegar in the adobo sauce.

PAN-ROASTING

You will see this term throughout the book. We use pan-roasting a lot at Mesa Grill and it is a great technique for thicker cuts of meat and fish. This method involves starting the food out in a hot sauté pan on top of the stove to get a good, flavorful crust and finishing it in a very hot oven to cook it evenly. If cooked entirely on the stove, thicker cuts will burn on the outside before cooking through on the inside. By finishing this kind of cut in the oven instead, where the heat is even and not just coming from underneath, the result is a perfectly cooked piece of meat or fish.

ROASTING CORN

Preheat the oven to 375 degrees F. Pull the husks back from each ear of corn, but do not pull them off entirely. Remove the silks and then replace the husks. Soak the ears in cold water for 5 minutes, then remove them and shake off the excess water. Place on a baking sheet and roast until the kernels are tender, 15 to 20 minutes. Let cool slightly before removing the kernels, if desired.

To remove the kernels from the cobs, whether raw or roasted, remove the husks and silks (if raw), stand the corn on end in a large bowl, and cut downward with a small sharp knife. Discard the cobs. One ear of corn will yield approximately ½ cup of kernels.

ROASTING GARLIC

Preheat the oven to 300 degrees F. Separate the cloves of a head of garlic, but do not peel. Drizzle the cloves with olive oil and season with salt and pepper. Wrap the garlic securely in aluminum foil and place on a baking sheet. Roast in the oven for 45 minutes to 1 hour, until very soft. Squeeze the pulp from the skins, discarding the skins. Roasted garlic will keep covered and stored in the refrigerator for up to 5 days.

REDUCING TO SAUCE CONSISTENCY

In the majority of sauce recipes in this book, you will notice that I say to cook until reduced to a sauce consistency. This simply means boiling the liquid until it thickens. I prefer to achieve a sauce consistency naturally, instead of adding a thickening agent such as cornstarch or a roux that would change the flavor and texture of the final sauce. The way to test for a "sauce consistency" is to dip a spoon into the sauce. If the sauce clings, that's a good sign. Next, draw your finger through the sauce. If the line your finger made stays, and the sauce doesn't run back into it, you have reached a sauce consistency. Whenever possible, use homemade stock *(see page 38)* for your sauces. Store-bought canned broths, while convenient, are not always made with bones and as such do not have natural gelatin in them. As a result, they do not thicken as well or give you the richest possible flavor.

MAKING SIMPLE SYRUP

Essentially predissolved sugar, simple syrup is great for sweetening cold drinks or using in fruit salads instead of gritty sugar. Combine equal parts water and sugar in a saucepan, bring to a simmer, and cook for a minute or two, until the sugar has completely dissolved. Let cool completely and store, nearly indefinitely, in the refrigerator.

TOASTING NUTS, SEEDS, AND SPICES

Toasting brings out the flavor of these ingredients. Preheat the oven to 350 degrees F. Put a single layer of nuts or seeds in a skillet or on a baking sheet and toast for 5 to 7 minutes, until lightly golden brown and fragrant, shaking the pan every couple of minutes to prevent burning. For spices, proceed as above, but toast for only 3 to 4 minutes, until just fragrant. Transfer the nuts, seeds, or spices to a plate and let cool completely. Store, tightly covered, for up to 1 day.

INDOOR GRILLING

It's no secret that I love to grill, but I realize that because of the change of seasons and the fact that many people live in apartments, it isn't always possible to fire up the grill in your backyard. I recommend buying a cast-iron grill pan that can be used on top of the stove for year-round grilling. Cast iron has incredible heat retention and distribution and with proper care will last a lifetime. I prefer the Logic Pro Grid/Iron Griddle (see Sources, page 272).

Dining at Mesa Grill is about so much more than just the food; it's about the total experience. The energy at Mesa Grill is undeniable. There's something about how the bright colors in the room and the bright flavors on the plates come together and make Mesa a good-time kind of place. For most of my customers, that good time begins at the bar.

The bar at Mesa Grill is a destination unto itself. The cocktails we serve are fresh, delicious, and the perfect accompaniment to our food. I can't imagine a meal that wouldn't be made better with one of our signature drinks. Nothing gets things started like a Cactus Pear Margarita. You'll also find a recipe for our famous pretzel breadsticks in here to help tide you over until dinner.

Making and enjoying these dishes should be a festive occasion, and you'll definitely find help bringing the party home in this chapter.

DRINKS

DRINKS

TEQUILA GUIDE

Mesa Grill's Southwestern cuisine shares so many of its flavors and ingredients, and indeed its culinary heritage, with that of Mexico. So it's only natural that the drink that best complements Mesa's dishes is often tequila, Mexico's finest. There's nothing better to start off a boldly flavored Southwestern meal than a well-made margarita, and it seems that most of Mesa Grill's patrons agree. Tequila is by far our most poured liquor.

My friend and business partner Laurence Kretchmer put out a great book a few years ago called *The Mesa Grill Guide to Tequila*. It takes a really in-depth look at tequila's history and production, with tasting notes and, of course, great recipes for fabulous cocktails. It has a wealth of knowledge about one of my favorite spirits and is a great reference piece. What follows is just a little of that knowledge. There's a lot more to tequila than shots at the bar!

Tequila is a distilled spirit made from the blue agave plant—which is not, contrary to popular belief, a cactus. The blue agave is harvested, trimmed, and cooked before its juices are extracted and fermented with the addition of yeast. This is the recipe (greatly simplified) for the production of 100 percent pure tequila.

There are plenty of mixed tequilas out there in addition to those labeled 100 percent pure. These are a minimum of 51 percent tequila, while the remaining percentage is made up of sugars added at the time of fermentation. This tequila makes up the bulk of what is exported to the United States, and while it does have its place in mixed drinks, more and more consumers are seeking out the 100 percent pure. There is no one way of labeling a mixed tequila; some will say "mixed" or "blended," others nothing at all. But you can bet it's mixed if "100% pure" isn't on the label.

TYPES OF TEQUILA

BLANCO (ALSO KNOWN AS SILVER OR PLATA)

This is tequila in its purest form. Unaged, clear, and fresh, tequila blanco, or white tequila, is the closest in taste to the agave plant itself. This tends to be my favorite type (when 100 percent pure) for use in mixed drinks, for its great tequila flavor.

REPOSADA

This slightly aged tequila is given a *reposada* (rest) for at least 2 months in oak prior to release. This affects the color, aroma, and taste of the tequila, making for a slightly tan, more mellow overall drink.

AÑEJO

Even more mellow than the reposadas, this type of tequila is aged for at least a year, with some distilleries aging for up to three years. These tequilas have many of the same characteristics of other aged spirits such as whiskey and bourbon, as they take on the rich flavor and color of the wood barrels in which they are stored. While many añejo tequilas can be enjoyed in mixed drinks, of all tequilas, this is the type best suited to sipping straight or on the rocks.

JOVEN ABOCADO OR GOLD

Until recently, these were probably the tequilas you would see behind most bars and on liquor store shelves. Gold or *joven* (young) tequila is unaged tequila that has been fortified with added colors and flavors. This both gives it the golden color of an aged tequila and removes some of the perceived "harsh" taste. So, really, it's artificially aged blanco tequila. It's made only for the export market and we tend not to use much of it at Mesa Grill.

MEZCAL

Mezcal is distilled from a different species of agave from that of tequila. Also, the agave used to make mezcal is roasted over charcoal rather than baked in an oven, giving the spirit a smoky flavor. While it is gaining in popularity outside of Mexico, far less mezcal than tequila is exported for foreign consumption. We use Single Village Mezcal from Del Maguey at Mesa Grill. These very distinctive spirits are worth getting to know.

CACTUS PEAR MARGARITA
SERVES 1

WHEN SOMEONE ASKS ME WHAT COCKTAIL THEY SHOULD TRY FIRST, I ALWAYS RECOMMEND THIS ONE. IT'S BRIGHT IN TASTE AND COLOR—IT'S A VIBRANT PINK. SLIGHTLY SWEET AND TOTALLY UNUSUAL, THIS MARGARITA IS THE PERFECT ACCOMPANIMENT FOR MESA'S CUISINE. CACTUS PEAR SYRUP CAN BE PURCHASED ONLINE *(see Sources, page 272)*.

- 2 ounces silver tequila
- 1 ounce orange liqueur, such as Cointreau or Triple Sec
- 1 ounce cactus pear syrup
- ½ ounce fresh lime juice
- Ice cubes
- Kosher salt (optional)
- 1 lime slice

Pour the tequila, orange liqueur, cactus pear syrup, and lime juice into a cocktail shaker, add ice, and shake for 10 seconds. Strain into a chilled martini glass with or without a salt rim and garnish with the lime slice.

NOTE You can also serve over ice in a rocks glass or you can blend with ice in a blender for a frozen cactus pear margarita.

MESA GRILL MARGARITA
SERVES 1

ON THE ROCKS, STRAIGHT UP, WITH OR WITHOUT SALT, THIS IS IT, MY ULTIMATE MARGARITA. THE KEY TO THIS MARGARITA IS TO KEEP IT SIMPLE AND TO KEEP IT TART. FRESH LIME JUICE CREATES A BRIGHTER, MORE AUTHENTIC MARGARITA THAN ANY SOUR MIX COULD. I STAY AWAY FROM THE GREEN STUFF!

- 2 ounces silver tequila
- 1 ounce orange liqueur, such as Cointreau or Triple Sec
- 1 ounce fresh lime juice
- Ice cubes
- 1 lime slice
- Kosher salt (optional)

Pour the tequila, orange liqueur, and lime juice into a cocktail shaker, add ice, and shake for 10 seconds. Rub the rim of a rocks glass with the lime slice and dip in a plate of salt. Strain the mixture into the glass and garnish with the lime slice.

Cranberry Margarita

Prepare Mesa Grill Margarita, adding 1 ounce thawed cranberry juice concentrate to the cocktail shaker.

Clockwise from left: Cactus Pear Margarita, Spicy Bloody Mary (page 31), and Mesa Grill Margarita

PINEAPPLE-CHILE MARGARITA

SERVES 4

THIS MARGARITA IS ONE OF OUR NEWEST CREATIONS. THE HEAT FROM THE CHILE SHOULD BE SUBTLE, BARELY MAKING ITSELF KNOWN IN THE BACK OF YOUR THROAT AFTER YOU SWALLOW.

- 2 cups fresh pineapple juice
- 1 cup coarsely chopped pineapple
- 1 Fresno chile, coarsely chopped
- 6 ounces reposada tequila, such as Hornitos

 Ice cubes

Combine the pineapple juice, pineapple, chile, and tequila in a blender and blend until smooth. Serve over ice.

TANGERINE MARGARITA

SERVES 4

TANGERINES JUST MIGHT BE MY FAVORITE CITRUS FRUIT. I LOVE USING THEM IN SAUCES AND VINAIGRETTES AND EVERY WINTER AT MESA GRILL WE FEATURE A TANGERINE MARGARITA ON THE COCKTAIL MENU. THE HONEY IN THE RECIPE NOT ONLY ADDS A TOUCH OF SWEETNESS THAT BALANCES OUT THE SLIGHTLY TART FLAVOR OF THE TANGERINE BUT ALSO ADDS A BIT OF BODY TO THE DRINK.

- 8 ounces silver tequila
- 4 ounces orange liqueur, such as Cointreau or Triple Sec
- 4 ounces fresh lime juice
- 4 ounces frozen tangerine concentrate, thawed
- 1 tablespoon honey

 Grated zest of 1 tangerine

 Ice cubes

- 4 tangerine slices
- 4 mint sprigs, for garnish (optional)

Combine the tequila, orange liqueur, lime juice, tangerine concentrate, honey, and zest in a blender and blend until smooth. Pour over ice in rocks glasses and garnish each with a tangerine slice and a mint sprig.

MESA GRILL SMOKY FLOATER
SERVES 1

IF YOU'RE LOOKING TO GET MORE FAMILIAR WITH MEZCAL, TRY THIS COCKTAIL. THE MEZCAL RESTS ATOP A MARGARITA-LIKE CONCOCTION, WHICH TEMPERS ITS SMOKY FLAVOR WITH THAT OF THE BRIGHTER TEQUILA.

- 2 ounces silver tequila
- 1 ounce orange liqueur, such as Cointreau or Triple Sec
- 1 ounce fresh lime juice
- 1 teaspoon simple syrup (see page 19)
  Ice cubes
- ½ ounce Del Maguey Chichicapa Single Village Mezcal

Pour the tequila, orange liqueur, lime juice, and simple syrup into a cocktail shaker, add ice, and shake until combined. Strain over ice in a rocks glass and pour the mezcal on top. Do not stir the mezcal into the drink; it should "float" on top.

SPICY BLOODY MARY
SERVES 2

COULD YOU SERVE BRUNCH WITHOUT ONE? I GUESS SO, BUT I WOULDN'T ADVISE IT. MY RECIPE IS FAIRLY TRADITIONAL—JUST AMPED UP A BIT, BECAUSE WHEN IT COMES TO THIS DRINK, SPICIER = BETTER. THERE ARE SOME PEPPER-FLAVORED VODKAS OUT THERE THAT WOULD BE A GREAT SUBSTITUTE FOR THE PLAIN VODKA.
See photograph on page 26.

- 1½ cups tomato juice (12 ounces)
- 4 ounces vodka
  Juice of 1 lemon
- 2 tablespoons prepared horseradish, drained
- 2 to 4 dashes Mesa Hot Sauce (page 226) or Tabasco sauce
- 2 dashes Worcestershire sauce
- ¼ teaspoon celery salt
- ¼ teaspoon freshly ground black pepper
  Ice cubes
  Celery spears and jalapeño chiles, for garnish (optional)

1. Whisk together the tomato juice, vodka, lemon juice, horseradish, hot sauce, Worcestershire, celery salt, and pepper in a small pitcher and refrigerate until cold, at least 30 minutes.

2. Pour the mixture into 2 large glasses filled with ice and garnish each with a celery spear and a jalapeño.

MESA GRILL PRETZELS

MAKES 20 PRETZELS

MY PASTRY STAFF DEVELOPED THESE PRETZELS TO BE SERVED AT THE BAR. AND TRUE TO THE PRETZELS' DESIGN, THEIR CRUNCHY TEXTURE AND SALTY AND SPICY JALAPEÑO FLAVOR ARE A GREAT ACCOMPANIMENT TO COCKTAILS— ESPECIALLY THOSE FEATURING TEQUILA.

Nonstick cooking spray (optional)

¼ cup yellow cornmeal

¾ cups warm water

¼ ounce fresh yeast

2 teaspoons light brown sugar

1 large egg

1 head roasted garlic, peeled (see page 19) and pureed

Kosher salt

1 teaspoon freshly ground black pepper

3 to 4 cups all-purpose flour, plus more for rolling

3 poblano chiles, roasted, peeled, seeded (see page 18), and finely diced

Jalapeño chile powder

1. Line 2 baking sheets with Silpat liners or parchment paper that has been lightly sprayed with nonstick cooking spray, and sprinkle an even layer of the cornmeal over each.

2. Combine the water and yeast in a large bowl and mix together with your fingertips until the yeast has dissolved. Whisk in the sugar, egg, and garlic until combined. Add 2 teaspoons salt, the pepper, 3 cups of flour (add more if necessary to form a smooth dough), and poblanos and mix until combined.

3. Transfer the dough to a lightly floured surface and knead until the dough is smooth. Place the dough in a lightly greased large bowl, cover the top with plastic wrap or a clean kitchen towel, and let rise in a warm area until doubled in size, about 1½ hours.

4. Preheat the oven to 350 degrees F.

5. Remove the dough from the bowl and divide in half. On a floured work surface, roll each half out into a 12 x 12-inch square about 1 inch thick. Cut each square into 10 even strips. Hold the dough by the ends; stretch it to the length of one of the baking sheets, keeping the shape as uniform as possible. Place the pretzels on the baking sheets, spacing 1 inch apart. Let rise, uncovered, in a warm place for 30 minutes. Season the tops with a combination of kosher salt and jalapeño powder. Bake until crisp and golden brown, 20 to 25 minutes. Remove to baking racks and let cool.

Mesa's soup selection changes with every season, but each soup is distinctly "Mesa Grill"—all are inspired by the traditional ingredients of the Southwest and all are delicious. You'll find homey, one-bowl meals such as Chicken and Mushroom Posole Soup and elegant starters for the most upscale dinner parties, like the refined Green Pea and Green Chile Soup. I hold texture second only to taste, and these soups are no exception. They are dynamic in every possible way, with layers of flavor and toppings that are just as vital to the finished dish as any other component. More than garnishes, I think you'll find that additions such as roasted pumpkin seeds, fried plaintain strips, and cool relishes elevate what is already great to spectacular. From the hearty black bean to silky pumpkin, there's got to be a Mesa soup that will find its way onto your table.

SOUPS

ENRICHED CHICKEN STOCK

ROASTED CAULIFLOWER AND GREEN CHILE SOUP
with Blue Corn–Goat Cheese Taquitos

BLACK BEAN SOUP
with Toasted Cumin Crema and Three Relishes

CHICKEN AND MUSHROOM POSOLE SOUP

GREEN PEA AND GREEN CHILE SOUP
with Crispy Serrano Ham and Mint-Cumin Crema

PUMPKIN SOUP
with Cinnamon Crema and Roasted Pumpkin Seeds

SWEET POTATO AND ROASTED PLANTAIN SOUP
with Smoked Chile Crema and Fried Plantain

ENRICHED CHICKEN STOCK

MAKES ABOUT 6 CUPS

THIS IS THE FULL-FLAVORED STOCK THAT WE USE AT MESA GRILL TO MAKE OUR SOUPS AND SAUCES. ITS RICH TASTE AND COLOR COME FROM ROASTING THE BONES BEFORE SIMMERING THEM IN WATER WITH AROMATICS AND THEN REDUCING THE STOCK TO CONCENTRATE THE FLAVORS.

- 5 pounds chicken pieces, such as wings, backs, and necks
- 3 tablespoons canola oil
- 2 medium Spanish onions, quartered
- 2 large stalks celery, plus leaves, coarsely chopped
- 2 large carrots, coarsely chopped
- 2 teaspoons black peppercorns
- 8 sprigs fresh thyme
- 12 sprigs fresh flat-leaf parsley
- 1 bay leaf

1. Preheat the oven to 400 degrees F.

2. Place the chicken parts in a large roasting pan and toss with the oil. Place in the oven and roast, turning once, until deep golden brown, 25 to 30 minutes.

3. Transfer the pieces to a large stockpot and add the onions, celery, carrots, peppercorns, thyme, parsley, bay leaf, and 3½ quarts of cold water. Bring the mixture to a boil over high heat, reduce the heat to medium, and let simmer, uncovered, for 3 hours. Strain the stock through a cheesecloth-lined strainer into a large saucepan and discard the solids.

4. Put the saucepan over high heat and boil the stock until reduced to approximately 6 cups, 35 to 40 minutes. Let cool to room temperature and then refrigerate until cold, at least 8 hours or overnight.

5. Once cold, remove the layer of fat that will have risen to the top and discard. The stock may be covered and refrigerated for up to 2 days or frozen for up to 3 months.

ROASTED CAULIFLOWER AND GREEN CHILE SOUP WITH BLUE CORN–GOAT CHEESE TAQUITOS

SERVES 4 TO 6

CAULIFLOWER IS AN UNDERRATED VEGETABLE, BUT IT DESERVES TO MAKE A COMEBACK. IT HAS A SOFT, SMOOTH FLAVOR AND CONSISTENCY THAT MAKES A GREAT BACKDROP TO GREEN CHILES AND TO TANGY GOAT CHEESE SPREAD OVER TORTILLA CHIPS AND BROILED.

2 heads cauliflower, cut into florets

3 tablespoons olive oil

Kosher salt and freshly ground black pepper

3 to 4 cups Enriched Chicken Stock (*opposite*) or low-sodium chicken broth or vegetable broth

½ cup heavy cream

2 poblano chiles, roasted (*see page 18*), and pureed

Blue Corn–Goat Cheese Taquitos (*recipe follows*)

Chopped fresh cilantro, for garnish (optional)

1. Preheat the oven to 350 degrees F. Put the cauliflower in a large baking dish, toss with the oil, and season with salt and pepper. Cover the pan with aluminum foil and using a paring knife, make a few slits in the foil.

2. Transfer the pan to the oven and roast until the cauliflower is soft, 25 to 30 minutes, removing the foil and stirring once during cooking.

3. Scrape the cauliflower into a medium saucepan and add the stock. Bring to a boil, then lower the heat and simmer for 15 minutes.

4. Carefully ladle the cauliflower into a blender or a food processor and add a few cups of the stock. Puree until smooth, adding more stock to reach a thick soup consistency. Strain the soup into a clean pot. The soup can be made up to this point 1 day in advance.

5. Bring to a simmer and whisk in the heavy cream and poblano puree and season with salt and pepper. Cook for about 5 minutes, or until just warmed through.

6. Ladle the soup into bowls and top each with 2 or 3 taquitos and a sprinkling of cilantro. Serve hot.

Blue Corn–Goat Cheese Taquitos

SERVES 4 TO 6

12 blue corn tortilla chips

4 ounces fresh goat cheese

1. Preheat the broiler.

2. Spread each tortilla chip with some goat cheese and arrange on a baking sheet. Place under the broiler and cook until the cheese begins to bubble and turn golden brown, 1 to 2 minutes. Serve immediately.

BLACK BEAN SOUP WITH TOASTED CUMIN CREMA AND THREE RELISHES

SERVES 6 TO 8

I LOVE THIS SOUP. THE SMOOTH BLACK BEANS MAKE A GORGEOUS CANVAS FOR THE CREMA AND RELISHES. THIS EXCITING DISH HAS SO MANY WONDERFUL TEXTURES AND FLAVORS, AND WHILE YOU COULD JUST MAKE THE SOUP, YOU'D REALLY BE MISSING OUT ON THE BEAUTY OF THIS COMBINATION IF YOU SKIPPED THE TOPPINGS, WHICH ARE EASY TO PUT TOGETHER. IF, BY CHANCE, YOU FIND YOURSELF WITH ANY LEFTOVER SOUP, IT MAKES A GREAT DIP, BECAUSE IT THICKENS WHEN IT COOLS. *See photograph on page 34.*

- 1 pound dried black beans, or 6 cups (3 15.5-ounce cans) canned black beans, drained and rinsed
- 2 tablespoons olive oil
- 1 medium carrot, peeled and coarsely chopped
- 1 medium Spanish onion, coarsely chopped
- 3 cloves garlic, coarsely chopped
- 1 cup red wine
- 3 jalapeño chiles, roasted, peeled, and seeded *(see page 18)*
- 1 poblano chile, roasted, peeled, and seeded *(see page 18)*
- 4 cups Enriched Chicken Stock *(page 38)*, low-sodium chicken broth, or water
- 2 tablespoons fresh lime juice

  Kosher salt and freshly ground black pepper

  Tomato-Serrano Relish *(recipe follows)*

  Toasted Cumin Crema *(recipe follows)*

  Avocado-Tomatillo Relish *(recipe follows)*

  Grilled Onion Relish *(recipe follows)*

1. If using dried beans, pick over them to remove any stones, put them in a large bowl, and add enough cold water to cover by at least 2 inches. Let soak for at least 8 hours or overnight. Drain well.

2. Heat the olive oil in a medium saucepan over medium heat. Add the carrot, onion, and garlic and cook for about 5 minutes, or until the onion is translucent. Add the wine, bring to a boil, and cook until reduced by half.

3. Add the beans and reduce the heat to medium. Add the jalapeños, poblano, and stock and simmer for 30 minutes if using canned beans, or 1 to 1½ hours if using dried, until the dried beans are cooked through.

4. Remove from the heat and add the lime juice, and salt and pepper to taste. Using a blender or food processor, puree half of the soup and return it to the pot (alternatively, use an immersion blender). Bring to a simmer before serving. Ladle the soup into individual bowls. Drizzle with the toasted cumin crema and top with a few tablespoons of each of the relishes. Serve immediately.

Tomato-Serrano Relish
MAKES ABOUT 1 CUP

- 2 ripe beefsteak tomatoes, seeded and finely diced
- 1 serrano chile, finely chopped

  Kosher salt and freshly ground black pepper

Combine the tomatoes and serrano in a bowl and season with salt and pepper to taste.

Toasted Cumin Crema
MAKES ABOUT 1 CUP

- 8 ounces crema, crème fraîche, or sour cream
- 1 tablespoon cumin seeds, toasted *(see page 19)* and ground
- 1 tablespoon fresh lime juice

  Kosher salt and freshly ground black pepper

Put the crema in a small bowl, add the cumin and lime juice, and season with salt and pepper to taste.

Avocado-Tomatillo Relish
MAKES ABOUT 2 CUPS

- 2 ripe Hass avocados, peeled, pitted, and coarsely chopped
- 2 tomatillos, husked, scrubbed, and coarsely chopped
- 3 tablespoons finely chopped red onion
- 1 small jalapeño chile, finely chopped
- 3 tablespoons fresh lime juice
- 2 tablespoons canola oil

  Kosher salt and freshly ground black pepper

Gently combine the avocados, tomatillos, onion, jalapeño, lime juice, and oil in a bowl and season with salt and pepper to taste.

Grilled Onion Relish
MAKES ABOUT 1 CUP

- 1 large red onion, sliced ½ inch thick
- 2 tablespoons olive oil

  Kosher salt and freshly ground black pepper

1. Preheat a grill to high or a grill pan over high heat.

2. Brush the onion slices with the olive oil, season with salt and pepper, and grill on each side for 4 to 5 minutes, until lightly charred and cooked through. Finely chop.

CHICKEN AND MUSHROOM POSOLE SOUP

SERVES 4 TO 6

WHILE IT COULD EASILY BE PORTIONED OUT AS A FIRST COURSE, THIS SOUP IS A PERFECT ALL-IN-ONE MEAL. THE CHEWY PUFFY HOMINY WILL BE A SURPRISE TO THOSE WHO ARE UNFAMILIAR WITH IT— BUT A GOOD ONE. IT ADDS A WONDERFUL TEXTURE AND SOAKS UP ALL OF THE AMAZING FLAVORS OF THE BROTH.

- 2 (8-ounce) boneless, skin-on chicken breast halves (*see Note*)
- 2 tablespoons canola oil

  Kosher salt and freshly ground black pepper
- 2 ancho chiles
- 1 ounce dried porcini mushrooms
- 6 cups Enriched Chicken Stock (*page 38*) or low-sodium chicken broth
- 1 cup canned posole (hominy), rinsed and drained
- 3 tablespoons chopped fresh cilantro
- ¾ cup shredded white Cheddar cheese (3 ounces)

  Fried Blue and White Corn Tortilla Strips (*recipe follows*), for garnish (*see Note*)

  Chopped fresh chives, for garnish (optional)

  Lime wedges, for garnish (optional)

1. Preheat the oven to 425 degrees F. Brush the chicken on both sides with the oil and season with salt and pepper.

2. Place the chicken on a baking sheet and roast until golden brown and just cooked through, 12 to 15 minutes. Remove from the heat and, when cool enough to handle, discard the skin and shred the meat. Set aside.

3. While the chicken is cooking, put the anchos and porcini in separate small bowls. Bring a small saucepan of water to a boil and pour the hot water over the anchos and porcini just to cover. Let soak for about 30 minutes, or until softened. Drain, seed, and thinly slice the anchos. Drain and chop the porcini.

4. Pour the stock into a medium saucepan and bring to a simmer over medium heat. Add the anchos, porcini, and posole and cook for 15 minutes. Add the chicken and cilantro and simmer for 5 minutes; season with salt and pepper.

5. Ladle the soup into bowls and top with the Cheddar cheese, some of the fried tortilla strips, chives, and lime.

NOTE If you have leftover roasted chicken, use it here—you'll need about 2 cups shredded. And if you don't feel like frying, substitute good-quality tortilla chips for the fried tortilla strips.

Fried Blue and White Corn Tortilla Strips
SERVES 4 TO 6

- 2 cups canola oil
- 2 (6-inch) blue corn tortillas, cut into thin strips
- 2 (6-inch) white corn tortillas, cut into thin strips

  Kosher salt

Heat the oil in a high-sided large sauté pan or shallow pot until it reaches 350 degrees F as measured on a deep-frying thermometer. Add the tortilla strips in 2 batches and cook, turning once, until just crisp, 15 to 20 seconds. Transfer to a plate lined with paper towels and season with salt immediately. These can be made up to 1 day ahead and stored in an airtight container.

GREEN PEA AND GREEN CHILE SOUP WITH CRISPY SERRANO HAM AND MINT-CUMIN CREMA

SERVES 4

THIS BRIGHT GREEN SOUP HAS SO MANY OF THE ELEMENTS THAT I LOVE TO HAVE IN A DISH. IT HAS CONTRASTING FLAVORS—THE SWEETNESS OF THE PEAS AND THE HEAT OF THE CHILES—AND CONTRASTING TEXTURES WITH THE CRISPY SERRANO HAM FLOATING IN THE SMOOTH SOUP. THE MINT-CUMIN CREMA ADDS THE RIGHT TOUCH OF FRESHNESS. SERRANO HAM IS SPAIN'S VERSION OF PROSCIUTTO, WHICH MAKES A FINE SUBSTITUTE SHOULD YOU NOT BE ABLE TO FIND SERRANO.

4 cups Enriched Chicken Stock (*page 38*) or low-sodium chicken broth

1 ham hock, rinsed and patted dry

3 cups frozen or shelled fresh peas

1 teaspoon kosher salt

2 teaspoons cumin seeds, toasted (*see page 19*) and ground, plus extra for garnish

2 poblano chiles, roasted (*see page 18*), peeled, seeded, and pureed

3 tablespoons crème fraîche

1 tablespoon honey

Mint-Cumin Crema (*recipe follows*)

Crispy Serrano Ham (*recipe follows*)

Fresh mint leaves, for garnish

1. Combine the stock and ham hock in a medium saucepan, bring to a simmer, and cook for 30 minutes.

2. Remove the ham hock and add the peas, salt, and cumin and cook until the peas are very soft, 15 to 20 minutes.

3. Using a slotted spoon, place the peas in a blender with 2 cups of the stock and blend until smooth. If the soup is too thick, add additional stock ¼ cup at a time.

4. Transfer the soup to a clean saucepan and place over medium heat. Whisk in the poblano puree, crème fraîche, and honey and cook until heated through, 4 to 5 minutes.

5. Ladle the soup into shallow bowls. Drizzle with the mint-cumin crema, sprinkle with a little cumin, and top with the crispy serrano ham and mint leaves.

Mint-Cumin Crema
MAKES ABOUT ¾ CUP

½ cup crema, crème fraîche, or sour cream

2 tablespoons chopped fresh mint

2 tablespoons cumin seeds, toasted (*see page 19*) and ground

Kosher salt and freshly ground black pepper

Whisk together all the ingredients in a small bowl.

Crispy Serrano Ham
SERVES 4

¼ cup olive oil

8 slices thinly sliced serrano ham

Heat the oil in a large sauté pan over high heat until it begins to shimmer. Carefully add 2 slices of the ham at a time and cook until crispy, about 30 seconds per side. Remove to a plate lined with paper towels and repeat with the remaining slices of ham.

PUMPKIN SOUP WITH CINNAMON CREMA AND ROASTED PUMPKIN SEEDS

SERVES 6 TO 8

IT'S ALMOST IMPOSSIBLE NOT TO HAVE THIS SOUP ON MESA'S MENU IN THE LATE FALL, BOTH BECAUSE I LOVE IT AND BECAUSE THE CUSTOMERS WOULDN'T LET ME LEAVE IT OFF. IT DOES HAVE ALL OF THOSE CLASSIC SPICES THAT YOU PAIR WITH PUMPKIN—CINNAMON, GINGER, ALLSPICE, NUTMEG—BUT THE ADDITION OF CHIPOTLES ADDS SOME NICE HEAT AND MAKES THIS SOUP ANYTHING BUT STANDARD OR SWEET. TO MAKE THIS RECIPE SPEEDY, I OPT FOR STORE-BOUGHT PUMPKIN PUREE AND RAW PUMPKIN SEEDS, WHICH ARE AVAILABLE AT HEALTH FOOD STORES, INSTEAD OF ROASTING THE PUMPKIN YOURSELF.

- 3 to 4 cups Enriched Chicken Stock (*page 38*) or low-sodium chicken broth or vegetable broth
- 3 cups pumpkin puree (not flavored pie filling)
- 2 teaspoons ground Mexican cinnamon, plus extra for garnish (optional)
- 1 teaspoon ground ginger
- ½ teaspoon ground allspice
- ¼ teaspoon freshly grated nutmeg
- 2 tablespoons honey
- 2 tablespoons pure maple syrup
- 2 teaspoons chipotle chile puree (*see page 18*)
- ¾ cup crema, crème fraîche, or sour cream
- Kosher salt and freshly ground black pepper
- Roasted Pumpkin Seeds (*recipe follows*)

1. Bring 3 cups of the stock to a boil in a large saucepan over high heat. Whisk in the pumpkin puree, 1 teaspoon of the cinnamon, the ginger, allspice, nutmeg, honey, maple syrup, and chipotle puree. Reduce the heat to low and simmer, stirring occasionally, for 15 to 20 minutes. Add more stock if the soup is too thick.

2. Remove from the heat and whisk in ¼ cup of the crema and season with salt and pepper to taste.

3. Mix together the remaining ½ cup crema and 1 teaspoon cinnamon until combined.

4. Ladle the soup into bowls. Drizzle with the cinnamon crema and sprinkle with the roasted pumpkin seeds and a little cinnamon.

Roasted Pumpkin Seeds
MAKES I CUP

- 1 cup raw pumpkin seeds
- 2 tablespoons vegetable oil
- Kosher salt

1. Preheat the oven to 325 degrees F.

2. Toss the seeds with the oil and season with salt to taste. Spread the seeds evenly on a baking sheet and bake, tossing occasionally, for 15 to 20 minutes, until they are lightly golden brown and crisp. Let cool. These can be made up to 2 days in advance and stored in an airtight container.

SWEET POTATO AND ROASTED PLANTAIN SOUP WITH SMOKED CHILE CREMA AND FRIED PLANTAIN

SERVES 4 TO 6

SWEET POTATOES AND PLANTAINS ARE A LOGICAL MATCH, BOTH HAVING AN OUTSTANDING NATURAL SWEETNESS. THEY ARE ALSO QUITE STARCHY, AND WHEN BLENDED TOGETHER, THEIR THICKNESS GIVES REAL BODY TO THIS SOUP, WHICH HAS A GREAT, LUXURIOUS CONSISTENCY. FRIED PLANTAIN LENDS A SUPERB CRUNCH—A PERFECT CONTRAST TO THE CREAMY SOUP. DOTS OF RED CHILE OIL *(page 228)* AND CILANTRO OIL *(page 222)* WOULD BE WELCOME IF YOU HAVE THEM ON HAND. *See photograph on page 37.*

2 large sweet potatoes

4 ripe plantains

½ cup pure maple syrup

About 3 cups Enriched Chicken Stock *(page 38)* or low-sodium chicken broth or vegetable broth

1 cup unsweetened coconut milk

2 teaspoons honey

Kosher salt and freshly ground black pepper

Smoked Chile Crema *(recipe follows)*

Fried Plantain *(recipe follows)*

Cilantro leaves, for garnish

1. Preheat the oven to 400 degrees F.

2. Put the sweet potatoes on a baking sheet and roast until soft, 50 to 60 minutes. Remove from the oven and let cool slightly. Once cool enough to handle, slice the potatoes in half lengthwise and scoop out their flesh into a bowl and mash until smooth.

3. While the sweet potatoes are roasting, place the plantains on a baking sheet and roast until their skins turn black and the plantains are slightly softened, 15 to 20 minutes. Remove from the oven and let cool, then peel *(see page 11)* and cut into chunks.

4. Heat the maple syrup in a medium sauté pan over medium heat. Add the plantain chunks and sauté until caramelized, 4 to 5 minutes. Remove the plantains using a slotted spoon and transfer to a food processor or blender and process until smooth. Set aside.

5. Combine the potatoes, plantains, and stock in a medium saucepan and cook for 30 minutes. Add the coconut milk and honey and cook for 5 minutes; season with salt and pepper.

6. Transfer the mixture to a food processor or blender and process until smooth, strain into a clean pot, and return to medium heat to heat through, if needed. If the mixture seems too thick, thin with some additional stock, or water.

7. Ladle the soup into bowls and drizzle with some of the smoked chile crema. Place a small mound of the fried plantain in the center of the soup and garnish with a few cilantro leaves.

Smoked Chile Crema
MAKES ABOUT ½ CUP

½ cup crema, crème fraîche, or sour cream

1 teaspoon chipotle chile puree (*see page 18*)

Kosher salt

Whisk together the crema and chipotle puree in a small bowl and season with salt. This can be made up to 1 day in advance and stored in an airtight container in the refrigerator.

Fried Plantain
MAKES ABOUT I CUP

2 cups canola oil

1 green plantain, peeled (*see page 11*) and cut into matchsticks or thinly sliced

Kosher salt

1. Heat the oil in a medium skillet to 365 degrees F as measured on a deep-frying thermometer.

2. Add a handful of plantain and cook until golden brown, 45 to 60 seconds. Using a slotted spoon, remove to a plate lined with paper towels and season with salt. Repeat with the remaining plantain.

WINTER MENU

Sweet Potato and Roasted Plantain Soup with Smoked Chile Crema and Fried Plantain *(opposite)*

Frisée Salad with Chorizo and Roasted Garlic Vinaigrette *(page 55)*

Pan-Roasted Venison with Tangerine–Roasted Jalapeño Sauce *(page 182)*

Green Onion Smashed Potatoes *(page 191)*

Milk Chocolate–Peanut Butter Crème Brûlée *(page 242)*

It would be a mistake to regard any of these salads as little more than a stepping-stone to the highlight of your meal. The salads that we serve at Mesa Grill are as exciting as anything else you'd find on the menu. Some, in fact, are meals on their own. There are Southwestern takes on French classics, such as the Frisée Salad with Chorizo and Roasted Garlic Vinaigrette and the Poached Salmon Salad with Warm Potatoes, Red Chile–Spiked Deviled Eggs, and Smoked Chile Dressing; vegetarian starters; and even a Caesar.

For me, it's all about mixing textures and flavors, fresh ingredients and hearty ones, all the while keeping everything in balance. I often find myself incorporating chilled and warm ingredients into the same salad to create another contrast—something that's unexpected but certainly not uninvited. There's no better place to play than on a salad plate.

SALADS

SALADS

GRILLED SQUID AND SWEET ONION SALAD
with Green Chile Vinaigrette

FRISEE SALAD with Chorizo and Roasted Garlic
Vinaigrette

POACHED SALMON SALAD
with Warm Potatoes, Red Chile–Spiked Deviled Eggs,
and Smoked Chile Dressing

SOPHIE'S CHOPPED SALAD

ROASTED ASPARAGUS AND MUSHROOM SALAD
with Toasted Pecans, Blue Cheese, and Red Chile–Mustard
Vinaigrette

CARAMELIZED APPLE SALAD
with Blue Cheese, Black Walnuts, and Spicy Orange
Vinaigrette

ROMAINE SALAD with Spicy Caesar Dressing, Hominy
Croutons, and Cheese Crisps

GRILLED SQUID AND SWEET ONION SALAD WITH GREEN CHILE VINAIGRETTE

SERVES 4

THIS IS A GREAT SALAD TO SERVE FOR A LARGE GROUP. NOT ONLY IS IT IMPRESSIVE IN TASTE AND APPEARANCE, BUT IT ALSO COMES TOGETHER QUICKLY AND EASILY. THE SQUID TAKES NO TIME AT ALL TO GRILL. HIT THIS WITH A LITTLE CILANTRO OIL *(page 222)* AND RED CHILE OIL *(page 228)* IF YOU HAVE THEM ON HAND. *See photograph on page 50.*

4 plum tomatoes, halved

¼ cup plus 2 tablespoons olive oil

Kosher salt and freshly ground black pepper

2 sweet onions, such as Vidalia or Walla Walla, sliced ¼ inch thick

1 pound medium squid, including tentacles, cleaned

4 ounces arugula

4 ounces frisée, torn into bite-sized pieces

Green Chile Vinaigrette *(page 223)*

Chopped fresh chives, for garnish (optional)

1. Preheat the oven to 350 degrees F.

2. Rub the tomatoes with the 2 tablespoons olive oil, season with salt and pepper, and place, cut side up, on a baking sheet. Roast for 25 to 35 minutes, until soft. Remove from the oven. When cool enough to handle, seed and dice the tomatoes.

3. Preheat a grill to high or a grill pan over high heat.

4. Brush the onions and squid with the ¼ cup olive oil and season with salt and pepper. Grill the onions for 3 to 4 minutes per side, until slightly charred and just cooked through. Remove from the grill and coarsely chop.

5. Grill the squid on each side for 2 to 3 minutes, until just cooked through. Cut crosswise into 1-inch pieces.

6. Combine the onions, squid, arugula, and frisée in a large serving bowl. Toss with some of the green chile vinaigrette. Transfer to a platter and top with the roasted tomatoes and chives and drizzle with the remaining vinaigrette.

FRISEE SALAD WITH CHORIZO AND ROASTED GARLIC VINAIGRETTE

SERVES 4

THE FRENCH HAVE THEIR FRISÉE AUX LARDONS; MESA GRILL HAS THIS SALAD, WHERE SPICY CHORIZO REPLACES THE BACON, AND SHAVED ASIAGO CHEESE TRUMPS THE STANDARD POACHED EGG. THIS MAY LOOK LIKE A LOT OF GARLIC, BUT ROASTING IT MAKES IT SWEET, NOT OVERWHELMING.

- 1 tablespoon olive oil
- 12 ounces Spanish chorizo sausage, sliced ¼ inch thick
- 8 ounces frisée, torn into bite-sized pieces

  Roasted Garlic Vinaigrette (recipe follows)

  Kosher salt and freshly ground black pepper
- 3 plum tomatoes, quartered

  Thinly shaved Asiago cheese or Parmigiano-Reggiano, for garnish

  Chopped fresh cilantro, for garnish (optional)

1. Heat the oil in a large skillet over high heat. Add the sausage and cook until lightly browned on both sides, 4 to 5 minutes. Remove with a slotted spoon to a plate lined with paper towels.

2. Place the frisée in a large bowl, add ¼ cup of the vinaigrette, season with salt and pepper, and toss to coat. Place the tomatoes in a bowl, add a few tablespoons of the dressing, season with salt and pepper, and toss to coat.

3. Divide the frisée among 4 large plates, arrange 3 of the tomato quarters and 5 slices of the chorizo around the perimeter of each plate. Garnish with shaved cheese and chopped cilantro and drizzle with the remaining vinaigrette.

Roasted Garlic Vinaigrette
MAKES ABOUT I CUP

- 8 cloves roasted garlic, peeled (see page 19)
- 3 tablespoons red wine vinegar
- 1 tablespoon chopped red onion
- 1 tablespoon honey
- 1 tablespoon fresh lime juice

  Kosher salt and freshly ground black pepper
- ½ cup olive oil

Combine the garlic, vinegar, onion, honey, lime juice, and salt and pepper to taste in a blender and blend until smooth. With the motor running, slowly add the oil and blend until emulsified. This can be made up to 1 day ahead and refrigerated.

POACHED SALMON SALAD WITH WARM POTATOES, RED CHILE–SPIKED DEVILED EGGS, AND SMOKED CHILE DRESSING

SERVES 4

THIS SALAD IS PERFECT FOR LUNCH OR A LIGHT DINNER. I'VE TAKEN SOME OF THE ELEMENTS THAT MAKE THE CLASSIC NIÇOISE SALAD SO SATISFYING—OLIVES, CAPERS, EGGS, POTATOES—AND MIXED THEM UP WITH SALMON AS OPPOSED TO TUNA. DEVILING THE EGGS IS AN ESPECIALLY DECADENT TOUCH.

Kosher salt

1 tablespoon black peppercorns

2 tablespoons fresh lemon juice

12 sprigs fresh flat-leaf parsley

1½ pounds salmon fillet, skin removed

¼ cup Kalamata olives, pitted and coarsely chopped

3 green onions, white and green parts, thinly sliced

2 tablespoons capers, drained

3 tablespoons finely chopped fresh cilantro

Smoked Chile Dressing (*page 230*)

3 medium red potatoes (about 1 pound), scrubbed

Red Chile–Spiked Deviled Eggs (*recipe follows*)

1. Combine 4 cups of water, 1 tablespoon of salt, the peppercorns, lemon juice, and parsley in a 9-inch high-sided sauté pan or shallow pot and bring to a simmer over medium heat. Place the salmon in the pan, cover, and simmer until just cooked through, about 15 minutes. Remove with a slotted spoon to a plate and let cool slightly.

2. Using a fork, flake the salmon into bite-sized pieces and place in a large bowl. Fold in the olives, green onions, capers, chopped cilantro, and ½ cup of the smoked chile dressing and stir until combined; season with salt. Cover and refrigerate for at least 30 minutes and up to 1 day before serving.

3. Put the potatoes in a medium saucepan of salted cold water and bring to a boil over high heat. Cook until tender when pierced with a knife, 12 to 15 minutes. Drain, set aside to cool slightly, and slice ¼ inch thick.

4. To serve, mound the salad in the center of 4 dinner plates. Arrange the potato slices and deviled eggs around the perimeter of the plates and drizzle everything with the remaining ½ cup dressing.

Red Chile–Spiked Deviled Eggs
SERVES 4

- 6 large eggs
- ¼ cup prepared mayonnaise
- 2 teaspoons chipotle chile puree *(see page 18)*
- 2 teaspoons ancho chile powder, plus extra for garnish
- 2 tablespoons finely chopped fresh chives
- 2 tablespoons finely chopped fresh cilantro

  Kosher salt and freshly ground black pepper

1. Put the eggs in a medium saucepan and add enough cold water to cover them by 1 inch. Bring just to a boil over high heat, then turn off the heat, cover the pot, and let sit for 15 minutes.

2. Drain the eggs and run under cold water to cool. Remove the shell from each egg. Slice each egg in half lengthwise and carefully remove the yolk. Place the yolks in a medium bowl and mash with a fork. Add the mayonnaise, chipotle puree, ancho powder, chives, and cilantro and stir until combined; season with salt and pepper.

3. Carefully spoon the mixture back into the egg white halves. These can be made up to 8 hours in advance. Dust with ancho powder before serving.

SOPHIE'S CHOPPED SALAD
SERVES 4 TO 6

THIS SALAD IS NAMED FOR MY
BEAUTIFULLY ENERGETIC DAUGHTER,
SOPHIE. IT HAS SO MUCH GOING ON
THAT YOU CAN'T HELP BUT LOVE IT—
JUST LIKE THE GIRL. CREAMY BEANS,
TWO KINDS OF CHEESE, CRISPY
TORTILLA CHIPS . . . IT ALL MAKES
FOR ONE GREAT SALAD.

¼ cup balsamic vinegar

1 heaping tablespoon Dijon mustard

1 teaspoon kosher salt

½ teaspoon freshly ground black pepper

½ cup canola oil

3 cups finely chopped romaine lettuce

2 ripe beefsteak tomatoes, seeded and finely diced

½ cup canned red beans, rinsed and drained

½ cup canned chickpeas, rinsed and drained

½ cup Niçoise olives, pitted and coarsely chopped

¾ cup ½-inch-cubed white Cheddar cheese (3 ounces)

¾ cup ½-inch-cubed Monterey Jack cheese (3 ounces)

Fried Blue and White Corn Tortilla Strips (*page 43*), made with tortillas cut into ½-inch squares

Chopped fresh chives, for garnish (optional)

1. In a blender, or, if making by hand, in a bowl with a wire whisk, blend the vinegar, mustard, salt, and pepper until smooth. With the motor running, slowly add the oil and blend until emulsified.

2. Toss the lettuce, tomatoes, beans, chickpeas, olives, and cheeses together in a large bowl and dress lightly with the balsamic vinaigrette. Garnish with the tortilla chips and chives.

ROASTED ASPARAGUS AND MUSHROOM SALAD WITH TOASTED PECANS, BLUE CHEESE, AND RED CHILE–MUSTARD VINAIGRETTE

SERVES 4

IF YOU ALREADY HAVE THE GRILL FIRED UP FOR ANOTHER DISH, THE ASPARAGUS FOR THIS SALAD WOULD ALSO BE TERRIFIC GRILLED. THE NUTS AND BLUE CHEESE MAKE THIS HEARTY SALAD A GREAT VEGETARIAN OPTION FOR ANY MEAL. *See photograph on page 53.*

- 20 medium spears asparagus, trimmed
- 1 pound assorted mushrooms, such as cremini, shiitake, and oyster, coarsely chopped
- ¼ cup olive oil
  Kosher salt and freshly ground black pepper
- 4 ounces mesclun greens
  Red Chile–Mustard Vinaigrette *(recipe follows)*
- 1 cup crumbled blue cheese, preferably Cabrales (4 ounces)
- ¼ cup pecans, toasted *(see page 19)* and coarsely chopped

1. Preheat the oven to 425 degrees F.

2. Spread out the asparagus and mushrooms on separate baking sheets and drizzle each with 2 tablespoons of oil and season with salt and pepper. Place the mushrooms on the bottom rack of the oven and the asparagus on the top rack. Roast the asparagus until just cooked through, 8 to 10 minutes, depending on size. Roast the mushrooms, stirring once, until golden brown, 20 to 25 minutes. Remove from the oven and let cool slightly.

3. Combine the mesclun greens and mushrooms in a large bowl and toss with about half of the dressing. Mound the mixture on 4 plates and top each with 5 asparagus spears. Drizzle with more of the dressing and sprinkle with the cheese and pecans.

Red Chile–Mustard Vinaigrette
MAKES ABOUT ¾ CUP

- ¼ cup red wine vinegar
- 1 heaping tablespoon Dijon mustard
- 1 tablespoon ancho chile powder
- 2 teaspoons honey
  Kosher salt and freshly ground black pepper
- ½ cup canola oil

Whisk together the vinegar, mustard, ancho powder, honey, and salt and pepper to taste in a small bowl. Slowly whisk in the oil until emulsified. This can be made up to 1 day in advance and refrigerated.

CARAMELIZED APPLE SALAD WITH BLUE CHEESE, BLACK WALNUTS, AND SPICY ORANGE VINAIGRETTE

SERVES 4

THE STANDARD WALDORF SALAD, MESA STYLE. THE APPLES ARE CARAMELIZED IN THE ORANGE VINAIGRETTE THAT LATER DRESSES THE SALAD SO THAT THE FLAVORS ARE CARRIED THROUGHOUT THE WHOLE DISH. I CALL FOR MAYTAG BLUE CHEESE BECAUSE I LOVE ITS TANGY, PIQUANT FLAVOR AND HOW IT COMPLEMENTS THE SPICY VINAIGRETTE. I DO LOVE BLACK WALNUTS, WHICH ARE PLENTIFUL IN PARTS OF THE MIDWEST, BUT IF YOU CAN'T FIND THEM OR AREN'T A FAN, REGULAR WALNUTS ARE A FINE SUBSTITUTION.

Spicy Orange Vinaigrette (recipe follows)

3 Granny Smith apples, peeled, quartered, and cored

8 ounces watercress

4 ounces frisée, torn into bite-sized pieces

Kosher salt and freshly ground black pepper

¼ cup black walnuts, toasted (see page 19)

1 cup crumbled blue cheese, preferably Maytag (4 ounces)

1. Heat ½ cup of the vinaigrette in a medium nonreactive sauté pan over medium-high heat. Add the apples, cut side down, and sauté until golden brown, 3 to 4 minutes; turn over and sauté until just cooked through, 2 to 3 minutes.

2. Combine the watercress and frisée in a medium bowl and toss with a few tablespoons of the remaining vinaigrette, season with salt and pepper, and divide among 4 large plates. Arrange 3 apple quarters on each plate, garnish with the walnuts and blue cheese, and drizzle with some of the remaining vinaigrette.

Spicy Orange Vinaigrette
MAKES ABOUT 1 CUP

1 quart orange juice (not from concentrate)

2 tablespoons red wine vinegar

2 tablespoons coarsely chopped red onion

1 jalapeño chile, coarsely chopped

1 tablespoon ancho chile powder

1 teaspoon kosher salt

¼ teaspoon freshly ground black pepper

¾ cup olive oil

1 tablespoon honey

1. Pour the orange juice into a medium nonreactive saucepan over high heat and cook, stirring occasionally, until thickened and reduced to about ¼ cup, 25 to 30 minutes.

2. Combine the reduced orange juice, the vinegar, onion, jalapeño, ancho powder, salt, and pepper in a blender and blend until smooth. With the motor running, slowly add the olive oil and blend until emulsified. Add the honey and blend for a few more seconds. This can be made up to 1 day in advance and refrigerated.

ROMAINE SALAD WITH SPICY CAESAR DRESSING, HOMINY CROUTONS, AND CHEESE CRISPS

SERVES 4

JUST ABOUT EVERYONE—MYSELF INCLUDED—LOVES CAESAR SALAD. TO MAKE A MESA GRILL–STYLE CAESAR, I PUNCHED UP THE DRESSING WITH HOT SAUCE AND LOTS OF ROASTED GARLIC AND SMOKY CHIPOTLES, AND COOKED UP LIGHT, CRISPY, AND CHEWY CROUTONS FROM HOMINY. AT THE RESTAURANT, WE TOP THE SALAD WITH A COUPLE OF ANCHOVY FILLETS—DO THE SAME IF YOU'RE A LOVER OF THEM.

- 3 tablespoons prepared mayonnaise
- 1 tablespoon Dijon mustard
- 2 teaspoons Worcestershire sauce
- 2 tablespoons red wine vinegar
- ¼ small red onion, coarsely chopped
- 6 cloves roasted garlic, peeled (*see page 19*)
- 11 anchovy fillets
- 1 chipotle chile in adobo sauce
- 2 dashes Tabasco sauce
  Kosher salt and freshly ground black pepper
- ½ cup canola oil
- ¼ cup grated Parmesan cheese (1 ounce)
- 8 ounces green romaine lettuce hearts
- 8 ounces red romaine lettuce leaves
  Hominy Croutons (*recipe follows*)
  Cheese Crisps (*recipe follows*)

1. Combine the mayonnaise, mustard, Worcestershire, vinegar, onion, garlic, 3 of the anchovy fillets, chipotle, and Tabasco in a blender, season with salt and pepper, and blend until smooth. With the motor running, slowly add the oil and blend until emulsified.

Add the Parmesan and blend for a few seconds more. Pour into a bowl, cover, and refrigerate. This can be made up to 1 day in advance.

2. Place the romaine hearts and leaves in a large bowl and toss with half of the dressing. Divide among 4 large plates and sprinkle with some of the hominy croutons. Drizzle with more dressing and top each serving with 2 anchovy fillets and a cheese crisp.

Hominy Croutons
MAKES ABOUT 4 CUPS

Nonstick cooking spray

2 cups plus 2 tablespoons canola oil

1 small Spanish onion, finely chopped

2 cloves garlic, finely chopped

1 cup dry white wine

1 cup white cornmeal

Kosher salt and freshly ground black pepper

1. Line a 12 x 17-inch rimmed baking sheet with parchment paper and lightly spray with cooking spray.

2. Heat the 2 tablespoons oil in a medium saucepan over high heat. Add the onion and cook until soft, 3 to 4 minutes. Add the garlic and cook for 1 minute. Add the wine and cook until reduced by half, 3 to 4 minutes.

3. Stir in 4 cups of cold water and bring to a boil. Slowly whisk in the cornmeal and continue whisking until slightly thickened, 2 to 3 minutes. Reduce the heat to medium and continue cooking, whisking occasionally, until thickened, 10 to 12 minutes. Season with salt and pepper. Spread the mixture evenly onto the prepared pan. Cover with plastic wrap and refrigerate until firm, at least 2 hours or up to 24 hours. Cut the polenta into 1-inch squares.

4. Heat the 2 cups oil in a medium saucepan over medium heat until it reaches 360 degrees F as measured on a deep-frying thermometer. Fry the croutons in batches until golden brown, 1 to 2 minutes; drain on a plate lined with paper towels; and season with salt and pepper.

Cheese Crisps
MAKES 4 CRISPS

Nonstick cooking spray

6 tablespoons grated Asiago cheese (1½ ounces)

6 tablespoons grated Parmesan cheese (1½ ounces)

1. Combine the Asiago and Parmesan cheeses in a bowl.

2. Lightly spray a 9-inch nonstick sauté pan with cooking spray and heat over medium heat. Sprinkle about 3 tablespoons of the cheese over the bottom of the pan and shake the pan to evenly distribute, as though making an omelet. Cook over medium heat until the cheese has melted and formed a light crust, 3 to 4 minutes. Continue to cook the cheese until the edges have set and a golden crust has developed on the bottom. Carefully lift and turn the layer of cheese with a spatula and cook until lightly golden on the second side, about 30 seconds.

3. Carefully remove from the pan and immediately drape over a rolling pin or empty wine bottle to bend slightly, like a taco. Repeat with the remaining cheese to make 4 crisps. Let cool completely and store in an airtight container for up to 1 day.

When I go out to dinner with a group of friends, I always make sure that we order tons of appetizers to share and I don't let one go by without a taste. I love to see the guests at Mesa Grill doing the same, passing around Queso Fundido, fighting over the last shrimp in the Shrimp and Roasted Garlic Corn Tamales . . . getting a taste of what we have to offer. Add a round or two of margaritas, and you've got yourself a party at the table!

That same festive atmosphere can happen in your home. Whether you're making a first course for dinner or preparing more than one starter for a cocktail party, there are bound to be recipes in this chapter that will wow your guests. Cornmeal-Crusted Oysters with Mango Vinaigrette and Red Chile Horseradish, with their crispy coating and silky interior, are luxurious party fare. And for a more casual get-together, eat-with-your-hands dishes such as Yucatán Chicken Skewers with Red Cabbage Slaw and Peanut–Red Chile BBQ Sauce set the tone for the rest of your night.

QUESO FUNDIDO with Roasted Poblano Vinaigrette

YELLOW CORN–CRUSTED CHILES RELLENOS
with Crushed Chickpeas and Morel Mushroom Sauce

Yellow Corn Crusted Chiles Rellenos
with Roasted Eggplant and Tomato–Red Pepper Sauce

CORNMEAL-CRUSTED OYSTERS with Mango Vinaigrette
and Red Chile Horseradish

FRIED SQUASH BLOSSOMS with Ricotta, Roasted Corn,
and Sweet and Hot Yellow Pepper Sauce

WILD MUSHROOM QUESADILLAS with Red Chile Jack Cheese
and White Truffle Oil

SPICY HUMMUS AND ZUCCHINI QUESADILLAS
with White Bean–Poblano Relish

COTIJA-CRUSTED QUESADILLAS with Basil, Red Chiles,
and Charred Corn Relish

GRILLED ASPARAGUS AND GOAT CHEESE QUESADILLAS
with Tomato Jam and Cilantro Yogurt

**SPICY CHICKEN, EGGPLANT, AND CARAMELIZED ONION
QUESADILLAS** with Mixed Tomato Salsa

**GRILLED SWEET CORN, ZUCCHINI, AND GOAT CHEESE
QUESADILLAS** with Fresh Tomato-Basil Salsa

OVEN-ROASTED RIBS with Peanut-Chipotle Sauce
and Peanut–Green Onion Relish

YUCATAN CHICKEN SKEWERS with Red Cabbage Slaw and
Peanut–Red Chile BBQ Sauce

BBQ-DUCK-FILLED BLUE CORN PANCAKES with Habanero Sauce

SPICY SALMON TARTARE ON CRISP HOMINY CAKES
with Avocado Relish and Mesa Hot Sauce

BAY SCALLOP AND SQUID CEVICHE ON TOSTONES
with Avocado and Radish

BLUE CORN SQUID with Green Chile Vinaigrette and
Lemon-Habanero Tartar Sauce

MUSSELS IN RED CHILE PESTO BROTH

YELLOW CORN PANCAKES with Smoked Salmon
and Mango-Serrano Crema

SHRIMP AND ROASTED GARLIC CORN TAMALES

QUESO FUNDIDO WITH ROASTED POBLANO VINAIGRETTE
SERVES 4

THIS IS ONE OF THE ALL-TIME MOST REQUESTED RECIPES AT MESA GRILL. AND IT'S EASY TO UNDERSTAND WHY. I MEAN, WHAT'S NOT TO LIKE ABOUT MELTED, BUBBLY CHEESE TOPPED WITH A GREEN CHILE VINAIGRETTE? THE COMBINATION OF TANGY GOAT CHEESE AND SMOOTH MONTEREY JACK IS IRRESISTIBLE. SERVE THIS WITH PILES OF CHIPS, BECAUSE THE DIPPING WON'T STOP UNTIL THE LAST DREGS ARE GONE.

- 1 tablespoon unsalted butter
- 1 tablespoon all-purpose flour
- 1 cup whole milk
- 3 cups grated Monterey Jack cheese (12 ounces)
- ¼ teaspoon kosher salt
- ⅛ teaspoon freshly ground black pepper
- 8 ounces fresh goat cheese, cut into 8 slices

  Roasted Poblano Vinaigrette *(recipe follows)*

- 2 tablespoons chopped fresh cilantro

  Fried Blue and White Corn Tortilla Strips *(page 43)*, made with tortillas cut into 1-inch strips (make a double batch), or one 9-ounce bag good-quality tortilla chips

1. Preheat the broiler.

2. Melt the butter in a medium saucepan over medium heat. Whisk in the flour and cook for 1 minute. Whisk in the milk and cook until slightly thickened. Remove from the heat and stir in the grated Monterey Jack cheese; season with the salt and pepper.

3. Scrape the mixture into an 8-inch cast-iron pan and place the slices of goat cheese over the top. Put the pan under the broiler and broil until the goat cheese is golden brown on top. Remove from the oven, drizzle with the poblano vinaigrette or spoon it over the top, and sprinkle with the chopped cilantro. Serve with chips for dipping.

Roasted Poblano Vinaigrette
MAKES ABOUT ¾ CUP

- 2 poblano chiles, roasted, peeled, seeded *(see page 18)*, and chopped
- 1 tablespoon red wine vinegar
- 1 clove garlic, chopped
- 1 teaspoon honey
- ¼ cup canola oil

  Kosher salt and freshly ground black pepper

Combine the poblanos, 2 tablespoons cold water, the vinegar, garlic, honey, canola oil, and salt and pepper in a blender or food processor and puree until smooth. This can be made up to 8 hours in advance and refrigerated.

YELLOW CORN-CRUSTED CHILES RELLENOS WITH CRUSHED CHICKPEAS AND MOREL MUSHROOM SAUCE

SERVES 4

I THINK IT'S IMPORTANT TO HAVE A VEGETARIAN OPTION ON MY MENUS, AND AT MESA GRILL I ALMOST ALWAYS FEATURE A CHILE RELLENO FOR THAT REASON. THEY TAKE SO WELL TO SO MANY FILLINGS AND I ESPECIALLY LOVE THIS CLASSIC COMBINATION OF EGGPLANT, TOMATOES, AND RED PEPPERS. POBLANOS ARE THE PERFECT CHILE FOR THIS DISH NOT ONLY BECAUSE OF THEIR GENEROUS SIZE, BUT ALSO BECAUSE OF THEIR GOOD PEPPERY—BUT NOT OVERLY SPICY—FLAVOR.

DIPPING THE CHILES IN CORNMEAL AND THEN FRYING THEM MAKES FOR A MUCH MORE INTERESTING TEXTURE THAN IF YOU WERE TO JUST BAKE THEM. THIS WAY, THE CRUST SURROUNDING THE SMOOTH, CHEESY FILLING IS NICE AND CRISPY. MOREL MUSHROOMS ARE A GREAT SUMMERTIME PRODUCE TREAT AND MAKE FOR AN EARTHY, SEDUCTIVE SAUCE. AT MESA, WE TAKE THIS DISH OVER THE TOP BY DRIZZLING IT WITH SMOKED RED PEPPER SAUCE, WHICH I HIGHLY RECOMMEND IF YOU HAVE TIME.

1 cup canned chickpeas, rinsed and drained

¾ cup crumbled fresh goat cheese (3 ounces)

1¼ cups grated Monterey Jack cheese (5 ounces)

¼ cup finely chopped fresh cilantro

Kosher salt and freshly ground black pepper

4 poblano chiles, roasted, carefully peeled, and seeded (*see page 18*)

1 (12-ounce) bottle dark beer (1½ cups)

3 large eggs

½ cup plus 2 tablespoons all-purpose flour

1½ cups white or yellow cornmeal

4 cups peanut oil

Morel Mushroom Sauce (*recipe follows*)

Smoked Red Pepper Sauce (*page 230*) (optional)

1. Put the chickpeas in a medium bowl and crush them with a fork into a chunky puree. Gently stir the goat and Monterey Jack cheeses and cilantro into the chickpeas and season with salt and pepper.

2. Divide the filling among the chiles, compressing it into the shape of each chile. The roasted chiles are very delicate and may begin to tear but will be fine.

3. Whisk together the beer, eggs, and the 2 tablespoons flour in a medium bowl.

4. Spread the ½ cup flour on a plate and season with salt and pepper. Spread out the cornmeal on a second plate and season with salt and pepper.

5. Dredge the chiles completely in the flour and tap off any excess. Dip the chiles into the beer batter and allow the excess to drain off before dredging the chiles in the cornmeal.

6. In a large frying pan or shallow pot, heat the oil to 370 degrees F as measured on a deep-frying thermometer. Fry the chiles in batches, if needed, turning until lightly brown, about 4 minutes. Drain on paper towels.

7. Place a chile in the center of each of 4 large plates and spoon some of the morel mushroom sauce around the chile.

Morel Mushroom Sauce
MAKES ABOUT 3 CUPS

- 3 tablespoons olive oil
- 1 pound morel mushrooms, coarsely chopped
- 1 large shallot, finely diced
- 2 cloves garlic, finely diced
- ½ cup balsamic vinegar
- 1 cup low-sodium vegetable broth or water
- Kosher salt and freshly ground black pepper
- 2 teaspoons chopped fresh thyme
- 2 tablespoons chopped fresh cilantro

1. Heat the oil in a large sauté pan over high heat until almost smoking. Add the morels, shallot, and garlic and cook, stirring occasionally, until the mushrooms are golden brown.

2. Add the vinegar to deglaze the pan, and cook until reduced by half. Add the broth and cook until the mixture is slightly thickened and the mushrooms are soft. Season with salt and pepper and stir in the thyme and cilantro. This can be made up to 1 day in advance and refrigerated. Reheat before serving.

YELLOW CORN CRUSTED CHILES RELLENOS WITH ROASTED EGGPLANT AND TOMATO–RED PEPPER SAUCE

Prepare Yellow Corn Crusted Chiles Rellenos *(opposite)* omitting the chickpeas in the filling and substituting instead 1 small eggplant cut into ½-inch dice, tossed with 3 tablespoons olive oil and salt and pepper to taste, and roasted in a 425 degrees F oven until golden brown and just cooked through, 20 to 25 minutes. Serve with Tomato–Roasted Red Pepper Sauce (recipe follows) instead of the morel mushroom sauce.

Tomato–Roasted Red Pepper Sauce
MAKES ABOUT 2 CUPS

- 2 tablespoons olive oil
- 1 small Spanish onion, finely chopped
- 2 cloves garlic, finely chopped
- 1 cup plum tomatoes and their juice, pureed
- 2 large red bell peppers, roasted, peeled, seeded *(see page 18)*, and chopped
- 2 tablespoons chopped fresh cilantro
- 1 tablespoon honey
- Kosher salt and freshly ground black pepper

1. Heat the oil in a medium saucepan over medium heat. Add the onion and garlic and cook until soft.

2. Add the tomatoes and cook over high heat until the sauce is thickened and reduced by half, 20 to 25 minutes. Place the red peppers and tomatoes in a blender and blend until smooth. Add the cilantro and honey and season with salt and pepper. This can be made up to 1 day in advance and refrigerated. Reheat before serving.

CORNMEAL-CRUSTED OYSTERS WITH MANGO VINAIGRETTE AND RED CHILE HORSERADISH

SERVES 4

THIS IS AN INCREDIBLY ELEGANT DISH, ESPECIALLY WITH THE OYSTERS SERVED ON THE HALF SHELL. WE'VE BEEN KNOWN TO TOP THESE OFF WITH A TOUCH OF CAVIAR TO PUSH THE OYSTERS OVER THE TOP FOR FESTIVE OCCASIONS SUCH AS NEW YEAR'S EVE. IT'S IMPORTANT NOT TO OVERCOOK THE OYSTERS SO THAT THE PLAY OF TEXTURES IS JUST RIGHT—YOU WANT THE CORNMEAL CRISPY AND THE OYSTER STILL SILKY AND TENDER.

MANGO VINAIGRETTE

¼ cup plus 2 tablespoons canola oil

3 tablespoons coarsely chopped red onion

1 clove garlic, coarsely chopped

2 ripe mangoes, peeled, pitted, and coarsely chopped

¼ cup fresh lime juice (2 to 3 limes)

1 to 2 tablespoons honey, depending on the sweetness of the mangoes

1 teaspoon chipotle chile puree (see page 18)

Kosher salt and freshly ground black pepper

CORNMEAL-CRUSTED OYSTERS

20 oysters

¾ cup canola oil

2 cups fine yellow cornmeal

2 teaspoons cayenne pepper

Kosher salt and freshly ground black pepper

½ cup prepared horseradish, drained

1½ tablespoons ancho chile powder

Chopped fresh chives, for garnish (optional)

1. To make the mango vinaigrette, heat the 2 tablespoons oil in a small saucepan over medium heat. Add the onion and garlic and cook until soft, 3 to 4 minutes. Add the mangoes and cook until soft, 8 to 10 minutes.

2. Transfer the mango mixture to a food processor, add the lime juice, honey, and chipotle puree and the remaining ¼ cup oil, and blend until smooth; season with salt and pepper to taste.

3. Shuck the oysters, reserving the best 20 half shells. Place 5 oyster shells on each of 4 plates and place 1 teaspoon of the mango vinaigrette in each shell.

4. In a medium nonstick sauté pan over high heat, heat 6 tablespoons of the oil. Mix the cornmeal with the cayenne and salt and pepper. Coat the oysters on both sides with the cornmeal mixture and sauté 10 at a time for about 45 seconds on each side, or until golden brown and crisp. Transfer to a plate lined with paper towels while you repeat with the remaining 6 tablespoons oil and oysters. When all of the oysters have been cooked, place 1 oyster in each shell.

5. Stir together the horseradish and ancho powder in a small bowl, spoon a small dollop on top of each oyster, and garnish with chives.

FRIED SQUASH BLOSSOMS WITH RICOTTA, ROASTED CORN, AND SWEET AND HOT YELLOW PEPPER SAUCE

SERVES 4

WHEN SQUASH BLOSSOMS ARE IN SEASON, THIS DISH IS A TOTAL MUST-MAKE. PRETTY SIMPLE BUT COMPLETELY IMPRESSIVE, IT'S A PLAY ON AN ITALIAN CLASSIC. THE ROASTED CORN AND THE YELLOW PEPPER SAUCE GIVE THE BLOSSOMS A SOUTHWESTERN KICK. KEEP THE BATTER THIN—YOU WANT IT TRANSLUCENT SO THAT YOU CAN SEE THE VEINS OF THE DELICATE SQUASH BLOSSOMS. *See photograph on page 64.*

1½ cups whole milk ricotta

½ cup roasted corn kernels *(see page 18)*

3 tablespoons grated cotija cheese

3 tablespoons finely chopped fresh basil

Kosher salt and freshly ground black pepper

16 squash blossoms

1 cup rice flour

2 cups vegetable oil

1½ cups baby greens

Citrus Vinaigrette *(page 223)*

Sweet and Hot Yellow Pepper Sauce *(page 231)*

1. Line a fine-mesh strainer with cheesecloth or a coffee filter. Scrape the ricotta into the strainer and set it over a bowl. Place the ricotta in the refrigerator for at least 4 hours or up to 8 hours to allow the excess liquid to drain and the ricotta to thicken.

2. Transfer the drained ricotta to a medium bowl and stir in the corn, cheese, and basil and season with salt and pepper. Carefully spoon about 2 tablespoons of the mixture into each squash blossom. Gently press the filling into the base of the flower. Cover with the petals and pinch the top to seal. Refrigerate for at least 30 minutes or up to 2 hours.

3. In a small bowl, whisk the rice flour with ½ cup of cold water. Add up to ¼ cup of additional cold water, if needed, to make a thin batter with the consistency of heavy cream. Let the batter sit for 15 minutes.

4. Heat the oil in a large high-sided sauté pan or shallow pot until it reaches 375 degrees F as measured on a deep-frying thermometer. Holding each squash blossom by the stem, dip into the batter, making sure to coat completely. Let any excess batter drip off. Place the blossoms in the oil in batches of 4 and fry, turning to brown evenly, until golden brown, 1 to 2 minutes. Remove to a paper-towel-lined plate.

5. Put the baby greens in a large bowl, toss with ¼ cup of the citrus vinaigrette, and season with salt and pepper. Spread 3 to 4 tablespoons of the yellow pepper sauce on the bottom of each of 4 plates, top with the blossoms, and place some of the baby greens in the center.

WILD MUSHROOM QUESADILLAS WITH RED CHILE JACK CHEESE AND WHITE TRUFFLE OIL

SERVES 4

THESE RICH AND SPICY QUESADILLAS ARE A GREAT ADDITION TO YOUR FALL TABLE. A DRIZZLE OF TRUFFLE OIL, WHILE NOT A NECESSITY, IS A DELICIOUS, DECADENT TOUCH. ADD THE TRUFFLE OIL AT THE LAST MOMENT SO THAT NONE OF ITS INTENSITY IS LOST BEFORE YOU GET THE QUESADILLAS TO THE TABLE. SERVE WITH CREMA, CRÈME FRAÎCHE, OR SOUR CREAM MIXED WITH GRATED LIME ZEST AND A PINCH OF SALT, IF DESIRED.

- ¼ cup olive oil
- ½ small red onion, finely diced
- 2 cloves garlic, finely diced
- 1½ pounds assorted mushrooms, such as cremini, shiitake, and portobello, chopped

  Kosher salt and freshly ground black pepper
- 2 ancho chiles, soaked (*see page 18*)
- 2 cups shredded Monterey Jack cheese (8 ounces)
- 12 (6-inch) flour tortillas
- ¼ cup grated cotija cheese or Romano cheese (1 ounce)
- 4 teaspoons white truffle oil

1. Preheat the oven to 425 degrees F.

2. Heat 2 tablespoons of the olive oil in a large sauté pan over medium-high heat. Add the onion and cook until soft, 3 to 4 minutes. Add the garlic and cook for 30 seconds more. Add the mushrooms, season with salt and pepper, and cook until golden brown and all of their liquid has evaporated, 8 to 10 minutes.

3. Remove the anchos from their soaking liquid, reserving ¼ cup of the liquid. Stem, seed, and finely chop the anchos and put them in a bowl. Add the reserved soaking liquid and the cheese and mix to combine.

4. Place 8 of the tortillas on a flat work surface. Divide the cheese mixture and mushrooms among the tortillas and season with salt and pepper. Stack the tortillas to make four 2-layer tortillas and cover each with one of the remaining tortillas. Brush the tops with the remaining 2 tablespoons oil and sprinkle with the cotija cheese.

5. Transfer to a baking sheet (you may need 2). Bake for 8 to 10 minutes, until lightly golden brown and the cheese has melted.

6. Cut into quarters and drizzle with the truffle oil.

SPICY HUMMUS AND ZUCCHINI QUESADILLAS WITH WHITE BEAN–POBLANO RELISH

SERVES 4

WE MAKE OUR QUESADILLAS A LITTLE DIFFERENTLY AT MESA GRILL. I LAYER THREE TORTILLAS TOGETHER, WITH TWO LAYERS OF FILLING AS OPPOSED TO THE CLASSIC TWO TORTILLA–ONE FILLING COMBO, AND INSTEAD OF FRYING THEM IN OIL OR LARD, WE BAKE THEM IN A VERY HOT OVEN. THE RESULT IS A LIGHTER, CRISPIER VERSION, AND IS DEFINITELY WORTH TRYING. THIS PARTICULAR QUESADILLA IS INSPIRED BY THE FLAVORS OF THE MIDDLE EAST, ALBEIT WITH A SOUTHWESTERN KICK.

SPICY HUMMUS

- 1½ cups canned chickpeas (1 15.5-ounce can), rinsed and drained
- 6 cloves roasted garlic (*see page 19*)
- ½ teaspoon chile de árbol powder
- 2 tablespoons fresh lemon juice
- 2 tablespoons tahini
- 2 tablespoons olive oil
  Kosher salt and freshly ground black pepper
- 3 tablespoons finely chopped fresh cilantro

QUESADILLAS

- 12 (6-inch) flour tortillas
- 1½ cups grated white Cheddar cheese (6 ounces)
- 1 medium zucchini, cut into matchsticks
- 8 ounces fresh goat cheese, crumbled
  Kosher salt and freshly ground black pepper
- 2 tablespoons canola oil
- 1 tablespoon ancho chile powder
  White Bean–Poblano Relish (*recipe follows*)

1. To make the hummus, combine the chickpeas, garlic, chile de árbol powder, lemon juice, and tahini in the bowl of a food processor and process until smooth. Slowly add the olive oil, process until combined, and season with salt and pepper to taste.

2. Transfer the hummus to a bowl and stir in the cilantro. This can be made up to 1 day in advance and refrigerated.

3. Preheat the oven to 425 degrees F.

4. To make the quesadillas, place 8 of the tortillas on a work surface. Spread 3 tablespoons of the hummus on each tortilla. Divide, in order, the Cheddar cheese, zucchini, and goat cheese among the tortillas and season with salt and pepper to taste. Stack the tortillas to make four 2-layer tortillas and top each with one of the remaining tortillas. Brush the tops of the tortillas with the oil and sprinkle with the ancho powder.

5. Transfer the tortillas to a baking sheet (you may need 2). Bake for 8 to 10 minutes, until the tortillas are lightly golden brown and the cheese has melted.

6. Cut into quarters and top each quarter with a large spoonful of the white bean–poblano relish.

White Bean–Poblano Relish
MAKES ABOUT 1 CUP

- 1 cup canned white beans, rinsed and drained
- 1 poblano chile, roasted, peeled, seeded (*see page 18*), and finely chopped
- 2 tablespoons fresh lemon juice
- ¼ cup olive oil
- 2 tablespoons finely chopped fresh thyme
- Kosher salt and freshly ground black pepper

Combine the beans, poblano, lemon juice, oil, and thyme in a medium bowl and season with salt and pepper to taste; let sit at room temperature for 30 minutes before serving. This can be made up to 8 hours in advance and stored in an airtight container in the refrigerator. Bring to room temperature before serving.

SPRING MENU

Green Pea and Green Chile Soup with Crispy Serrano Ham and Mint-Cumin Crema *(page 44)*

Spicy Hummus and Zucchini Quesadillas with White Bean–Poblano Relish *(opposite)*

Grilled Lamb Porterhouse with Cascabel-Fig Sauce and Red Chile–Fig Marmalade *(page 174)*

Mesa Grill Spinach *(page 210)*

Spicy Coconut Tapioca with Mango and Blackberries *(page 246)*

COTIJA-CRUSTED QUESADILLAS WITH BASIL, RED CHILES, AND CHARRED CORN RELISH

SERVES 4

YOU HAVE TO TAKE ADVANTAGE OF LOCAL CORN WHEN IT'S IN SEASON, AND THIS IS ONE TERRIFIC WAY TO DO SO. THE COTIJA CHEESE BROWNS BEAUTIFULLY ON TOP OF THE QUESADILLA WHEN IT BAKES. IF YOU CAN'T FIND COTIJA, YOU MIGHT WANT TO GIVE PARMESAN A TRY.

12 (6-inch) flour tortillas

1½ cups grated Monterey Jack cheese (6 ounces)

8 ounces fresh goat cheese, crumbled

2 large red jalapeño chiles, finely diced

¼ cup fresh basil leaves, cut into thin ribbons

Kosher salt and freshly ground black pepper

2 tablespoons canola oil

¼ cup grated cotija cheese or Parmesan cheese (1 ounce)

2 teaspoons ancho chile powder

Charred Corn Relish *(recipe follows)*

Smoked Red Pepper Sauce *(page 230)*, for garnish (optional)

1. Preheat the oven to 425 degrees F.

2. Place 8 of the tortillas on a flat surface and divide, in order, the Monterey Jack, goat cheese, jalapeños, and basil among the tortillas. Season with salt and pepper to taste. Stack the tortillas to make four 2-layer tortillas and top each with one of the remaining tortillas. Brush the tops of the tortillas with the oil and sprinkle with the cotija cheese and the chile powder.

3. Transfer the tortillas to a baking sheet (you may need 2). Bake for 8 to 10 minutes, until the tortillas are lightly golden brown and the cheese has melted. Cut into quarters and top each quarter with some of the corn relish.

Charred Corn Relish
MAKES ABOUT 2¼ CUPS

4 ears fresh corn, roasted, kernels removed from the cobs *(see page 18)*

½ small red onion, thinly sliced

2 tablespoons balsamic vinegar

1 tablespoon honey

2 tablespoons canola oil

2 tablespoons chopped fresh basil

Kosher salt and freshly ground black pepper

Combine the corn, onion, vinegar, honey, oil, basil, and salt and pepper to taste in a bowl. Let sit at room temperature for at least 15 minutes and up to 1 hour before serving.

GRILLED ASPARAGUS AND GOAT CHEESE QUESADILLAS WITH TOMATO JAM AND CILANTRO YOGURT

SERVES 4

THE TOMATO JAM IS SAVORY, SLIGHTLY SPICY, AND THE PERFECT COMPANION TO THE COOL CILANTRO YOGURT. THIS IS ONE QUESADILLA WHERE THE TOPPINGS REALLY MAKE IT SPECIAL. *See photograph on page 67.*

- 20 thin spears asparagus, trimmed
- ¼ cup canola oil
- Kosher salt and freshly ground black pepper
- 12 (6-inch) flour tortillas
- ¾ cup grated Monterey Jack cheese (3 ounces)
- ¾ cup grated white Cheddar cheese (3 ounces)
- 8 ounces fresh goat cheese, crumbled
- 2 teaspoons ancho chile powder
- ¼ cup grated cotija cheese (1 ounce)
- Tomato Jam (*recipe follows*)
- Cilantro Yogurt (*recipe follows*)
- Chopped fresh chives, for garnish (optional)

1. Preheat a grill to high or a grill pan over high heat.

2. Brush the asparagus with 2 tablespoons of the oil and season with salt and pepper. Grill, turning once, for 3 to 4 minutes, until almost cooked through (the asparagus will continue to cook in the oven).

3. Preheat the oven to 425 degrees F.

4. Place 8 of the tortillas on a work surface. Divide the Monterey Jack, Cheddar, and goat cheeses among the tortillas. Place 5 spears of the asparagus on 4 of the tortillas and season each layer with salt and pepper. Stack the asparagus layers on top of the cheese-only layers to make four 2-layer tortillas and cover each with one of the remaining tortillas.

5. Transfer the tortillas to a baking sheet (you may need 2). Brush the tops with the remaining 2 tablespoons oil and sprinkle with the ancho powder and cotija cheese. Bake for 8 to 10 minutes, until the tortillas are lightly golden brown and crisp and the cheese has melted.

6. Cut into quarters and top each quarter with some of the tomato jam, cilantro yogurt, and chives.

Tomato Jam
MAKES ABOUT ¾ CUP

- 2 tablespoons canola oil
- 1 small red onion, finely diced
- 1 clove garlic, finely chopped
- 1 teaspoon ground allspice
- ¼ teaspoon ground cloves
- 2 cups canned plum tomatoes, drained and squeezed
- ¼ cup ketchup
- ½ habanero chile, chopped
- 2 tablespoons molasses
- 2 tablespoons balsamic vinegar
- 1 tablespoon honey
- Kosher salt and freshly ground black pepper

1. Heat the oil in a medium saucepan over high heat. Add the onion and cook until soft, 3 to 4 minutes. Add the garlic and cook for 30 seconds. Add the allspice and cloves and cook for 30 seconds.

2. Stir in the tomatoes, ketchup, habanero, molasses, vinegar, and honey and cook, stirring occasionally, until the tomatoes are soft and the mixture has thickened, 25 to 30 minutes.

3. Transfer to a food processor and process until smooth; season with salt and pepper. Let cool to room temperature before serving. This can be made up to 1 day in advance and stored in an airtight container in the refrigerator. Bring to room temperature before serving.

Cilantro Yogurt
MAKES ABOUT I CUP

- 1 cup Greek yogurt or plain full-fat yogurt
- Juice of ½ lime
- 3 tablespoons finely chopped fresh cilantro
- Kosher salt and freshly ground black pepper

Whisk together all the ingredients in a small bowl. This can be made up to 1 day in advance and refrigerated.

SPICY CHICKEN, EGGPLANT, AND CARAMELIZED ONION QUESADILLAS WITH MIXED TOMATO SALSA

SERVES 4

EACH ELEMENT OF THIS QUESADILLA WOULD BE GOOD ON ITS OWN, BUT WHEN YOU PUT THEM ALL TOGETHER, IT MAKES FOR SOMETHING OUTSTANDING. AND WHEN YOU'RE THINKING ABOUT FILLINGS, JUST REMEMBER THAT IF IT WORKS FOR A SANDWICH, IT WORKS FOR A QUESADILLA.

SPICY CHICKEN AND EGGPLANT

- ¼ cup plus 3 tablespoons olive oil
- ¼ cup fresh lime juice (2 to 3 limes)
- 2 jalapeño chiles, coarsely chopped
- 3 tablespoons chopped fresh cilantro
- 3 cloves garlic, coarsely chopped
- 1 (8-ounce) boneless, skinless chicken breast halves

  Kosher salt and freshly ground black pepper
- 2 medium Japanese eggplants, halved lengthwise

CARAMELIZED ONIONS

- 2 tablespoons olive oil
- 2 large red onions, halved and thinly sliced
- 2 tablespoons balsamic vinegar
- 2 tablespoons finely chopped fresh cilantro

  Kosher salt and freshly ground black pepper

QUESADILLAS

- 12 (6-inch) flour tortillas
- ¾ cup grated Monterey Jack cheese (3 ounces)
- ¾ cup grated white Cheddar cheese (3 ounces)

  Kosher salt and freshly ground black pepper
- 2 tablespoons canola oil
- 2 teaspoons ancho chile powder
- ¼ cup grated cotija cheese (1 ounce)

  Mixed Tomato Salsa (page 218)

1. To marinate the chicken, in a blender, combine the ¼ cup oil, the lime juice, jalapeños, cilantro, and garlic and blend until smooth.

2. Put the chicken in a medium bowl, pour the marinade over it, cover, and refrigerate for at least 1 hour and up to 4 hours.

3. Preheat a grill to high or a grill pan over high heat.

4. To cook the chicken and the eggplant, remove the chicken from the marinade and pat dry with paper towels; discard the marinade. Season the breast halves on both sides with salt and pepper. Grill for about 4 minutes per side, until golden brown and just cooked through. Remove to a cutting board, let rest for 5 minutes, and then slice into ¼-inch-thick slices on the bias.

5. Keep the grill on, or if using a grill pan, wipe it out and return to high heat. Brush the eggplant on both sides with the 3 tablespoons oil and season with salt and pepper. Grill for 3 to 4 minutes on each side, until just cooked through. Remove to a cutting board and coarsely chop.

6. To caramelize the onions, heat the oil in a medium sauté pan over medium heat. Add the onions and cook, stirring occasionally, until soft and caramelized, 20 to 25 minutes. Add the balsamic vinegar and cilantro and cook until the liquid has evaporated, about 5 minutes; season with salt and pepper.

7. Preheat the oven to 425 degrees F.

8. To make the quesadillas, place 8 of the tortillas on a flat surface. Divide, in order, the Monterey Jack and Cheddar cheeses, chicken, onions, and eggplant among the tortillas and season with salt and pepper. Stack the tortillas to make four 2-layer tortillas and top each with one of the remaining tortillas.

9. Transfer to a baking sheet (you may need 2). Brush the tops with the oil and sprinkle with the ancho powder and cotija cheese. Bake for 8 to 10 minutes, until the tortillas are lightly golden brown and the cheese has melted.

10. Cut into quarters and garnish with the mixed tomato salsa.

GRILLED SWEET CORN, ZUCCHINI, AND GOAT CHEESE QUESADILLAS WITH FRESH TOMATO-BASIL SALSA

SERVES 4

I CAN'T THINK OF ANY BETTER WAY TO MAKE USE OF SUMMER'S FARM-STAND BOUNTY THAN WITH THIS FRESH QUESADILLA.

- 12 (6-inch) flour tortillas
- ¾ cup grated Monterey Jack cheese (3 ounces)
- ¾ cup grated white Cheddar cheese (3 ounces)
- 8 ounces goat cheese, crumbled
- ¼ cup finely chopped red onion
- ½ medium zucchini, cut into matchsticks
- ½ cup fresh corn kernels (see page 9)
  Kosher salt and freshly ground black pepper
- 3 to 4 tablespoons canola oil
  Tomato-Basil Salsa (recipe follows)

1. Preheat a grill to medium or a grill pan over medium heat.

2. Place 8 of the tortillas on a work surface. Divide, in order, the Monterey Jack, Cheddar, and goat cheeses, the onion, zucchini, and corn among the tortillas and season with salt and pepper to taste. Stack the tortillas to make four 2-layer tortillas and cover each with one of the remaining 4 tortillas. Brush the tops with about 2 tablespoons of the oil.

3. Grill, oil side down, for 3 to 4 minutes, until golden brown. Brush the tops of the tortillas with a tablespoon or two of the remaining oil, carefully flip over, and continue grilling until golden brown on the other side and the cheese has melted, 2 to 3 minutes. Cut into wedges and garnish with the tomato-basil salsa.

Tomato-Basil Salsa
MAKES ABOUT 2 CUPS

- 3 ripe tomatoes, seeded and coarsely chopped
- ¼ cup finely chopped red onion
- 2 cloves garlic, finely chopped
- 1 tablespoon finely chopped jalapeño chile
- 2 tablespoons red wine vinegar
- 2 tablespoons olive oil
- 2 tablespoons finely chopped fresh basil
  Kosher salt and freshly ground black pepper

Combine the tomatoes, onion, garlic, jalapeño, vinegar, oil, and basil in a medium bowl and season with salt and pepper. Let the relish sit at room temperature for at least 15 minutes. This can be made up to 1 day in advance and stored in an airtight container in the refrigerator. Bring to room temperature before serving.

OVEN-ROASTED RIBS WITH PEANUT-CHIPOTLE SAUCE AND PEANUT–GREEN ONION RELISH

SERVES 8 AS AN APPETIZER OR 4 AS AN ENTRÉE

THE THOUGHT OF PREPARING RIBS AT HOME CAN BE PRETTY INTIMIDATING FOR SOME PEOPLE. IT NEEDN'T BE, ESPECIALLY WITH THIS EASY RECIPE FOR BAKING THEM IN THE OVEN. THE PEANUT-CHIPOTLE SAUCE BECOMES A GLAZE AS IT COOKS DOWN AND SEEPS INTO THE MEAT OF THE RIBS, MAKING EACH BITE LUSCIOUS.

PEANUT-CHIPOTLE SAUCE

2 cups Mesa Grill BBQ Sauce (*page* 225)

½ cup smooth peanut butter, such as Jif

¼ cup soy sauce

1½ tablespoons rice wine vinegar

2 teaspoons chipotle chile puree (*see page* 18)

1½ tablespoons honey

RIBS

¼ cup canola oil

2 racks of pork ribs (12 ribs each)

Spice rub from Spice-Crusted New York Strip Steaks with Mesa Grill Steak Sauce (*page* 155)

Peanut–Green Onion Relish (*recipe follows*)

Kosher salt

1 cup soy sauce

¼ cup coarsely chopped fresh ginger

1. To make the sauce, whisk together the barbecue sauce, peanut butter, soy sauce, vinegar, chipotle puree, and honey until combined. The sauce can be stored in the refrigerator for up to 4 days.

2. Preheat the oven to 500 F.

3. Heat the oil in a large roasting pan over two burners over medium-high heat until shimmering. Season the racks on both sides with salt and season on the top side with the rub. Place in the pan, rub-side down, and cook until golden brown and a crust has formed, 3 to 5 minutes on each side. Remove the racks to a cutting board or baking sheet.

4. Pour any excess oil out of the roasting pan and return to medium-high heat. Combine the soy sauce, 4 cups of water, and the ginger in the roasting pan and bring to a boil. Put a rack into the roasting pan and place the ribs on the rack. Brush with the peanut-chipotle puree.

5. Place in the oven and bake for 1¼ to 1½ hours, basting every 15 minutes, until the meat is falling-off-the-bone tender. Remove from the oven and cut into single ribs; arrange on a platter and sprinkle with the peanut–green onion relish.

Peanut–Green Onion Relish
MAKES ABOUT 1½ CUPS

1 cup roasted peanuts, coarsely chopped

¼ cup finely sliced green onions, white and green parts (about 3)

2 teaspoons light brown sugar

¼ teaspoon ground cinnamon

¼ teaspoon ground ginger

Combine all the ingredients in a bowl just before serving.

YUCATAN CHICKEN SKEWERS WITH RED CABBAGE SLAW AND PEANUT–RED CHILE BBQ SAUCE

SERVES 4

THIS IS A GREAT PARTY DISH—IT LOOKS FABULOUS ON THE PLATE, IS FULL OF FLAVOR, AND IS INTERACTIVE. HAVE YOUR GUESTS MAKE THEIR OWN WRAPS (THINK OF A THAI SUMMER ROLL FOR INSPIRATION), PILING CHICKEN, SLAW, BARBECUE SAUCE, AND FRESH MINT AND CILANTRO INTO WARM FLOUR TORTILLAS. IT'S A GREAT CONTRAST OF FLAVORS AND TEXTURES. RED CHILE OIL *(page 228)* AND CILANTRO OIL *(page 222)* WOULD TAKE THIS OVER THE TOP.

½ cup fresh orange juice (about 2 oranges)

¼ cup fresh lime juice (2 to 3 limes)

2 tablespoons canola oil

2 tablespoons ancho chile powder

3 cloves garlic, coarsely chopped

6 (6-ounce) boneless, skinless chicken thighs, cut in half lengthwise

24 wooden skewers, soaked in water for 30 minutes

Kosher salt and freshly ground black pepper

12 (6-inch) four tortillas

Red Cabbage Slaw *(recipe follows)*

Peanut–Red Chile BBQ Sauce *(recipe follows)*

Fresh mint leaves, for garnish

Fresh cilantro leaves, for garnish (optional)

Finely chopped roasted peanuts, for garnish (optional)

1. To marinate the chicken, in a large shallow baking dish, whisk together the orange and lime juices, oil, chile powder, and garlic until combined.

2. Skewer each chicken thigh half with 2 skewers running lengthwise through the chicken so that it lies flat. Put the chicken in the baking dish and turn to coat with the marinade. Cover and refrigerate for at least 1 hour and up to 4 hours.

3. Preheat a grill to high or a grill pan over high heat.

4. Remove the thighs from the marinade (discard the marinade) and season with salt and pepper on both sides. Grill for 4 to 5 minutes on each side, until just cooked through.

5. Place the tortillas on the grill and grill for 10 seconds per side to heat through.

6. Serve the skewers on a platter accompanied by the cabbage slaw, peanut–red chile barbecue sauce, tortillas, mint and cilantro leaves, and peanuts for everyone to assemble his own wrap.

Red Cabbage Slaw
MAKES ABOUT 2 CUPS

¼ cup rice wine vinegar

½ cup fresh orange juice (about 2 oranges)

¼ cup canola oil

1 tablespoon honey

½ head red cabbage, finely shredded

1 small red onion, halved and thinly sliced

¼ cup fresh cilantro leaves

Kosher salt and freshly ground black pepper

Whisk together the vinegar, orange juice, oil, and honey in a medium bowl. Add the cabbage, onion, and cilantro and season with salt and pepper. Toss to combine. Let sit at room temperature for at least 20 minutes or up to 1 hour before serving.

Peanut–Red Chile BBQ Sauce
MAKES ABOUT 2 CUPS

- 1 tablespoon canola oil
- 2 tablespoons finely chopped fresh ginger
- 1½ cups Mesa Grill BBQ Sauce *(page 225)*
- 2 cups Enriched Chicken Stock *(page 38)* or low-sodium chicken broth
- 2 tablespoons soy sauce
- ¼ cup smooth peanut butter, such as Jif

  Kosher salt and freshly ground black pepper

1. Heat the oil in a medium saucepan over medium heat. Add the ginger and cook until soft, 1 to 2 minutes. Raise the heat to high, add the barbecue sauce and chicken stock, and cook, stirring occasionally, until reduced by half.

2. Whisk in the soy sauce and peanut butter and cook over medium heat until thickened, 12 to 15 minutes. Season with salt and pepper. This can be made up to 2 days in advance and refrigerated. Reheat before serving.

BBQ-DUCK-FILLED BLUE CORN PANCAKES WITH HABANERO SAUCE

SERVES 8

THIS MESA CLASSIC HAS BEEN ON THE MENU SINCE THE BEGINNING. THE SWEET AND SPICY DUCK IS THE PERFECT FILLING FOR THE NUTTY, CREPELIKE BLUE CORN PANCAKES. IT'S ONE OF MY FAVORITE COMBINATIONS, ESPECIALLY WHEN DRIZZLED WITH SMOKED RED PEPPER SAUCE, AS WE DO AT THE RESTAURANT.

BBQ DUCK

2 pounds duck legs (about 6), skin removed

1 cup Mesa Grill BBQ Sauce (*page 225*) or your favorite store brand

3 cups Enriched Chicken Stock (*page 38*) or low-sodium chicken broth

Habanero Sauce (*recipe follows*)

3 tablespoons coarsely chopped fresh cilantro

Kosher salt and freshly ground black pepper

BLUE CORN PANCAKES

½ cup blue cornmeal

½ cup all-purpose flour

1 teaspoon baking powder

Pinch of kosher salt

1 large egg, beaten

¾ cup whole milk

2 tablespoons honey

1 tablespoon unsalted butter, melted

Nonstick cooking spray

Smoked Red Pepper Sauce (*page 230*)

Fresh cilantro leaves, for garnish (optional)

1. Preheat the oven to 325 degrees F.

2. Generously brush the duck legs with the barbecue sauce and place them in a baking pan. Pour the stock and ½ cup of the habanero sauce around them. Cover the pan, place in the oven, and cook for about 2 hours, or until the meat begins to fall off the bone.

3. To make the pancakes, combine the cornmeal, flour, baking powder, and salt in a medium bowl. In a separate bowl, whisk together the egg, milk, honey, and butter; add the wet ingredients to the dry ingredients and mix until combined.

4. Place a 6-inch nonstick pan over high heat. Spray with cooking spray and reduce the heat to medium. Ladle ¼ cup of the pancake mixture into the pan, swirling to evenly coat the pan with the mixture. Cook the pancake until just set on the first side, about 1 minute. Flip over and cook for an additional 20 to 30 seconds. Remove to a plate and repeat with the remaining mixture, stacking the pancakes and covering them with aluminum foil to keep warm. You should have 8 pancakes.

5. Remove the duck from the braising liquid and set aside to cool slightly. Strain the braising liquid and reserve. When the duck is cool enough to handle, shred the duck meat into bite-sized pieces and discard the bones.

6. Combine the shredded meat with ½ cup of the reserved braising liquid in a sauté pan over medium heat until heated through. Add the chopped cilantro and season with salt and pepper to taste.

7. Mound some of the duck mixture in the center of each pancake. Fold the pancake over the filling to make a semicircle and drizzle with the remaining habanero sauce and the smoked red pepper sauce. Garnish with cilantro leaves.

Habanero Sauce
MAKES ABOUT 1 CUP

- 10 cups Enriched Chicken Stock *(page 38)* or low-sodium chicken broth
- 1 cup apple juice concentrate, thawed
- 3 tablespoons dark brown sugar
- 2 star anise
- 1 cinnamon stick
- ½ habanero chile, coarsely chopped
- 1 tablespoon fennel seeds, toasted *(page 19)*

  Kosher salt and freshly ground black pepper

1. Combine the stock, apple juice, brown sugar, star anise, cinnamon, habanero, and fennel seeds in a large saucepan; place over high heat and boil, stirring occasionally, until reduced to 1 cup, about 1 hour.

2. Strain into a bowl and season with salt and pepper to taste. This can be made up to 2 days in advance and refrigerated. Warm over low heat before serving.

SPICY SALMON TARTARE ON CRISP HOMINY CAKES WITH AVOCADO RELISH AND MESA HOT SAUCE

SERVES 8

MAKING THESE HOMINY CAKES IS WORTH THE EFFORT, WITHOUT A DOUBT. THEY ARE CRISPY OUTSIDE WITH A CREAMY INTERIOR. THEY MAKE A FABULOUS BASE FOR THE SPICY AND FLAVORFUL TARTARE.

HOMINY CAKES

8 tablespoons (1 stick) unsalted butter, plus extra for the pan

Kosher salt

2 cups white cornmeal

½ cup grated cotija cheese (2 ounces)

Freshly ground black pepper

Canola oil

SALMON TARTARE

2 tablespoons Dijon mustard

1 tablespoon chipotle chile puree (see page 18)

3 tablespoons olive oil

1 pound fresh salmon, cut into ¼-inch dice

3 tablespoons capers, drained

¼ cup thinly sliced green onion, white and green parts (about 3)

3 tablespoons finely chopped fresh cilantro

Kosher salt and freshly ground black pepper

Avocado Relish (page 216)

Mesa Grill Hot Sauce (page 226) or Tabasco sauce

Fresh cilantro leaves, for garnish (optional)

1. To make the hominy cakes, butter a rimmed 12 x 17-inch baking sheet, line it with parchment paper, and butter the parchment paper. Set aside.

2. Combine 4 cups of water and 2 teaspoons of salt in a medium saucepan and bring to a boil over high heat. Slowly whisk in 1 cup of the cornmeal until smooth. Reduce the heat to medium and continue cooking, stirring frequently with a wooden spoon and adding more water if the mixture appears too thick, until the gritty texture is gone and the mixture is smooth and has thickened.

3. Remove from the heat and stir in the 8 tablespoons butter and the cotija cheese until melted; season with salt and pepper. Spread the mixture evenly into the prepared sheet pan, cover, and place in the refrigerator until chilled and firm, at least 1 hour and up to 24 hours.

4. Heat 2 inches of oil in a large skillet to 365 degrees F as measured on a deep-frying thermometer. Remove the cornmeal mixture from the refrigerator and cut into eight 3-inch circles with a cookie cutter. Spread the remaining 1 cup cornmeal on a plate and season with salt and pepper. Dredge each circle in the cornmeal, tapping off any excess. Fry the cakes until golden brown, about 1 to 2 minutes per side, and remove to a plate lined with paper towels.

5. To make the tartare, whisk together the mustard, chipotle puree, and oil in a medium bowl. Fold in the salmon, capers, green onion, and cilantro until combined; season with salt and pepper. The tartare can be made only up to 10 minutes before serving.

6. Spread some of the avocado relish on each cake, top with salmon tartare, and drizzle with some of the hot sauce. Garnish with cilantro leaves.

BAY SCALLOP AND SQUID CEVICHE ON TOSTONES WITH AVOCADO AND RADISH

SERVES 4 TO 6

MAKE SURE THAT YOUR SEAFOOD IS VERY FRESH BEFORE GOING AHEAD WITH THIS RECIPE. WHILE YOU COULD SAY THE SQUID AND SCALLOPS ARE "COOKED" AS THEY BATHE IN HERBED CITRUS JUICES, THEY'RE STILL ESSENTIALLY RAW. IT'S NOT ONLY ABOUT SAFETY BUT ALSO ABOUT FLAVOR. CRISP TOSTONES (FLATTENED FRIED PLANTAINS) ADD A NICE TEXTURAL CONTRAST.

Kosher salt

8 ounces squid, bodies cleaned and sliced into ½-inch-thick rings and tentacles kept whole

8 ounces bay scallops

1 tablespoon grated lemon zest

1 tablespoon grated lime zest

1 cup fresh orange juice (about 2 oranges)

1 cup fresh lime juice (about 10 limes)

¼ cup finely diced red onion

¼ cup finely diced tomatillo

¼ cup finely diced tomato

¼ cup finely diced mango

¼ cup finely diced yellow or green bell pepper, or a combination

1 serrano chile, finely diced

¼ cup coarsely chopped fresh cilantro

1 tablespoon chopped fresh chives

Freshly ground black pepper

1 small orange

3 cups peanut oil or canola oil

3 green plantains, peeled (see page 11) and quartered crosswise

Avocado Relish (page 216)

3 black or red radishes, thinly sliced

1. Bring a medium pot of salted water to a boil. Have ready a bowl of ice water nearby. Add the squid and cook for 2 minutes. Drain and plunge into the ice water; drain again.

2. Combine the squid, scallops, lemon and lime zests, orange and lime juices, onion, tomatillo, tomato, mango, bell pepper, serrano chile, cilantro, and chives in a large nonreactive bowl and stir to combine; season with salt and pepper. Cover and refrigerate for at least 1 hour and up to 3 hours.

3. Using a sharp knife, remove all of the peel and pith of the orange so the juicy flesh is exposed. Cut between the membranes to remove the sections. Cut the sections into 2 or 3 pieces each.

4. Heat the oil in a heavy frying pan to 325 degrees F as measured on a deep-frying thermometer. Add the plantain quarters in 3 batches and fry, turning once, until soft, about 2 minutes per side. Transfer with a slotted spoon to a plate lined with paper towels to drain. Repeat with the remaining plantains.

5. Heat the oil to 375 degrees F. Using a tostone maker, tortilla press, meat pounder, or the bottom of a heavy skillet, flatten each plantain piece until ⅛ inch thick. Fry the plantains again, this time until crisp and golden brown, about 1 minute per side. Drain on paper towels. Sprinkle with salt.

6. Place 3 of the hot tostones on each of 4 plates. Using a slotted spoon, place a few tablespoons of the ceviche on top of each tostone and top with some diced orange. Serve with dollops of avocado relish topped with radish, to spoon over the ceviche.

BLUE CORN SQUID WITH GREEN CHILE VINAIGRETTE AND LEMON-HABANERO TARTAR SAUCE

SERVES 4

THIS IS THE SOUTHWESTERN VERSION OF THE CLASSIC SPANISH DISH CALAMARES A LA ROMANA, FRIED SQUID WITH AIOLI. I ONCE AGAIN TURN TO BLUE CORNMEAL TO ADD GREAT TEXTURE, AND I PUMP UP THE VOLUME OF THE TARTAR SAUCE BY ADDING LOTS OF LEMON FOR FRESHNESS, CORNICHON FOR CRUNCH, AND HABANERO FOR SOME HEAT.

About 3 cups peanut oil

1½ cups rice flour

Kosher salt and freshly ground black pepper

2 cups blue cornmeal

1½ pounds squid rings and tentacles

½ cup Green Chile Vinaigrette (*page 223*)

Lemon-Habanero Tartar Sauce (*recipe follows*)

1. Fill a medium pot with enough oil to come halfway up the side of the pot with the oil and heat until the oil reaches 360 degrees F as measured on a deep-frying thermometer. Line a large plate or baking sheet with paper towels and set aside.

2. Whisk together the flour and 1½ cups of cold water in a large bowl and season with salt and pepper. The mixture should resemble heavy cream; if it is too thick, add more water a few tablespoons at a time.

3. Place the cornmeal in a large bowl and season with salt and pepper.

4. Season the squid with salt and pepper and working in batches, put a third of the squid into the rice flour batter; remove with a slotted spoon and allow the excess to drip off, then dredge in the cornmeal. Transfer the

squid into the pot and fry until lightly golden brown and crisp. Remove with a slotted spoon, drain on the paper-towel-lined plate, and season immediately with salt.

5. Drizzle the green chile vinaigrette on a platter, top with the squid, and serve the lemon-habanero tartar sauce on the side.

Lemon-Habanero Tartar Sauce
MAKES ABOUT 1¾ CUPS

Finely grated zest of 1 lemon

3 cups fresh lemon juice (12 to 14 lemons)

2 teaspoons honey

1½ cups prepared mayonnaise

3 anchovy fillets

¼ habanero chile, chopped

½ teaspoon kosher salt

2 tablespoons capers, drained

6 cornichons, finely diced

2 tablespoons finely chopped fresh cilantro

1. Bring the lemon zest and juice to a boil in a small saucepan over high heat and cook until reduced to about ¼ cup, 20 to 25 minutes. Whisk in the honey and let cool.

2. Combine the mayonnaise, anchovies, habanero, salt, and the reduced lemon juice in a food processor and process until smooth. Scrape the mixture into a bowl and stir in the capers, cornichons, and cilantro. Cover and refrigerate for at least 1 hour and up to 24 hours before serving.

MUSSELS IN RED CHILE PESTO BROTH

SERVES 4

MUSSELS TAKE NO TIME AT ALL TO COOK AND THIS RED CHILE PESTO COMES TOGETHER QUICKLY AS WELL. THIS FAST AND EASY DISH BECOMES A FULL MEAL WITH THE ADDITION OF A SALAD AND SOME BREAD TO SOAK UP THE FRUITY, SPICY, BRINY RED CHILE–MUSSEL SAUCE.

- 2 ancho chiles, soaked *(see page 18)*
- 2 New Mexico red chiles, soaked *(see page 18)*
- ¼ cup plus 2 tablespoons chopped fresh cilantro
- 3 cloves garlic, chopped
- 2 tablespoons pine nuts
- ½ cup extra-virgin olive oil
  Kosher salt and freshly ground black pepper
- 2 cups dry white wine
- 2 pounds cultivated mussels, scrubbed
- 2 teaspoons honey
  Fresh cilantro leaves, for garnish (optional)

1. Remove both kinds of chiles from their soaking liquid, reserving the liquid, and seed and coarsely chop. Put the chiles in the bowl of a food processor along with ¼ cup of the soaking liquid, the ¼ cup cilantro, the garlic, and pine nuts and process until smooth. With the motor running, slowly add the oil and process until emulsified; season with salt and pepper. This can be made 1 day in advance and stored in the refrigerator.

2. Bring the wine to a boil in a large pot over high heat. Add the mussels, and cover and steam until opened, 3 to 5 minutes, discarding any that do not open. Transfer the mussels to 4 large bowls with a slotted spoon.

3. Return the cooking liquid to a boil and let reduce by half, 8 to 10 minutes. Whisk in the red chile pesto and honey. Season with salt and pepper to taste and stir in the 2 tablespoons cilantro. Pour the mixture over the mussels and serve immediately, topped with cilantro leaves, if desired.

YELLOW CORN PANCAKES WITH SMOKED SALMON AND MANGO-SERRANO CREMA

SERVES 4

THIS IS AN APPETIZER THAT TAKES BEAUTIFULLY TO BEING PASSED ON A PLATTER OR SERVED INDIVIDUALLY—MESA-STYLE BLINI WITH SMOKED SALMON. THAT BEING SAID, SMOKED SABLEFISH OR WHITEFISH COULD BE SUBSTITUTED FOR THE SALMON. AND, PLEASE, FEEL FREE TO "LUXURIATE" THIS DISH WITH A DAB OR TWO OF YOUR FAVORITE CAVIAR.

½ cup yellow cornmeal

½ cup all-purpose flour

1 teaspoon baking powder

½ teaspoon kosher salt

2 tablespoons honey

1 large egg, beaten

½ cup plus 2 tablespoons whole milk

1 tablespoon unsalted butter, melted

Nonstick cooking spray

Mango-Serrano Crema (recipe follows)

24 paper-thin slices smoked salmon

Fresh cilantro leaves, for garnish (optional)

1. In a medium bowl, combine the cornmeal, flour, baking powder, salt, and honey. In a separate bowl, whisk together the egg, milk, and butter. Add the dry ingredients to the wet ingredients, and mix until just combined.

2. Heat a large nonstick sauté pan over high heat and spray with nonstick cooking spray. Working in batches, drop the batter by spoonfuls to make 3-inch pancakes. Cook the pancakes until light brown, 1 to 2 minutes per side. Wipe out the pan with a paper towel and spray with nonstick cooking

spray between batches. Set the pancakes aside, stacked and covered with aluminum foil to keep warm. You should have about 12 pancakes.

3. Place 3 pancakes on each of 4 plates, spread some of the mango-serrano crema over each pancake, and place 2 slices of salmon on top of each pancake. Top with a little more crema and garnish with a cilantro leaf.

Mango-Serrano Crema
MAKES ABOUT 1 CUP

½ cup crema, crème fraîche, or sour cream

1 serrano chile, roasted, peeled, seeded (see page 18), and finely diced

1 ripe mango, peeled, pitted, and finely diced

2 tablespoons finely diced red onion

Kosher salt and freshly ground black pepper

Combine the crema, serrano, mango, and red onion in a small bowl and season with salt and pepper. Cover and refrigerate for at least 30 minutes and up to 8 hours.

SHRIMP AND ROASTED GARLIC CORN TAMALES
SERVES 8 TO 10

THESE TAMALES WERE ON THE MENU THE DAY MESA GRILL OPENED AND HAVEN'T BEEN OFF SINCE. THE FIRST TIME THE NEW YORK TIMES REVIEWED MESA GRILL IN 1991, THIS DISH WAS CALLED ONE OF THE BEST THINGS ON THE MENU AND IT CONTINUES TO BE ONE OF THE MOST POPULAR DISHES IN BOTH NEW YORK CITY AND LAS VEGAS. THE SHRIMP IS TENDER, THE ROASTED GARLIC SAUCE IS CREAMY AND FLAVORFUL, AND THE MASA IS SWEET AND MOIST. LISTEN, IT'S NOT STAYING ON THERE FOR SENTIMENTALITY; IT'S THERE BECAUSE EVERYONE LOVES IT.

TAMALES

24 dried corn husks

4 cups fresh corn kernels *(see page 9)*

1 small red onion, chopped

9 tablespoons (1 stick plus 1 tablespoon) unsalted butter, melted

Kosher salt and freshly ground black pepper

2/3 cup yellow cornmeal

2 tablespoons honey

SHRIMP AND ROASTED GARLIC SAUCE

1 tablespoon canola oil

1 small onion, finely diced

1 head roasted garlic, peeled *(see page 19)*

1 cup dry white wine

3 cups heavy cream

Kosher salt and freshly ground black pepper

1/4 cup olive oil

24 large shrimp, shelled and deveined

1 cup fresh corn kernels *(see page 9)*

Finely chopped fresh chives, for garnish

Cilantro Oil (*page 222*), for garnish (optional)

Red Chile Oil (*page 228*), for garnish (optional)

Fresh cilantro leaves, for garnish (optional)

1. Two hours before you form the tamales, clean the husks under running water. Soak them in warm water for 2 hours, or until softened.

2. Puree the corn and onion with 1½ cups of water in a food processor or blender. Transfer the masa mixture to a large bowl, stir in the butter, and season with salt and pepper. Add the cornmeal and honey and mix until there are no visible lumps. The mixture will be loose.

3. Remove the corn husks from the water, and set aside the best 20 husks. Pat dry. Tear the remaining husks into 1-inch-wide strips to be used for tying. Lay 2 husks flat on a work surface with the tapered ends facing left and right and the broad centers overlapping each other by about 3 inches. Place about ⅓ cup of the masa mixture in the center. Bring the long sides up over the masa, slightly overlapping, and pat down to close. Tie each end of the bundle with a strip of corn husk, pushing the filling toward the middle as you tie. Trim the ends of the strip to about ½ inch beyond the tie. The tamales can be assembled up to 4 hours ahead and refrigerated.

4. Bring a couple of inches of water to a boil in the bottom of a steamer. Arrange the tamales in a single layer on the rack, cover tightly with aluminum foil, and steam over boiling water for 45 to 75 minutes, until firm to the touch.

5. While the tamales are steaming, make the sauce. Heat the canola oil in a medium saucepan over high heat. Add the onion and cook until soft, 3 to 4 minutes. Add the garlic and wine and cook until the wine is almost evaporated, 3 to 4 minutes. Add the cream, bring to a boil, reduce the heat to low, and cook until reduced by half, 15 to 20 minutes.

6. Transfer to a food processor or blender and process until smooth; season with salt and pepper.

7. To cook the shrimp, heat 2 tablespoons of the olive oil in a large sauté pan over high heat. Season the shrimp on both sides with salt and pepper. Sauté half of the shrimp until lightly golden brown on both sides and just cooked through, 2 to 3 minutes. Remove to a plate and repeat with the remaining 2 tablespoons oil and shrimp.

8. Add the corn to the pan that you sautéed the shrimp in and cook for 3 to 4 minutes. Add the garlic sauce and bring to a simmer. Return the shrimp to the pan and cook just to heat through, about 1 minute; season with salt and pepper to taste.

9. To serve, arrange one tamale on each plate. Cut off one end of the tamale to open it up, so the masa flows out of the husk and onto the plate. Spoon 3 shrimp and a generous portion of the sauce over each tamale. Garnish with chives, cilantro oil, red chile oil, and cilantro and serve immediately. Husks are not edible.

The primarily landlocked Southwest may not seem like the most natural choice for inspirational seafood dishes, but I beg to differ. To begin with, much of Southwestern cooking is directly inspired by the dishes of Mexico, a seafood-loving culture. I have also found that many of the flavors of Southwestern cooking make incredibly good matches with the fish and shellfish of the Atlantic and Pacific coasts, such as in Smoked Chile Shellfish and Posole Stew and Smoked Shrimp Cakes with Roasted Corn and Poblano Relish and Cilantro Vinaigrette.

In fact, I would say that fish and shellfish are some of my most favorite things to cook—and eat. The cooking time of fish tends to be short, making it a great choice for quick cooking. The real skill and joy in cooking seafood lies in not overcooking it and in pairing it with just the right herbs and spices, relishes, vinaigrettes, glazes, and sauces to maximize its natural flavors.

SHELLFISH AND FISH

SAUTEED SHRIMP with Garlic–Red Chile Oil and Tomatillo Brandade

SAUTEED SHRIMP with Sweet Potato and Smoked Chile Grits and Green Onion–Cilantro Sauce

SMOKED SHRIMP CAKES with Roasted Corn and Poblano Relish and Cilantro Vinaigrette

GRILLED SHRIMP BRUSHED with Smoked Chile Butter and Tomatillo Salsa

SMOKED CHILE SHELLFISH AND POSOLE STEW

GRILLED PRAWNS with Habanero–Toasted Garlic Vinaigrette

BLUE CORN CRAB CAKES with Mango–Green Onion Relish

RED CHILE–HONEY GLAZED SALMON with Black Bean Sauce and Jalapeño Crema

BLUE CORN–CRUSTED RED SNAPPER with Warm Tomato Relish

GRILLED RED SNAPPER with Tomato–New Mexico Red Chile Sauce

GRILLED TUNA with Red Tomatillo Sauce

GRILLED TUNA with Apricot-Mustard-Mint Glaze

SEARED TUNA TOSTADA with Black Bean–Mango Salsa

"BBQ" MARLIN with Avocado Vinaigrette

STRIPED BASS with Roasted Poblano Vinaigrette and Yellow Pepper Grits

GRILLED SWORDFISH with Pineapple-Mustard Glaze and Cilantro-Mint Chimichurri

ARCTIC CHAR AND MUSSELS IN GREEN GARLIC BROTH

CRISPY WHOLE FISH with Five Pepper–Ginger Sauce

SAUTEED SHRIMP WITH GARLIC–RED CHILE OIL AND TOMATILLO BRANDADE

SERVES 4

YOU CAN THINK OF THIS AS A SOUTH-WESTERN VERSION OF GRILLED SHRIMP WITH REALLY FLAVORFUL MASHED POTATOES. IN CASE YOU AREN'T FAMILIAR WITH BRANDADE, IT IS BASICALLY MASHED POTATOES MIXED WITH SALT COD AND LOTS OF GARLIC, HEAVY CREAM, AND OLIVE OIL. IT SOUNDS STRANGE, BUT IT'S A CLASSIC BY REASON OF ITS AMAZING TASTE. OF COURSE, IF YOU CAN'T FIND SALT COD OR DON'T HAVE THE TIME TO PREPARE IT (IT HAS TO SOAK FOR TWO DAYS IN ADVANCE), THESE TASTY SHRIMP WOULD BE JUST AS GOOD SERVED WITH GARLIC MASHED POTATOES.

- 1 pound salt cod
- 2 cups whole milk
- 3 large Idaho potatoes, peeled and cut into 1-inch cubes
- 8 cloves garlic, coarsely chopped
- ¾ cup olive oil
- ½ cup heavy cream
  Kosher salt and freshly ground black pepper
- 24 large shrimp, shelled and deveined
- 2 tablespoons ancho chile powder
  Garlic–Red Chile Oil (recipe follows)
  Tomatillo-Jalapeño Salsa (page 221)
  Chopped fresh cilantro, for garnish

1. Put the salt cod in a large bowl and cover it with cold water. Place in the refrigerator for 48 hours, changing the water twice during this time.

2. Drain the cod and break it into pieces. Put it in a medium saucepan, add the milk, and simmer over medium heat until very soft, 30 to 45 minutes.

3. While the cod is cooking, put the potatoes in a medium saucepan and cover with cold water. Bring to a boil over high heat and cook until the potatoes are really tender, 25 to 30 minutes; drain well.

4. Drain the cod, discarding the milk. Flake the cod with a fork and transfer to the bowl of a food processor. Add the potatoes and garlic and pulse 4 or 5 times. With the motor running, slowly add the oil and heavy cream until the mixture is smooth; season with salt and pepper. This can be made 4 hours ahead and refrigerated. Reheat in a bowl set over a pan of simmering water.

5. Toss the shrimp with the ancho powder in a medium bowl and season with salt and pepper.

6. Heat half of the garlic–red chile oil in a large sauté pan over high heat. Add half of the shrimp to the pan and cook until golden brown and just cooked through, 1 to 2 minutes per side. Use a slotted spoon to transfer the shrimp to a plate. Discard the oil in the pan, wipe out the pan with a paper towel, and repeat with the remaining oil and shrimp.

7. Spoon some of the brandade in the center of each of 4 plates. Arrange the shrimp around the brandade, spoon the tomatillo-jalapeño salsa around the shrimp, and garnish with chopped cilantro

Garlic–Red Chile Oil
MAKES ABOUT ½ CUP

  2 guajillo chiles, toasted and seeded *(see page 18)*

  ½ cup canola oil

  4 cloves garlic, chopped

  ½ teaspoon kosher salt

Combine the chiles and oil in a blender and blend for 5 minutes. Strain the mixture through a fine-mesh strainer into a bowl, add the garlic, and season with salt. This can be made 1 day ahead and stored in the refrigerator. Bring to room temperature before using.

SAUTEED SHRIMP WITH SWEET POTATO AND SMOKED CHILE GRITS AND GREEN ONION–CILANTRO SAUCE

SERVES 4

I SEE THIS AS A SUNDAY DINNER FOR THE FAMILY, WITH THE GRITS PILED IN THE MIDDLE OF THE PLATE SURROUNDED BY THE SHRIMP. BUT THE GRITS ARE SO GOOD, YOU COULD ALSO SERVE THEM AS A SIDE DISH TO AN ELABORATE MEAL.

1 large sweet potato

2 tablespoons canola oil

1 small Spanish onion, finely chopped

2 cloves garlic, finely chopped

2½ cups Enriched Chicken Stock *(page 38)* or low-sodium chicken broth

1 cup whole milk

2 teaspoons chipotle chile puree *(see page 18)*

Kosher salt

1½ cups quick-cooking grits

2 tablespoons unsalted butter

2 to 3 teaspoons honey

6 tablespoons olive oil

1 pound large shrimp, shelled and deveined

Freshly ground black pepper

Green Onion–Cilantro Sauce *(recipe follows)*

Red Chile Oil *(page 228)* (optional)

Thinly sliced green onion, white and green parts, for garnish (optional)

1. Preheat the oven to 400 degrees F.

2. Roast the sweet potato on a rack in the oven until tender when pierced with a knife, 45 to 60 minutes.

3. Peel the sweet potato and puree the flesh in a food processor or pass it through a ricer; set aside.

4. Heat the canola oil in a medium saucepan over medium-high heat. Add the onion and cook until soft, 3 to 4 minutes. Add the garlic and cook for 30 seconds. Add the stock, milk, chipotle puree, and 2 teaspoons salt and bring to a boil. Slowly whisk in the grits, reduce the heat to medium-low, and simmer for 10 minutes.

5. Stir in the sweet potato puree and cook, stirring frequently, for 5 to 10 minutes, until smooth and thickened. Remove from the heat and whisk in the butter and honey to taste. Cover and keep warm.

6. Heat 3 tablespoons of the olive oil in a large sauté pan over high heat. Season the shrimp with salt and pepper. Cook half of the shrimp until lightly golden brown and just cooked through, 1 to 2 minutes per side. Transfer to a plate and repeat with the remaining 3 tablespoons oil and shrimp.

7. Spoon the grits into 4 shallow bowls and arrange the shrimp around the grits. Drizzle with the green onion–cilantro sauce and red chile oil and sprinkle with green onion.

Green Onion–Cilantro Sauce
MAKES ABOUT ¾ CUP

- 1 cup sliced green onions, white and green parts (about 12)
- ¼ cup coarsely chopped fresh cilantro
- ¼ cup rice wine vinegar
- 1 tablespoon Dijon mustard
- 2 teaspoons honey
- Kosher salt and freshly ground black pepper
- ½ cup canola oil

Combine the green onions, cilantro, vinegar, ¼ cup cold water, the mustard, and honey in a blender and blend until smooth. Season with salt and pepper. With the motor running, slowly add the oil and blend until emulsified. This can be made up to 8 hours in advance and refrigerated.

SMOKED SHRIMP CAKES WITH ROASTED CORN AND POBLANO RELISH AND CILANTRO VINAIGRETTE

SERVES 4

EVERYONE'S FAVORITE—SWEET SHRIMP—GETS EVEN BETTER WHEN SMOKED. KEEP THE SHRIMP PIECES BIG BECAUSE YOU REALLY WANT TO BE ABLE TO TASTE THEM. THE RELISH AND VINAIGRETTE ARE KEY ELEMENTS HERE, PROVIDING TEXTURE AND GREAT FLAVORS FOR THE CAKES TO SOAK UP. *See photograph on page 103.*

¾ cup canola oil

1 pound large shrimp, cold-smoked (*see page 17*), peeled, and deveined

Kosher salt and freshly ground black pepper

1 small red onion, finely diced

2 cloves garlic, finely chopped

1 cup prepared mayonnaise

¼ cup prepared horseradish, drained

1 tablespoon chipotle chile puree (*see page 18*)

¼ cup finely chopped fresh cilantro

2½ cups panko bread crumbs

Cilantro Vinaigrette (*page 222*)

Smoked Red Pepper Sauce (*page 230*) (optional)

Roasted Corn and Poblano Relish (*recipe follows*)

1. Heat 2 tablespoons of the oil in a large sauté pan over high heat until almost smoking. Season the shrimp with salt and pepper. Add half of them to the pan and cook for 1 minute on each side (they will be slightly undercooked but will finish cooking later). Remove the cooked shrimp to a plate, and repeat with 2 more tablespoons of the oil and the remaining shrimp. Let the shrimp cool slightly, then cut into large chunks and transfer to a large bowl.

2. Return the pan to medium-high heat and add the onion. Cook until soft, 3 to 4 minutes, then add the garlic and cook for 30 seconds. Scrape the onion and garlic into the bowl with the shrimp.

3. Stir together the mayonnaise, horseradish, chipotle puree, and cilantro in a small bowl and season with salt and pepper. Pour the mayonnaise mixture over the shrimp and stir until just combined. Add ¼ cup of the bread crumbs and stir until combined; if the mixture appears too loose to form cakes, add more bread crumbs, a tablespoon at a time, until the mixture just holds together but is still moist. Cover the mixture and place in the refrigerator for at least 1 hour and up to 8 hours.

4. Form the shrimp mixture into 8 cakes about 2 inches in diameter. Spread the remaining bread crumbs on a large plate and season with salt and pepper. Dredge each cake in the bread crumbs on both sides and tap off any excess.

5. Heat ¼ cup of the oil in a large nonstick sauté pan over medium-high heat. Sauté 4 cakes at a time until golden brown on each side and just cooked through, 2 to 3 minutes per side. Remove to a plate lined with paper towels. Discard the oil, wipe out the pan with a paper towel, and repeat with the remaining ¼ cup oil and cakes.

6. Spoon cilantro vinaigrette onto plates, drizzle with red pepper vinaigrette, and top with 2 cakes per person. Spoon some corn and poblano relish on top.

Roasted Corn and Poblano Relish
MAKES ABOUT 1½ CUPS

- 4 ears fresh corn, roasted, kernels removed from the cobs (*see page 9*)
- 1 poblano chile, roasted, peeled, seeded (*see page 18*), and finely diced
- ½ small red onion, finely diced
- 2 tablespoons chopped fresh cilantro
- Juice of 1 lime
- 1 tablespoon honey
- 2 tablespoons canola oil
- Kosher salt and freshly ground black pepper

Combine the corn, poblano, onion, cilantro, lime juice, honey, and oil in a medium bowl and season with salt and pepper. Let the relish sit at room temperature for at least 15 minutes to allow the flavors to meld. This can be made up to 8 hours ahead and stored in the refrigerator. Bring to room temperature before serving.

GRILLED SHRIMP BRUSHED WITH SMOKED CHILE BUTTER AND TOMATILLO SALSA

SERVES 4

THIS IS ACTUALLY A VERY SIMPLE DISH, ESPECIALLY IF YOU MAKE THE FLAVORED BUTTER AHEAD OF TIME. THE HEAT OF THE SHRIMP MELTS THE BUTTER AS YOU BRUSH IT ON—YUM. I THINK THAT THIS TOMATILLO SALSA IS A GOOD ACCOMPANIMENT TO THE SHRIMP, BUT FEEL FREE TO SUBSTITUTE ALMOST ANY SALSA OF YOUR LIKING.

- 10 tomatillos, husked and scrubbed, 5 cut in half and 5 diced
- 3 tablespoons fresh lime juice
- ¼ cup finely chopped red onion
- 1 serrano chile, finely chopped
- 2 tablespoons olive oil
- 1 tablespoon honey

  Kosher salt and freshly ground black pepper
- ¼ cup coarsely chopped cilantro
- 1½ pounds large shrimp, shelled and deveined
- 32 (6-inch) wooden skewers, soaked in water for 30 minutes
- 3 tablespoons canola oil

  Smoked Chile Butter *(recipe follows)*

1. Place the halved tomatillos and the lime juice in a blender and blend until smooth. Put the coarsely chopped tomatillos, the onion, and serrano in a medium bowl, add the pureed tomatillo mixture, and stir to coat.

2. Add the olive oil and honey and season with salt and pepper. Fold in the cilantro just before serving. This can be made up to 4 hours in advance and kept in the refrigerator.

3. Preheat a grill to high or a grill pan over high heat.

4. Spear 2 shrimp onto each skewer by pushing a skewer through the thick end and the tail, then smoothing the shrimp along the skewer to help it lie flat. Brush the shrimp with the canola oil, then season on both sides with salt and pepper. Grill the shrimp, brushing with the smoked chile butter every 30 seconds, for 1 to 2 minutes on each side, until cooked through.

5. Remove the shrimp from the skewers, place on a platter, and immediately brush with the remaining chile butter. Serve the shrimp over tomatillo salsa with any melted chile butter spooned around the shrimp.

Smoked Chile Butter
MAKES ABOUT ¾ CUP

- 1 tablespoon olive oil
- 3 cloves garlic, chopped
- 1 small shallot, chopped
- 12 tablespoons (1½ sticks) unsalted butter, at room temperature
- 2 canned chipotle chiles in adobo sauce

  Juice of 1 lime

  Kosher salt and freshly ground black pepper

1. Heat the oil in a small sauté pan over medium heat. Add the garlic and shallot and cook until soft, about 2 minutes. Remove from the heat and let cool slightly.

2. Put the butter in a food processor and add the shallot mixture, chipotle chiles, and lime juice. Season with salt and pepper and process until smooth. Scrape the chile butter into a bowl. This can be made up to 2 days in advance and refrigerated.

SMOKED CHILE SHELLFISH AND POSOLE STEW

SERVES 4

POSOLE IS TWO THINGS: IT'S AN INGREDIENT (HOMINY) AND A DISH—A STEW OF PORK, BROTH, GREEN CHILES, AND HOMINY OFTEN WITH CABBAGE OR RADISHES FOR CRUNCH. THIS PARTICULAR STEW IS MORE OF A SOUTHWESTERN TWIST ON A MEDITERRANEAN CLASSIC, BOUILLABAISSE. SERVE WITH MESA GRILL BLUE AND YELLOW CORN MUFFINS *(page 211)*.

- 2 tablespoons unsalted butter
- 1 medium red onion, chopped
- 2 cloves garlic, chopped
- 1 cup dry white wine
- 4 cups lobster stock, bottled clam juice, or low-sodium vegetable broth
- 2 teaspoons chipotle chile puree *(see page 18)*
- 2 ancho chiles, soaked, seeded, and pureed *(see page 18)*
- Kosher salt and freshly ground black pepper
- 2½ pounds small clams, such as littleneck or Manila, scrubbed
- 2 tablespoons honey
- 1 cup canned posole (hominy), rinsed and drained
- ¼ cup olive oil
- 8 large sea scallops
- 12 large shrimp, shelled and deveined
- Fresh cilantro leaves, for garnish

1. Melt the butter in a medium saucepan over medium heat. Add the onion and cook until soft, 3 to 4 minutes. Add the garlic and cook for 1 minute. Stir in the wine, raise the heat to high, and boil until reduced by half. Add the stock and the chipotle and ancho purees and simmer until reduced slightly, 15 to 20 minutes.

2. Strain the broth into a large clean saucepan, season lightly with salt and pepper, and bring to boil over high heat. Add the clams and cook until the clams open, 4 to 5 minutes. Remove the clams with a slotted spoon to a bowl, discarding any unopened clams; cover and keep warm.

3. Add the honey and posole to the broth and keep warm over low heat while you prepare the scallops and shrimp.

4. Heat 2 tablespoons of the oil in a large saucepan over high heat until almost smoking. Season the scallops on both sides with salt and pepper and cook until golden brown on both sides and just cooked through, about 2 minutes per side. Remove to a plate.

5. Heat the remaining 2 tablespoons oil in the pan over high heat. Season the shrimp with salt and pepper and sauté until just cooked through, 1 to 2 minutes per side.

6. Ladle the broth and posole into 4 bowls and divide the clams, scallops, and shrimp among the bowls. Garnish with cilantro leaves.

GRILLED PRAWNS WITH HABANERO– TOASTED GARLIC VINAIGRETTE

SERVES 4

THIS DISH MAKES FOR AN IMPRESSIVE ENTRÉE, BUT IT WOULD ALSO WORK REALLY WELL AS A PASSED APPETIZER. HABANEROS ARE THE SPICIEST CHILES OUT THERE, AND THE COMBINATION OF THESE WITH THE TOASTED GARLIC REALLY WAKES UP THE PRAWNS—AND YOUR APPETITE!

½ cup plus 3 tablespoons canola oil

6 cloves garlic, peeled

Kosher salt

¼ cup white wine vinegar

½ habanero chile, chopped

2 teaspoons honey

1 tablespoon chopped fresh thyme, plus whole sprigs for garnish

1¼ pounds large prawns, shells on

Freshly ground black pepper

1. Heat 1 tablespoon of the oil in a small sauté pan over medium heat. Add the garlic, season with salt, and cook until golden brown on both sides, 4 to 5 minutes.

2. Transfer the garlic to a blender and add the vinegar, habanero, honey, and chopped thyme; blend until smooth. With the motor running, slowly add the ½ cup oil and blend until emulsified. This can be made up to 8 hours in advance and refrigerated. Bring to room temperature before using.

3. Preheat a grill to high or a grill pan over high heat.

4. Toss the prawns with the remaining 2 tablespoons oil and season with salt and pepper. Grill for about 2 minutes on each side, or until just cooked through.

5. Transfer the prawns to a platter and immediately drizzle with the vinaigrette. Garnish with thyme sprigs.

SUMMER MENU

Sophie's Chopped Salad
(page 59)

Grilled Prawns with Habanero– Toasted Garlic Vinaigrette
(this page)

Spice-Crusted New York Strip Steaks with Mesa Grill Steak Sauce *(page 155)*

Southwestern Potato Salad
(page 195)

Tropical Fruit Salad with Pineapple-Tequila Sherbet
(page 248)

BLUE CORN CRAB CAKES WITH MANGO–GREEN ONION RELISH

SERVES 4

THE SECRET TO A GREAT-TASTING CRAB CAKE ISN'T MUCH OF A SECRET—YOU'VE GOT TO USE THE BEST-QUALITY CRAB YOU CAN GET. I HATE A CRAB CAKE THAT'S MORE ABOUT THE BREAD CRUMBS THAN THE CRAB. NUTTY BLUE CORN GOES REALLY WELL WITH THE SWEET CRAB, AND BLUE CORNMEAL IS AVAILABLE EVERYWHERE NOW, BUT FEEL FREE TO SUBSTITUTE YELLOW CORNMEAL. THE SERRANO CHILE GIVES A NICE DASH OF HEAT TO THE RELISH.

- 6 tablespoons olive oil
- 1 medium red onion, diced
- 2 cloves garlic, finely chopped
- 2 jalapeño chiles, diced
- ¼ cup sour cream or crème fraîche
- ¼ cup prepared horseradish, drained
- 3 tablespoons Dijon mustard
- 2 pounds lump crabmeat
- 3 tablespoons Wondra flour
  Kosher salt and freshly ground black pepper
- 2 cups blue cornmeal
  Mango–Green Onion Relish *(recipe follows)*
  Smoked Red Pepper Sauce *(page 230),* for garnish (optional)
  Chopped fresh chives, for garnish (optional)

1. Heat 2 tablespoons of the oil in a medium sauté pan over medium-high heat. Add the onion and cook until soft, 3 to 4 minutes. Add the garlic and jalapeños and cook for 1 minute. Remove from the heat and set aside to cool slightly.

2. In a large mixing bowl, whisk together the sour cream, horseradish, mustard, and onion mixture until combined. Pick over the crabmeat to remove any bits of shell. Add the crab and the flour to the bowl and gently fold to combine; season with salt and pepper. Refrigerate, covered, for 1 hour and up to 24 hours.

3. Divide the chilled crab mixture into 8 patties about ½ inch thick. Dredge each cake in the cornmeal and tap off any excess.

4. Heat the remaining 4 tablespoons olive oil in a large nonstick sauté pan over high heat and fry the cakes until crusty and lightly golden brown, about 3 minutes on each side.

5. Place 2 crab cakes on each of 4 dinner plates and top each cake with mango–green onion relish and red pepper sauce. Garnish with chives.

Mango–Green Onion Relish
MAKES ABOUT 1½ CUPS

- 2 ripe mangoes, peeled, pitted, and diced
- 2 green onions, white and green parts, thinly sliced
- 1 serrano chile, thinly sliced
- 2 tablespoons fresh lime juice
- 1 tablespoon honey
- 2 tablespoons olive oil
  Kosher salt and freshly ground black pepper

Combine the mangoes, green onions, serrano chile, lime juice, honey, and oil in a medium bowl and season with salt and pepper. Let the relish sit at room temperature for at least 15 minutes before serving to allow the flavors to meld. This can be made up to 24 hours in advance and refrigerated. Bring to room temperature before serving.

RED CHILE–HONEY GLAZED SALMON WITH BLACK BEAN SAUCE AND JALAPEÑO CREMA

SERVES 4

THIS DISH IS A MESA GRILL CLASSIC. THE RICH SALMON HOLDS ITS OWN BEAUTIFULLY AGAINST THE BIG SPICY AND SWEET FLAVOR OF THE GLAZE AS WELL AS THAT OF THE SAVORY BLACK BEAN SAUCE. CREMA SPIKED WITH JALAPEÑOS PROVIDES THE PERFECT COOL FINISHING TOUCH.

BLACK BEAN SAUCE

- 1½ cups dried black beans
- 1 small red onion, coarsely chopped
- 2 cloves garlic, peeled
- 2 chipotle chiles in adobo sauce, chopped
- 1 teaspoon ground cumin
- Kosher salt

RED CHILE–HONEY GLAZED SALMON

- ⅓ cup honey
- 1 tablespoon ancho chile powder
- 1 tablespoon Dijon mustard
- Kosher salt and freshly ground black pepper
- Four (8-ounce) skin-on salmon fillets
- 2 tablespoons canola oil
- Jalapeño Crema (recipe follows)
- Thinly sliced green onions, white and green parts, for garnish (optional)

1. Pick over the beans and discard any stones. Put in a bowl, cover with water, and let soak overnight.

2. Drain the beans and combine with the onion, garlic, chipotles, and cumin in a medium saucepan and add just enough cold water to cover by an inch; bring to a boil over high heat. Reduce the heat and simmer, adding more water if the beans appear dry, until the beans are tender, 1 to 1½ hours.

3. Transfer the mixture to a food processor or blender (in batches, if needed) with a slotted spoon, add 1 cup of the cooking liquid, and process until almost smooth; the sauce should be a little chunky. Season with salt. If the sauce is too thick, thin with more of the cooking liquid or with water. This can be made up to 4 hours in advance and refrigerated. Reheat before serving.

4. To make the glaze for the salmon, whisk together the honey, ancho powder, and mustard in a small bowl and season with salt and pepper.

5. Preheat a grill pan or large nonstick sauté pan over high heat. Brush the salmon with the oil on both sides and season with salt and pepper. Place the salmon in the pan, skin side down, and cook until golden brown and a crust has formed, 3 to 4 minutes. Brush the top of the salmon with some of the glaze, flip over the fillets, and continue cooking until a crust has formed and the salmon is cooked to medium, about 2 minutes more. The salmon will be pink in the center.

6. Spoon some of the black bean sauce onto 4 plates and drizzle with some of the jalapeño crema. Set the salmon in the center, glazed side up, brush with more of the glaze, and garnish with green onion.

Jalapeño Crema
MAKES ABOUT ½ CUP

- ½ cup crema, crème fraîche, or sour cream
- 1 large or 2 small jalapeño chiles, roasted, peeled, seeded *(see page 18)*, and chopped

  Kosher salt and freshly ground black pepper

Combine the crema and jalapeños in a food processor and process until smooth. (Alternatively, you can finely chop the jalapeños by hand and then stir them into the crema.) Season with salt and pepper and refrigerate for 30 minutes before serving. This can be made and refrigerated up to 1 day in advance.

BLUE CORN-CRUSTED RED SNAPPER WITH WARM TOMATO RELISH

SERVES 4

THIS WARM, FRESH TOMATO SAUCE IS MY TAKE ON THE TRADITIONAL MEXICAN RECIPE, SAUCE VERACRUZ. AS THE TOMATOES, OLIVE OIL, AND CAPERS ARE ALSO MEDITERRANEAN INGREDIENTS, THE ADDITION OF BASIL AND PICHOLINE OLIVES IS A NATURAL CHOICE AND GREAT PAIRING WITH RED SNAPPER IN A CRISP BLUE CORN COATING.

WARM TOMATO RELISH

- 2 tablespoons olive oil
- 1½ cups red cherry or grape tomatoes, halved
- 2 cloves garlic, finely chopped
- 2 serrano chiles, thinly sliced
- 1 cup V8 juice
- 2 teaspoons honey
- ½ cup picholine olives, pitted
- 2 tablespoons capers, drained
- 2 tablespoons chopped fresh basil
- 2 teaspoons chopped fresh oregano
  Kosher salt and freshly ground black pepper

BLUE CORN-CRUSTED SNAPPER

- 1 cup all-purpose flour
- 3 large eggs
- 2 cups coarsely crushed blue corn chips
  Kosher salt and freshly ground black pepper
- 4 (8-ounce) skinless red snapper fillets
- ¼ cup canola oil
  Smoked Red Pepper Sauce (*page 230*)

Fresh oregano leaves, for garnish (optional)

Sliced green onion, for garnish (optional)

1. To make the relish, heat the oil in a medium sauté pan over high heat. Add the tomatoes, garlic, and serranos and cook for 1 minute. Add the vegetable juice and honey, bring to a simmer, and cook for 2 to 3 minutes. Add the olives, capers, basil, and oregano and cook for 1 minute more. Season with salt and pepper to taste. This can be made up to 1 day ahead and refrigerated. Reheat before serving.

2. To prepare the snapper, put the flour in a shallow bowl. In another bowl, whisk the eggs with 2 tablespoons of water. Put the blue corn chips in a third bowl. Season the flour and eggs with salt and pepper.

3. Season each fillet on both sides with salt and pepper. Dredge one side of each fillet first in the flour, tapping off any excess flour, then in the egg, and finally in the crushed blue corn chips.

4. Heat the oil in a large nonstick sauté pan over medium-high heat. Place the fish in the pan, coated side down, and cook until a crust forms, 2 to 3 minutes. Flip the fish over and continue cooking for 4 to 5 minutes, until just cooked through.

5. Spoon some of the tomato relish in the bottom of 4 large shallow bowls. Place the fillets on top, garnish with more of the relish, and drizzle with red pepper sauce. Garnish with oregano leaves and green onion.

GRILLED RED SNAPPER WITH TOMATO–NEW MEXICO RED CHILE SAUCE

SERVES 4

I MODELED THIS SAUCE AFTER DISHES THAT I TRIED WHILE TRAVELING IN ALBUQUERQUE, NEW MEXICO. WHILE THEY MIGHT HAVE PAIRED IT WITH GRILLED OR BRAISED MEATS, I'VE CROSSED THE BORDER AND TEAMED THE TOMATO–NEW MEXICO RED CHILE SAUCE WITH WHAT IS PERHAPS MEXICO'S FAVORITE FISH, RED SNAPPER. ROUND THIS DISH OUT INTO A FULL-BLOWN DINNER-PARTY MAIN COURSE WITH CREAMY GREEN CHILE RICE *(page 201)* AND A DRIZZLE OF CILANTRO OIL *(page 222)*.

- 2 tablespoons olive oil
- 1 medium Spanish onion, coarsely chopped
- 4 cloves garlic, coarsely chopped
- 1 cup dry red wine
- 2 (14.5-ounce) cans plum tomatoes and their juice, pureed
- 3 New Mexico red chiles, stemmed and seeded
- 1 tablespoon honey

  Kosher salt and freshly ground black pepper
- 4 (8-ounce) skin-on red snapper fillets
- 2 tablespoons canola oil

  Fresh cilantro leaves, for garnish

1. Heat the olive oil in a medium saucepan over high heat. Add the onion and cook until soft, 3 to 4 minutes. Add the garlic and cook for 1 minute. Add the wine and cook until reduced by half, 3 to 4 minutes. Add the tomato puree, chiles, and 1 cup of water and cook, stirring occasionally, until the mixture is reduced by half and the chiles are soft, 15 to 20 minutes. Transfer to a food processor or blender and process until smooth.

2. Return the sauce to the pan and bring to a simmer; stir in the honey and salt and pepper. The sauce can be made up to 1 day ahead and refrigerated. Reheat before serving.

3. Preheat a grill to high or a grill pan over high heat.

4. Brush both sides of the snapper fillets with canola oil and season with salt and pepper. Grill for 3 to 4 minutes per side, until slightly charred and just cooked through.

5. Ladle some of the sauce onto 4 large plates and top each with a fillet; garnish with cilantro leaves.

GRILLED TUNA WITH RED TOMATILLO SAUCE
SERVES 4

DON'T EVEN TRY LOOKING FOR A RED TOMATILLO, BECAUSE THEY DON'T EXIST. CHILE POWDER MAKES THIS TART AND SPICY SAUCE RED. THIS DISH WAS MENTIONED IN ONE OF MESA GRILL'S FIRST REVIEWS AND I ACTUALLY HAD THE REVIEWER CALL ME TO ASK ME WHERE ONE COULD FIND RED TOMA-TILLOS! AFTER THAT, THERE WAS NO WAY I WOULD CHANGE ITS NAME. SERVE THIS WITH BLACK RICE *(page 201)*, WHICH ISN'T MADE WITH BLACK RICE (THOUGH THAT DOES EXIST).

- 8 large tomatillos, husked and scrubbed
- 1 medium red onion, coarsely chopped
- 3 cloves garlic, peeled
- 5 tablespoons canola oil

  Kosher salt and freshly ground black pepper
- ½ habanero chile, chopped
- 2 tablespoons New Mexico red chile powder
- ¼ cup red wine vinegar
- 2 tablespoons honey
- 3 tablespoons chopped fresh cilantro leaves
- 3 tablespoons chopped fresh mint leaves
- 4 (8-ounce) tuna steaks (each about 1 inch thick)

1. Preheat the oven to 400 degrees F.

2. Place the tomatillos, onion, and garlic on a baking sheet, toss with 3 tablespoons of the oil, and season with salt and pepper. Roast in the oven, stirring once, until the tomatillos are slightly charred and soft, 25 to 30 minutes.

3. Transfer the mixture to a food processor or blender and add the habanero, chile powder, vinegar, honey, cilantro, and mint. Season with salt and process until smooth. The sauce can be made up to 1 day ahead and refrigerated. Reheat before serving.

4. Preheat a grill to high or a grill pan over high heat.

5. Brush the tuna on both sides with the remaining 2 tablespoons oil and season with salt and pepper. Grill the tuna for 2 to 3 minutes, until golden brown and slightly charred. Turn over and continue cooking for 1 to 2 minutes for medium-rare. The tuna will be red in the center.

6. Ladle some of the sauce into the center of 4 large plates and top each with a tuna fillet.

GRILLED TUNA WITH APRICOT-MUSTARD-MINT GLAZE

SERVES 4

TUNA HAS GREAT TEXTURE, BUT IT OFTEN NEEDS SOME HELP IN THE FLAVOR DEPARTMENT. THIS GLAZE DELIVERS. THE DRIED APRICOTS GIVE A GREAT SWEET-TART FOUNDATION AND MUSTARD AND MINT ARE JUST THE RIGHT COMPLEMENTS. SERVE OVER GREEN CHILE–TOASTED PINE NUT COUSCOUS (*page 199*).

APRICOT-MUSTARD-MINT GLAZE

- 2 tablespoons canola oil
- 1 small Spanish onion, coarsely chopped
- 3 cloves garlic, chopped
- 2 Fresno chiles or jalapeño chiles, chopped
- 1 cup chopped dried apricots
- 2 cups dry white wine
- 3 tablespoons light brown sugar
- ¼ cup red wine vinegar
- 2 tablespoons Dijon mustard
- Kosher salt and freshly ground black pepper
- 3 tablespoons finely chopped fresh mint

GRILLED TUNA

- 1 tablespoon ground cumin
- 1 tablespoon ancho chile powder
- 1 tablespoon light brown sugar
- ¼ teaspoon ground cloves
- ¼ teaspoon ground allspice
- ¼ teaspoon ground cinnamon
- Four (8-ounce) tuna steaks (each about 1 inch thick)
- 2 tablespoons canola oil
- Kosher salt and freshly ground black pepper

Chopped fresh chives, for garnish (optional)

Red Chile Oil (*page 228*), for garnish (optional)

Cilantro Oil (*page 222*), for garnish (optional)

1. To make the glaze, heat the oil in a medium saucepan over high heat. Add the onion and cook until soft, 3 to 4 minutes. Add the garlic and chiles and cook for 1 minute. Add the apricots, wine, ¼ cup of water, and the sugar and bring to a boil. Reduce the heat to low and simmer, stirring occasionally, until the apricots are soft and most of the liquid has been absorbed, about 20 minutes. Remove from the heat and let cool slightly.

2. Transfer the apricot mixture to a blender, add the vinegar and mustard, and season with salt and pepper; blend until smooth. Add the mint, pulse a few times to incorporate, and transfer the glaze to a bowl. The glaze can be made up to 1 day ahead and refrigerated. Bring to room temperature before using.

3. Preheat a grill to high or a grill pan over high heat.

4. Whisk together the cumin, ancho powder, sugar, cloves, allspice, and cinnamon in a bowl.

5. Brush the tuna on both sides with the oil and season with salt and pepper. Rub one side of each steak with the spice rub. Place the tuna on the grill, rub side down, and cook until golden brown and a crust has formed, 2 to 3 minutes. Flip over, brush with some of the glaze, and continue cooking for 2 to 3 minutes for medium-rare. The tuna will be red in the center.

6. Remove from the grill and brush or drizzle with more of the glaze before serving. Garnish with chives, red chile oil, and cilantro oil.

SEARED TUNA TOSTADA WITH BLACK BEAN–MANGO SALSA

SERVES 4

THE TUNA TOSTADA HAS BEEN A FAN FAVORITE FOR YEARS. WE USE ONLY THE FRESHEST TUNA AND SERVE IT ALMOST RAW—JUST A QUICK SEAR FOR A NICE CRUST. THE SUBSTANTIAL BLACK BEAN–MANGO SALSA, WITH ITS SWEET AND SPICY NOTES, IS A CRUCIAL ELEMENT OF THE DISH, AS IS THE AVOCADO VINAIGRETTE. WHILE I FINISH THE TOSTADA WITH SMOKED RED PEPPER SAUCE AND CILANTRO OIL AT THE RESTAURANT, YOU CAN LEAVE THEM OUT WITHOUT SACRIFICING MUCH OF THE FINAL TASTE AND PRESENTATION. *See photograph on page 100.*

Peanut oil

4 (6-inch) flour tortillas

Kosher salt

2 tablespoons canola oil

4 (6-ounce) tuna steaks (each about ¾ inch thick)

Freshly ground black pepper

Black Bean–Mango Salsa *(page 217)*

Smoked Red Pepper Sauce *(page 230)*

Avocado Vinaigrette *(opposite)* (optional)

1 Hass avocado, peeled, pitted, and sliced

Fresh cilantro leaves, for garnish (optional)

1. Heat 1 inch of peanut oil in a medium high-sided sauté pan over medium heat until it reaches a temperature of 360 degrees F as measured on a deep-frying thermometer. Fry the tortillas, one at a time, until lightly golden brown, about 10 seconds per side. Remove to a plate lined with paper towels and immediately season with salt.

2. Heat the canola oil in a large nonstick sauté pan over high heat until almost smoking. Season each tuna steak with salt and pepper and cook for 2 minutes, or until golden brown. Turn the tuna over and continue cooking for 1 to 2 minutes for rare to medium-rare. The tuna will be red in the center.

3. Top each tortilla with some black bean–mango salsa and a piece of tuna. Drizzle with smoked red pepper sauce and avocado vinaigrette, top with sliced avocado, and garnish with cilantro leaves.

"BBQ" MARLIN WITH AVOCADO VINAIGRETTE

SERVES 4

THE "BBQ" IN THE TITLE IS PUT IN QUOTATION MARKS FOR A REASON: THERE'S NO BARBECUE SAUCE HERE, JUST ALL OF THOSE GREAT FLAVORS WE ASSOCIATE WITH BARBECUE MIXED UP IN A DRY RUB INSTEAD. IT MAKES FOR A TASTY PIECE OF FISH. WE SERVE MARLIN ON OCCASION AS A SPECIAL, BUT MEATY TUNA STEAKS WOULD BE THE PERFECT SUBSTITUTION. SERVE ON A BED OF SPICY YELLOW RICE WITH RED BEANS *(page 202)*, IF DESIRED.

2 tablespoons ancho chile powder

2 teaspoons light brown sugar

1 teaspoon ground fennel

1 teaspoon ground cumin

1 teaspoon kosher salt

½ teaspoon freshly ground black pepper

4 (8-ounce) skinless marlin fillets

2 tablespoons olive oil

Avocado Vinaigrette *(recipe follows)*

Cilantro Oil *(page 222)* (optional)

1. Combine the ancho powder, sugar, fennel, cumin, salt, and pepper in a small bowl. Season one side of each fillet with the spice mixture.

2. Heat the oil in a large sauté pan over high heat. Sear the fish, spice side down, until golden brown and a crust has formed, 2 to 3 minutes. Turn the fish over and cook for 3 to 4 minutes, until cooked through.

3. Serve drizzled with avocado vinaigrette and cilantro oil.

Avocado Vinaigrette
MAKES ABOUT 1 CUP

2 ripe Hass avocados, peeled, pitted, and coarsely chopped

¼ small red onion, coarsely chopped

¼ cup fresh lime juice (2 to 3 limes)

1 teaspoon kosher salt

¼ teaspoon freshly ground black pepper

½ cup canola oil

1 tablespoon honey

3 tablespoons chopped fresh cilantro

Place the avocados, onion, lime juice, salt, and pepper in a blender and process until smooth. With the motor running, add the oil until emulsified. Add the honey and cilantro and pulse until just combined, but there are still some flecks. This can be made up to 1 hour in advance and refrigerated.

STRIPED BASS WITH ROASTED POBLANO VINAIGRETTE AND YELLOW PEPPER GRITS

SERVES 4

THIS DISH WOULD BE JUST AS GOOD WITH RED SNAPPER OR HALIBUT— WHATEVER LOOKS FRESHEST AT THE MARKET. THE ROASTED POBLANO SAUCE HAS A GREAT CHILE FLAVOR—PEPPERY BUT NOT SPICY. AS FOR THE SUNNY GRITS, THEY'RE THE SOUTHWESTERN VERSION OF ITALIAN POLENTA.

3 large yellow bell peppers, roasted, peeled, and seeded *(see page 18)*

2 (16-ounce) cans posole (hominy), rinsed and drained

¼ cup olive oil

1 tablespoon unsalted butter

1 medium Spanish onion, finely chopped

3 cloves garlic, finely chopped

1 cup heavy cream

Kosher salt and freshly ground black pepper

1 cup grated white Cheddar cheese (4 ounces)

Four (8-ounce) skin-on striped bass fillets

Roasted Poblano Vinaigrette *(page 68)*

Chopped fresh cilantro, for garnish (optional)

1. Place 2 of the yellow peppers in a food processor and process until smooth. Add the posole and pulse until coarsely ground, 4 to 5 pulses (do not blend until smooth, or the posole will get gummy). Finely dice the remaining pepper and set aside.

2. Heat 2 tablespoons of the oil and the butter in a medium saucepan over medium heat. Add the onion and cook until soft, 3 to 4 minutes. Add the garlic and cook for 1 minute. Add the posole–yellow pepper puree and the cream and season with salt and pepper. Cook for about 10 minutes, or until thickened and the cream is absorbed; if the mixture appears too dry, add more heavy cream or water. Fold in the diced yellow pepper and Cheddar.

3. Heat a large nonstick sauté pan or grill pan over high heat until almost smoking. Brush the bass on both sides with the remaining 2 tablespoons olive oil and season with salt and pepper. Cook, skin side down, for 2 to 3 minutes, until golden brown. Turn over and continue cooking for 3 to 4 minutes, until just cooked through.

4. Place a heaping mound of yellow pepper grits on 4 dinner plates. Place a fillet on top of each mound, and drizzle with the roasted poblano vinaigrette. Garnish with cilantro.

GRILLED SWORDFISH WITH PINEAPPLE-MUSTARD GLAZE AND CILANTRO-MINT CHIMICHURRI

SERVES 4

CHIMICHURRI IS LIKE ARGENTINEAN KETCHUP IN THAT IT'S THE CONDIMENT USED ON EVERYTHING. THIS HERBACEOUS SAUCE IS A CLASSIC WITH STEAKS, PERFECT OVER CHICKEN, AND, IN THIS CASE, AMAZING OVER GRILLED SWORD-FISH. THE STRONG CHIMICHURRI CALLS FOR A MEATY FISH THAT WON'T BE OVERPOWERED BY IT, AND SWORDFISH REALLY FITS THE BILL.

- 3 cups fresh pineapple juice
- 1 cup white wine vinegar
- 2 tablespoons soy sauce
- 2 tablespoons finely chopped fresh ginger
- ¼ cup packed light brown sugar
- 2 tablespoons Dijon mustard
- 2 tablespoons fresh lime juice
- Kosher salt and freshly ground black pepper
- 4 (8-ounce) swordfish steaks (each about 1 inch thick)
- 2 tablespoons canola oil
- Cilantro-Mint Chimichurri (recipe follows)
- Fresh mint leaves, for garnish (optional)

1. Combine the pineapple juice, vinegar, soy sauce, ginger, and brown sugar in a medium saucepan and bring to a boil over high heat. Reduce the heat to medium and simmer, stirring occasionally, until the volume is reduced by half, 20 to 25 minutes.

2. Remove from the heat and whisk in the mustard and lime juice and season with salt and pepper. Let cool to room temperature. The glaze can be made up to 1 day in advance and refrigerated. Bring back to room temperature before using.

3. Preheat a grill to high or a grill pan over high heat.

4. Brush the fish with the oil and season with salt and pepper on both sides. Grill on one side until lightly golden brown, 2 to 3 minutes; then brush with some of the mustard glaze and flip over. Brush with more of the glaze, and continue grilling for 3 to 4 minutes, for medium-well. The fish will be slightly pink in the center.

5. Remove the swordfish from the grill, brush with more of the glaze, and top with the chimichurri. Garnish with fresh mint leaves.

Cilantro-Mint Chimichurri
MAKES ABOUT 1 CUP

- ½ cup finely chopped fresh cilantro
- ¼ cup finely chopped fresh mint
- 3 cloves garlic, finely chopped
- 3 tablespoons red wine vinegar
- ¼ cup olive oil
- Kosher salt and freshly ground black pepper

Combine the cilantro, mint, garlic, vinegar, and oil in a medium bowl and season with salt and pepper.

ARCTIC CHAR AND MUSSELS IN GREEN GARLIC BROTH

SERVES 4

WE RUN THIS AS A SPECIAL FROM TIME TO TIME AT MESA GRILL AND IT IS ANOTHER DISH THAT SELLS OUT IN A FEW HOURS. ARCTIC CHAR IS A VARIETY OF FISH BEST DESCRIBED AS A MIX BETWEEN SALMON AND TROUT. SINCE IT'S NOT ALWAYS READILY AVAILABLE, YOU CAN SUBSTITUTE SALMON IF YOU CAN'T FIND IT. AND ACTUALLY, THE GARLIC AND CILANTRO BROTH IS SO INTENSELY FLAVORFUL THAT THIS DISH IS PERFECT WITH JUST MUSSELS, TOO.

- 4 plum tomatoes, halved lengthwise
- 6 tablespoons olive oil

  Kosher salt and freshly ground black pepper
- 6 cloves garlic, coarsely chopped
- 1 cup dry white wine
- 2 cups fish stock, bottled clam juice, or low-sodium vegetable broth
- ½ cup chopped fresh cilantro, plus whole leaves for garnish
- 32 cultivated mussels, scrubbed
- 2 teaspoons honey
- ½ cup canned posole (hominy), rinsed and drained
- 4 (8-ounce) skin-on Arctic char fillets

1. Preheat a grill to high or a grill pan over high heat.

2. Brush the tomatoes with 2 tablespoons of the oil and season with salt and pepper. Grill until slightly charred and soft, 3 to 4 minutes per side. Coarsely chop and set aside.

3. Heat 2 tablespoons of the oil in a large saucepan over medium heat. Add the garlic and cook until soft, 2 to 3 minutes. Raise the heat to high, add the wine, and boil until almost completely reduced, 3 to 4 minutes. Add the chopped tomatoes and fish stock and simmer for 15 minutes over medium heat.

4. Transfer the mixture to a food processor, add the chopped cilantro, season lightly with salt and pepper, and process until smooth.

5. Return the tomato mixture to the saucepan and bring to a boil over high heat. Add the mussels and stir to combine with the broth. Cover and cook until the mussels have opened, 4 to 5 minutes. Remove the mussels to a bowl with a slotted spoon, discarding any unopened ones, and cover to keep warm.

6. Return the tomato mixture to a boil over high heat and cook until slightly reduced, 5 to 7 minutes. Add the honey and posole and season with salt and pepper. Cook for 2 to 3 minutes, to warm through the posole.

7. Once the mussels have been cooked and while the tomato mixture has been reducing, heat the remaining 2 tablespoons olive oil in a large sauté pan over high heat until almost smoking. Season the char on both sides with salt and pepper and sear, skin side down, until golden brown, 2 to 3 minutes. Turn over and continue cooking for 3 to 4 minutes, until just cooked through.

8. Divide the tomato mixture among 4 large shallow bowls. Top with the char and mussels and garnish with cilantro leaves.

CRISPY WHOLE FISH WITH FIVE PEPPER–GINGER SAUCE

SERVES 4

THIS DISH IS AMBITIOUS BUT INCREDIBLY REWARDING. IT'S WORTH THE ENERGY ON PRESENTATION VALUE ALONE: BRINGING WHOLE FISH TO THE TABLE NEVER FAILS TO IMPRESS. AND AS FOR FLAVOR, I HAVE TO SAY THIS SAUCE IS TOTALLY AMAZING. THE FIVE PEPPERS ARE A HOT AND SWEET MIX, AND WHEN YOU COMBINE THEM WITH GINGER AND TANGY VINEGAR, YOU'VE GOT A COMPLETELY ADDICTIVE SAUCE. REALLY—YOU WON'T BE ABLE TO STOP EATING IT.

FIVE PEPPER–GINGER SAUCE

3 cups red wine vinegar

1 cup distilled white vinegar

2½ cups sugar

½ habanero chile

3 tablespoons chopped fresh ginger

½ red bell pepper, finely diced

½ yellow bell pepper, finely diced

½ poblano chile, finely diced

1 serrano chile, finely diced

3 tablespoons finely chopped fresh mint

Kosher salt

CRISPY WHOLE FISH

2 cups rice flour

Kosher salt and freshly ground black pepper

6 cups peanut oil or canola oil

4 (1-pound) whole striped bass, scaled, gutted, rinsed, and patted dry

2 cups blue or yellow cornmeal

Chopped fresh cilantro, for garnish

1. Combine the red and white vinegars, sugar, habanero, and ginger in a medium saucepan and cook, stirring occasionally, over high heat until reduced to 1½ cups, 15 to 20 minutes. If the sauce becomes too thick, thin with a little bit of water.

2. Strain the sauce through a fine-mesh strainer into a bowl, stir in the red and yellow peppers, the poblano, serrano, and mint, and season with salt.

3. Mix together the rice flour and 1 cup of cold water in a medium baking dish until smooth. The mixture should have the consistency of whole milk; add more water if it is too thick. Season with salt and pepper. Let rest at room temperature for 15 minutes.

4. Heat the oil in a large pot until it reaches 365 degrees F as measured on a deep-frying thermometer.

5. Make 3 slits on each side of each fish with a knife just until you hit the bone. Season the outside and the cavity of each fish with salt and pepper. Dip each fish into the rice batter, shake off the excess, and dredge on both sides in the cornmeal. Fry the fish in batches of 2, turning once, until golden brown and just cooked through, 10 to 12 minutes. Drain on a plate lined with paper towels.

6. Place the fish on 4 serving plates and drizzle with the five pepper–ginger sauce. Garnish with chopped cilantro.

Poultry cries out for big flavors, spicy rubs, savory sauces, and sweet glazes. There is no reason why a piece of grilled chicken has to be boring. I have heard people say that chicken is one of the last things that they'd order when out to dinner for that very reason, and I have to say that would be a big mistake at Mesa Grill. We do everything we can to make poultry tasty, succulent, and anything but run of the mill.

Poultry has so many angles to play up. There're elegant Cornish game hens to grace your party table, little chicken taquitos sure to bring a smile to your guests' faces, as well as a pan-roasted chicken perfect for any night of the week. And there couldn't be a poultry chapter without the big one—the turkey. I have a recipe here for an outrageously good—yes, it can be juicy and flavorful—Thanksgiving turkey that will ensure that your house is cemented in place as Thanksgiving's home for years to come.

CUMIN-CRUSTED CHICKEN with Cotija and Mango-Garlic Sauce

GRILLED CHICKEN with Fresno Chile–Plum Sauce

PAN-ROASTED CHICKEN with Blackberry-Ancho Sauce

SIXTEEN-SPICE CHICKEN with Cilantro–Pumpkin Seed Sauce

FRY BREAD TAQUITOS with Jerk Chicken, Red Cabbage–Jicama Slaw, and Mango-Habanero Hot Sauce

TAMARIND–CRACKED BLACK PEPPER GLAZED CHICKEN

CORNISH GAME HENS with Wild Rice–Goat Cheese Stuffing

PAN-SEARED DUCK BREAST with Red Chile–Pear Sauce and Asian Pear Relish

ANCHO-MAPLE GLAZED ROAST TURKEY with Roasted Garlic–Cilantro Gravy and Cranberry-Mango Relish

CUMIN-CRUSTED CHICKEN WITH COTIJA AND MANGO-GARLIC SAUCE

SERVES 4

I LOVE THE TOASTED, SMOKY FLAVOR OF CUMIN. (YOU DO HAVE TO BE SURE THAT YOU KEEP AN EVEN HAND WITH IT, HOWEVER, AS TOO MUCH CAN QUICKLY OVERPOWER A DISH.) HERE TOASTED CUMIN SEEDS ADD NOT JUST FLAVOR BUT TEXTURE, COMBINING WITH PARMESAN-LIKE COTIJA CHEESE TO MAKE A GREAT CRUST FOR CHICKEN.

5 tablespoons cumin seeds, toasted *(see page 19)*

1 cup fresh lemon juice (3 to 4 lemons)

½ cup plus 3 tablespoons olive oil

2 tablespoons honey

Freshly ground black pepper

4 (8-ounce) bone-in, skin-on chicken breast halves

⅓ cup grated cotija cheese

Kosher salt

Mango-Garlic Sauce *(recipe follows)*

1. Whisk together 2 tablespoons of the cumin seeds, the lemon juice, the ½ cup olive oil, the honey, and pepper in a medium baking dish. Add the chicken and turn to coat. Cover, and marinate for at least 1 hour and up to 4 hours in the refrigerator.

2. Preheat the oven to 400 degrees F.

3. Grind the remaining 3 tablespoons cumin seeds in a coffee or spice grinder.

4. Remove the chicken from the marinade and wipe off any excess. Combine the ground cumin and cotija in a small bowl and season with salt and pepper. Season the chicken on the skin side with the ground cumin mixture.

5. Heat the 3 tablespoons olive oil in a large ovenproof sauté pan over medium-high heat. Place the chicken, skin side down, in the pan and cook until golden brown, 3 to 4 minutes. Carefully drain off the excess oil, turn over the chicken breasts, and place the pan in the oven. Bake for 8 to 10 minutes, until just cooked through.

6. Ladle some of the mango-garlic sauce onto 4 large plates and top with a breast.

Mango-Garlic Sauce
MAKES 2 CUPS

1 head roasted garlic, peeled
(see page 19)

6 cups Enriched Chicken Stock *(page 38)* or low-sodium chicken broth

3 tablespoons black peppercorns

3 cups red wine vinegar

1 cup white wine vinegar

2 cups sugar

2 large ripe mangoes, peeled and pitted
Kosher salt and freshly ground black pepper

1. Puree the roasted garlic in a food processor and transfer to a medium saucepan. Add the stock and peppercorns and bring to a boil, stirring occasionally, over high heat. Cook until reduced by half, 20 to 25 minutes.

2. While the stock is reducing, combine the red and white wine vinegars and sugar in a medium saucepan over high heat and cook, stirring occasionally, until the sugar has melted and the mixture has reduced to 1 cup, 20 to 25 minutes.

3. Puree the mangoes in a food processor. Add to the vinegar mixture and cook for 2 minutes.

4. Whisk the stock mixture into the mango mixture and cook until reduced to a sauce consistency, 25 to 30 minutes. Strain into a bowl and season with salt and pepper. This can be made up to 1 day in advance and refrigerated. Reheat before serving.

GRILLED CHICKEN WITH FRESNO CHILE–PLUM SAUCE

SERVES 4

GRILLED CHICKEN—EASY, GOOD FOR YOU—IT'S NO SURPRISE IT'S SUCH A STAPLE IN OUR DIETS. THIS SAUCE SAVES IT FROM MONOTONY WITH MY FAVORITE COMBINATION OF SPICY AND SWEET ELEMENTS. YOU COULD USE PEACHES OR NECTARINES IN PLACE OF THE PLUMS, BUT I THINK THAT PLUMS HAVE A SOMEWHAT RICHER FLAVOR. THIS DISH IS GREAT WITH MESA GRILL SPINACH *(page 210)* AND SOUTHWESTERN POTATO SALAD *(page 195)*.

- 6 cups Enriched Chicken Stock *(page 38)* or low-sodium chicken broth
- 4 Fresno chiles, chopped
- 1 cup rice wine vinegar
- 1 cup distilled white vinegar
- 1½ cups granulated sugar
- 4 ripe plums, pitted and chopped
  Kosher salt
- 1 teaspoon freshly ground black pepper
- 2 teaspoons light brown sugar
- 4 (8-ounce) bone-in, skin-on chicken breast halves
- 2 tablespoons canola oil

1. Combine the chicken stock and Fresno chiles in a large saucepan, bring to a boil over high heat, and cook until reduced by half, 20 to 25 minutes. Strain the mixture into a medium bowl.

2. While the stock is reducing, combine the vinegars, granulated sugar, and plums in a medium saucepan and cook over medium-high heat until the mixture is thickened and the plums are very soft, 15 to 20 minutes. Puree the mixture in a food processor until smooth and strain into a clean medium saucepan.

3. Add the reduced stock to the plum mixture and cook over medium-high heat, stirring occasionally, until reduced to a sauce consistency, 12 to 15 minutes; season with salt.

4. Preheat a grill to high or a grill pan over medium heat.

5. Combine 2 teaspoons salt, the pepper, and brown sugar in a small bowl. Brush the chicken with the oil and season with the spice mixture on both sides.

6. Grill the chicken, skin side down, until golden brown and slightly charred, 4 to 5 minutes. Turn the chicken over and continue cooking until just cooked through, 6 to 7 minutes more.

7. Ladle some of the sauce onto each of 4 plates, and top with a breast.

PAN-ROASTED CHICKEN WITH BLACKBERRY-ANCHO SAUCE

SERVES 4

THIS DEEP, FLAVORFUL, JAMMY SAUCE IS PERFECT WITH CHICKEN, BUT IT'S TOO GOOD TO LEAVE JUST FOR THAT ALONE. IT IS ALSO A GREAT SAUCE FOR OTHER ROASTED MEATS, SUCH AS LAMB AND VENISON. SERVE THIS DISH WITH GREEN ONION SMASHED POTATOES *(see page 191)*.

- 3 ancho chiles, soaked *(see page 18)*
- 1 clove garlic, smashed
- 2 tablespoons chopped fresh cilantro
  Kosher salt
- 1 cup ruby port
- 1 cup red wine
- 1 cup thawed cranberry juice concentrate
- ½ cup packed dark brown sugar
- 6 cups Enriched Chicken Stock *(page 38)* or low-sodium chicken broth
- 1 tablespoon black peppercorns
- 1 cup fresh or frozen blackberries
- 2 tablespoons cold unsalted butter
  Freshly ground black pepper
- 1 cup all-purpose flour
- 2 tablespoons cascabel chile powder
- 4 (8-ounce) bone-in, skin-on chicken breast halves
- ¼ cup olive oil

1. Drain the anchos well, reserving the soaking liquid. Stem and seed the anchos, place in a food processor with the garlic, cilantro, 1 teaspoon salt, and ¼ cup of the soaking liquid, and process until smooth; set the ancho puree aside for the moment.

2. Preheat the oven to 400 degrees F.

3. Bring the port and red wine to a boil in a medium saucepan over high heat. Cook until reduced to about ¼ cup, about 10 minutes. Add the ancho puree, cranberry juice concentrate, brown sugar, stock, and peppercorns and boil, stirring occasionally, until reduced by half, 20 to 25 minutes.

4. Strain the mixture into a clean saucepan, return to the heat, and cook until reduced by half again. Fold in the blackberries and cook until softened, 3 to 4 minutes. Stir in the butter and season with salt and pepper. Keep warm.

5. In a medium bowl, combine the flour and cascabel powder. Season the chicken breasts with salt and pepper, dredge in the flour, and tap off any excess.

6. Heat the oil in a large ovenproof sauté pan over high heat until almost smoking. Place the chicken in the pan, skin side down, and cook until golden brown, 3 to 4 minutes. Carefully drain off the excess oil, turn over the chicken breasts, and place the pan in the oven. Roast for 8 to 10 minutes, until just cooked through. Remove from the oven and let rest for 5 minutes before serving with the blackberry-ancho sauce.

SIXTEEN-SPICE CHICKEN WITH CILANTRO–PUMPKIN SEED SAUCE

SERVES 4

THIS HAS BECOME THE MESA GRILL POULTRY SPICE RUB. IT SOUNDS—AND LOOKS—LIKE A LOT OF INGREDIENTS, BUT IT TAKES SECONDS TO MIX AND WILL KEEP FOR MONTHS. THIS RUB CREATES ONE DISTINCT MESA GRILL FLAVOR AND WORKS EQUALLY WELL ON MEATY FISH SUCH AS FRESH TUNA AND SWORDFISH.

- 2 cups packed fresh cilantro leaves, plus extra for garnish
- ½ cup pumpkin seeds, toasted (*see page 47*), plus extra for garnish
- 1 small shallot, coarsely chopped
- 2 cloves garlic, chopped
- ¼ cup red wine vinegar
- ½ cup spinach leaves, coarsely chopped
- ½ cup extra-virgin olive oil
- 1 tablespoon honey

    Kosher salt and freshly ground black pepper

    Four 8-ounce bone-in, skin-on chicken breast halves
- ½ cup Sixteen-Spice Rub (*recipe follows*)
- 2 tablespoons olive oil

    Smoked Red Pepper Sauce (*page 230*) (optional)

1. Combine the cilantro, pumpkin seeds, shallot, garlic, vinegar, spinach, and ½ cup of water in a food processor or blender and process until smooth. With the motor running, slowly add the ½ cup extra-virgin olive oil and blend until emulsified. Add the honey and salt and pepper to taste. The mixture should be a slightly loose sauce consistency; if it is too thick to pour, begin adding water 1 tablespoon at a time. This can be made up to 1 day ahead and refrigerated. Bring to room temperature before serving.

2. Preheat the oven to 400 degrees F.

3. Rub each breast with 2 tablespoons of the spice mixture. Heat the 2 tablespoons olive oil in a large ovenproof sauté pan over medium-high heat until almost smoking. Sauté the breasts, skin side down, until golden brown, 2 to 3 minutes. Turn the breasts over and transfer the pan to the oven. Bake the chicken until cooked through, 8 to 10 minutes. Remove from the oven and let rest for 5 minutes before serving topped with the cilantro–pumpkin seed sauce, red pepper sauce, pumpkin seeds, and cilantro.

Sixteen-Spice Rub
MAKES ABOUT 2 CUPS

- 3 tablespoons ground cinnamon
- 3 tablespoons ancho chile powder
- 3 tablespoons pasilla chile powder
- 3 tablespoons ground cumin
- 3 tablespoons ground coriander
- 3 tablespoons ground ginger
- 3 tablespoons light brown sugar
- 2 tablespoons garlic powder
- 2 tablespoons onion powder
- 2 tablespoons kosher salt
- 2 tablespoons coarsely ground black pepper
- 1 tablespoon ground cloves
- 1 tablespoon ground fennel seeds
- 1 tablespoon ground allspice
- 1 teaspoon chile de árbol
- 1 teaspoon cayenne pepper

Combine all of the ingredients. Store in an airtight container for up to 6 months.

FRY BREAD TAQUITOS WITH JERK CHICKEN, RED CABBAGE–JICAMA SLAW, AND MANGO-HABANERO HOT SAUCE

SERVES 8

THIS DISH INTRODUCES THE CARIBBEAN TO THE SOUTHWESTERN. THE JERK CHICKEN AND ACCOMPANIMENTS REALLY TAKE TO THE DELICIOUS FRY BREAD TAQUITOS, A SOUTHWESTERN STAPLE. IT'S NOT A TRADITIONAL DISH BY ANY MEANS, BUT I THINK YOU'LL AGREE THAT IT JUST WORKS. *See photograph on page 135.*

FRY BREAD TAQUITOS

1½ cups all-purpose flour

1½ teaspoons baking powder

1 tablespoon dry milk powder

Kosher salt

¼ cup cold vegetable shortening or lard

2 cups canola oil

JERK-RUBBED CHICKEN BREASTS

2 tablespoons ground coriander

2 tablespoons ground ginger

2 tablespoons light brown sugar

1 tablespoon onion powder

1 tablespoon garlic powder

1 tablespoon kosher salt

1 tablespoon habanero chile powder

2 teaspoons coarsely ground black pepper

2 teaspoons dried thyme

1 teaspoon ground cinnamon

1 teaspoon ground allspice

1 teaspoon ground cloves

4 (8-ounce) boneless, skinless chicken breast halves

2 tablespoons canola oil

Red Cabbage–Jicama Slaw *(recipe follows)*

Mango-Habanero Hot Sauce *(page 224)*

1. To make the taquitos, combine the flour, baking powder, milk powder, and 1 teaspoon salt in a large bowl. Cut in the shortening with a pastry blender or 2 knives until the mixture is crumbly, add ¾ cup of cold water, and mix until the dough comes together. Place on a lightly floured surface and knead lightly until smooth. Cover with a kitchen towel and let sit at room temperature for 1 hour.

2. Heat the oil in a large high-sided sauté pan until it reaches 360 degrees F as measured on a deep-frying thermometer.

3. Divide the dough into 8 pieces and roll out each piece into a 4-inch circle about 1/8 inch thick. Fry the bread in batches in the oil until golden brown on both sides, 2 to 3 minutes. Remove to a sheet pan lined with paper towels and season with salt. The fry bread can be made up to 8 hours in advance and stored in an airtight container. Warm in a low oven before serving.

4. To make the jerk rub, combine the coriander, ginger, sugar, onion powder, garlic powder, salt, habanero powder, black pepper, thyme, cinnamon, allspice, and cloves in a small bowl. The rub will keep in an airtight container for up to 6 months.

5. Rub the top of each breast with 1 heaping tablespoon of the jerk rub.

6. Heat the oil in a large sauté pan over medium-high heat. Place the chicken in the pan, rub side down, and cook until golden brown and a crust has formed, about 3 minutes. Turn the breasts over and continue cooking until just cooked through, about 5 minutes.

7. Let the chicken rest for 5 minutes before slicing each breast on the bias into 1/4-inch-thick slices. Serve the chicken on top of the warm tacquitos, topped with red cabbage–jicama slaw and drizzled with mango-habanero hot sauce.

Red Cabbage–Jicama Slaw
MAKES ABOUT 3 CUPS

- 1/2 cup fresh lime juice (4 to 5 limes)
- 1 tablespoon ancho chile powder
- 1/2 teaspoon kosher salt
- 1/4 teaspoon freshly ground black pepper
- 2 teaspoons honey
- 1/4 cup canola oil
- 1/4 small head red cabbage, thinly shredded
- 1 small jicama, peeled and thinly shredded
- 1/4 cup coarsely chopped fresh cilantro

1. Whisk together the lime juice, ancho powder, salt, pepper, honey, and oil in a large bowl.

2. Add the cabbage, jicama, and cilantro and toss well to combine. Let sit at room temperature for at least 15 minutes and up to 4 hours in the refrigerator before serving.

TAMARIND–CRACKED BLACK PEPPER GLAZED CHICKEN

SERVES 4

TAMARIND HAS A UNIQUE SWEET-TART FLAVOR THAT I FIND DELICIOUS. YOU CAN FIND TAMARIND PASTE ONLINE AT WWW.MEXGROCER.COM AND AT SPECIALTY FOOD MARKETS ACROSS THE COUNTRY. THE CRACKED BLACK PEPPER IS JUST AS IMPORTANT AS THE TAMARIND, HOWEVER, AS ITS BITE REALLY PIERCES THE SWEETNESS OF THE GLAZE. TRY SERVING THIS DISH WITH AVOCADO-TOMATILLO RELISH (*page 216*) FOR A CREAMY, REFRESHING COUNTERPART.

- 3 tablespoons canola oil
- 1 small red onion, coarsely chopped
- 2 tablespoons coarsely chopped fresh ginger
- 1 quart orange juice (not from concentrate)
- 3 tablespoons tamarind paste
- 1 tablespoon honey
  Kosher salt
- 1 teaspoon cracked black pepper
- 4 (8-ounce) bone-in, skin-on chicken breast halves
  Freshly ground black pepper

1. Heat 1 tablespoon of the oil in a medium saucepan over high heat. Add the onion and ginger and cook until the onion is soft, 3 to 4 minutes. Add the orange juice and cook, stirring occasionally, until reduced to 1 cup, 20 to 25 minutes.

2. Whisk in the tamarind paste, honey, and 1 teaspoon salt and cook until the tamarind paste has dissolved, 3 to 4 minutes. Strain into a bowl and stir in the coarsely ground black pepper. Let cool to room temperature. This can be made up to 1 day in advance and refrigerated. Heat through to return the sauce to its original consistency before serving.

3. Preheat the oven to 425 degrees F.

4. Divide the glaze between 2 small bowls, one to be used for brushing the chicken as it cooks, the other reserved for serving. Heat the remaining 2 tablespoons oil in a large ovenproof sauté pan over high heat. Season the chicken on both sides with salt and freshly ground black pepper. Place in the pan, skin side down, and cook until golden brown, 3 to 4 minutes.

5. Turn over the chicken and brush with some of the glaze. Carefully drain off the excess oil, transfer the pan to the oven, and bake, brushing with some of the glaze every few minutes, until the chicken is just cooked through, 8 to 10 minutes. Remove from the oven, drizzle with the remaining glaze, and let rest for 5 minutes before serving.

CORNISH GAME HENS WITH WILD RICE–GOAT CHEESE STUFFING
SERVES 4

THIS RECIPE COULD MAKE A GREAT ENTREE FOR A SOUTHWESTERN-STYLE THANKSGIVING. THE INDIVIDUAL HENS ARE ELEGANT AS WELL AS DELICIOUSLY STUFFED; SERVE THEM WITH MESA GRILL SPINACH *(page 210)* AND RED CHILE GRAVY *(page 227)*, AND YOUR FRIENDS AND FAMILY MAY NEVER LET YOU MAKE TURKEY AGAIN! *See photograph on page 132.*

1 cup wild rice

Kosher salt

6 ounces Spanish chorizo sausage, finely diced

6 tablespoons unsalted butter, at room temperature

2 tablespoons olive oil

1 medium Spanish onion, finely diced

3 cloves garlic, finely chopped

2 teaspoons finely chopped fresh thyme

1½ cups Enriched Chicken Stock *(page 38)* or low-sodium chicken broth

6 ounces fresh goat cheese, cut into small pieces

¼ cup finely chopped fresh cilantro or flat-leaf parsley

¼ to ½ cup plain bread crumbs

Freshly ground black pepper

Four 1- to 1½-pound Cornish game hens

Coarsely ground black pepper

Chopped fresh chives, for garnish (optional)

1. Put the wild rice in a medium saucepan and add 5 cups cold water and 1 tablespoon salt. Bring to a boil over high heat and cook until the grains have opened (the rice should be very soft to the bite), 1 to 1½ hours. Drain the rice well and place in a large bowl.

2. Place a small sauté pan over medium heat, add the chorizo, and cook until golden brown and the fat has rendered, 8 to 10 minutes. Remove with a slotted spoon to a plate lined with paper towels.

3. Heat 2 tablespoons of the butter and the oil in a large sauté pan over high heat. Add the onion and cook until soft, 3 to 4 minutes. Add the garlic and thyme and cook for 1 minute. Add the stock and the chorizo and bring to a simmer. Pour the mixture over the rice and stir to combine. Fold in the goat cheese and cilantro and ¼ cup bread crumbs. The mixture should be wet, but if it appears to have too much liquid, add up to another ¼ cup bread crumbs, 1 tablespoon at a time, until the mixture just comes together but is still moist. Season with salt and freshly ground black pepper and let cool to room temperature. The stuffing can be made up to 1 day ahead and refrigerated. Bring to room temperature before filling the hens.

4. Preheat the oven to 400 degrees F.

5. Rinse the hens and pat dry with paper towels. Rub each hen with 1 tablespoon of the remaining 4 tablespoons butter and season generously with salt and coarsely ground black pepper, including the cavity. Loosely fill the cavity of each hen with about ½ cup of the wild rice stuffing and tie the legs together with butcher's twine.

6. Place the hens in a roasting pan, breast side up, and roast until the skin is golden brown and the thickest part of the breast meat registers 155 degrees F on an instant-read thermometer, 45 to 55 minutes.

7. Remove from the oven and let rest for 10 minutes before serving. Remove the twine before transferring the hens to plates. Garnish with the chives.

PAN-SEARED DUCK BREAST WITH RED CHILE–PEAR SAUCE AND ASIAN PEAR RELISH

SERVES 4

DUCK IS ONE OF THOSE THINGS THAT PEOPLE LOVE TO ORDER IN MY RESTAURANTS BUT TELL ME THEY SELDOM PREPARE AT HOME BECAUSE THEY THINK IT'S DIFFICULT TO COOK. HONESTLY, IT IS ACTUALLY JUST AS EASY TO COOK AS CHICKEN AND, UNLIKE CHICKEN, IS BEST SERVED AT MEDIUM DONENESS. THE NEW MEXICO RED CHILES, CINNAMON, AND STAR ANISE HAVE A GREAT AFFINITY FOR ONE ANOTHER AND TOGETHER CREATE A SPICY AND FRUITY SAUCE THAT PARTNERS SUPERBLY WITH THE RICH FLAVOR OF THE DUCK.

1 (2-pound) Muscovy duck breast

Kosher salt and freshly ground black pepper

2 tablespoons olive oil

1 medium red onion, finely diced

1 cup dry red wine

6 cups Enriched Chicken Stock *(page 38)* or low-sodium chicken broth

3 New Mexico red chiles

2 cinnamon sticks

2 star anise

2 ripe pears, cored and diced (not peeled)

2 tablespoons cold unsalted butter

Asian Pear Relish *(recipe follows)*

1. Preheat the oven to 400 degrees F.

2. Heat a medium ovenproof sauté pan over medium heat. Season the duck with salt and pepper to taste and place the duck, skin side down, in the pan. Cook until the skin is crisp and golden brown, 8 to 10 minutes. Drain the rendered fat and turn the breast over. Place the pan in the oven and roast for 12 to 15 minutes for medium doneness. The duck will be pink in the center.

3. While the duck is roasting, heat the oil in a medium saucepan over high heat. Add the onion and cook, stirring occasionally, until soft, 3 to 4 minutes. Add the wine and cook until completely reduced, 3 to 4 minutes. Add the stock, chiles, cinnamon, star anise, and pears and cook, stirring occasionally, until reduced by half, 25 to 30 minutes.

4. Strain the sauce into a clean medium saucepan and cook, stirring occasionally, over high heat until a sauce consistency, 15 to 20 minutes. Remove the pan from the heat, stir in the cold butter, and season with salt and pepper.

5. Transfer the duck to a cutting board to rest for 5 minutes. Slice thin on the bias and serve with some of the sauce and the Asian pear relish.

Asian Pear Relish
MAKES ABOUT I CUP

2 tablespoons unsalted butter

3 ripe Asian pears, peeled, cored, and diced

¼ teaspoon chile de árbol powder

½ teaspoon kosher salt

½ cup bourbon

3 tablespoons light brown sugar

3 tablespoons chopped fresh cilantro

1. Heat the butter in a large sauté pan over high heat. Add the pears, chile de árbol powder, and salt and cook until the pears are lightly golden brown on both sides.

2. Remove the pan from the heat and add the bourbon and brown sugar. Return the pan to the heat and cook until the bourbon has reduced and the pears are slightly glazed, 3 to 4 minutes. Stir in the cilantro. This can be made up to 1 day ahead and refrigerated. Reheat slightly before serving.

ANCHO-MAPLE GLAZED ROAST TURKEY WITH ROASTED GARLIC– CILANTRO GRAVY AND CRANBERRY- MANGO RELISH

SERVES 8

THIS IS HOW MESA GRILL DOES THANKS- GIVING. NOT ONLY IS THIS TURKEY MOIST AND INCREDIBLY FLAVORFUL (NOT SOMETHING MOST TURKEYS CAN LIVE UP TO), IT IS ALSO BEAUTIFUL TO LOOK AT. SLIPPING SAGE LEAVES UNDER THE TURKEY'S SKIN MAKES FOR AN INCREDIBLY DRAMATIC PRESENTATION. AS FOR THE GRAVY AND THE CRAN- BERRY RELISH, YOU DIDN'T THINK THIS BIRD COULD BE PAIRED WITH STANDARD GRAVY AND CRANBERRIES FROM A CAN, DID YOU? ROASTED GARLIC WAKES UP THE GRAVY—AND THE SWEET AND SPICY BIRD—AND THE RELISH PROVIDES THE PERFECT SWEET-TART FINISH.

TURKEY

- 1½ cups pure maple syrup
- 2 tablespoons Dijon mustard
- 3 tablespoons ancho chile powder
  Kosher salt
- 1 (18-pound) turkey
- 20 fresh sage leaves
- 8 tablespoons (1 stick) unsalted butter, melted
  Freshly ground black pepper
  Cranberry-Mango Relish (*page 217*)

ROASTED GARLIC–CILANTRO GRAVY

- 1 medium Spanish onion, finely chopped
- 1 large carrot, finely chopped
- 2 stalks celery, finely chopped
  Turkey neck and giblets
- 3 tablespoons all-purpose flour
- 1 cup dry white wine
- 6 cups Enriched Chicken Stock (*page 38*) or low-sodium chicken broth
- 1 head roasted garlic, peeled (*see page 19*)
  Kosher salt and freshly ground black pepper
- ¼ cup finely chopped fresh cilantro

1. Preheat the oven to 450 degrees F.

2. Whisk together the maple syrup, mustard, and ancho powder in a medium bowl and season with salt.

3. Remove the neck and giblets from the turkey and set aside for the gravy. Rinse the bird thoroughly with cold water and pat dry. Using your fingers, gently loosen the skin from the breasts and drumsticks and slip the sage leaves underneath. Rub the entire surface with half (¼ cup) of the melted butter. Lightly sprinkle the skin and cavity with salt and pepper.

4. Truss the turkey or simply tie the legs closed with butcher's twine and place on a rack in a large roasting pan. Roast, basting with the remaining butter every 10 minutes, for about 30 minutes, or until brown.

5. Reduce the oven temperature to 350 degrees F and continue roasting the turkey for another 1½ to 2 hours, until an instant-read thermometer inserted into the thigh registers 155 degrees F. Continue roasting, brushing with the glaze every 5 minutes, until the turkey reaches 165 degrees F, 20 to 30 minutes.

6. Transfer the turkey to a cutting board, brush with more of the glaze, and let rest for 20 minutes before carving. The temperature of the bird will rise to 180 degrees F as it rests.

7. While the turkey is resting, make the gravy. Place the roasting pan with the drippings over two burners on your stove. Turn the heat to high and bring the drippings to a simmer. Add the onion, carrot, celery, and turkey neck and giblets to the pan and cook until the mixture is golden brown, 8 to 10 minutes. Add the flour and cook, stirring, until lightly golden brown, 3 to 4 minutes. Whisk in the wine and the stock and bring to a boil.

8. Mash the roasted garlic cloves to a paste in a bowl using a fork. Whisk in the roasted garlic and continue cooking the gravy over high heat until the gravy is reduced by half, 15 to 20 minutes; season with salt and pepper to taste. Strain the gravy into a bowl and stir in the chopped cilantro.

Satisfying as little else is, a juicy steak or a tender piece of pork or lamb is what we showcase at Mesa Grill. While some of my other books contain recipes for simply grilled pieces of meat paired with relishes and other accompaniments, at Mesa Grill the dishes we serve are a bit more complex in technique and flavor. That doesn't necessarily mean complicated, but it does mean rewarding.

Pork and lamb are both very traditional meats in the Southwestern kitchen and I enjoy using them for that reason. They both naturally pair with the Southwestern flavors that grace Mesa Grill's table, such as in Pan-Roasted Pork Chops with Yellow Pepper Mole Sauce and Braised Lamb Tiwa Tacos with Ancho Chile Jam. I like to throw out a bit of the unexpected as well, and lean venison and rabbit make for such dishes. And as for beef, you can't go wrong with velvety short ribs, a spice-encrusted strip steak, or a classic (almost) steak au poivre. Come to the table hungry, because dinner is on!

SPICE-CRUSTED NEW YORK STRIP STEAKS with Mesa Grill Steak Sauce

GRILLED RIB-EYE STEAKS with Chipotle-Honey Glaze and Garlic Chips

BLACK PEPPER–CRUSTED FILETS MIGNONS and Ancho–Red Pepper Sauce and Toasted Goat Cheese

COFFEE-RUBBED FILETS MIGNONS with Ancho-Mushroom Sauce

CHILE-RUBBED SHORT RIBS with Creamy Polenta and Cotija Cheese

THE MESA GRILL BURGER with Double Cheddar Cheese, Grilled Vidalia Onion, and Horseradish Mustard

FIRE-ROASTED VEAL CHOPS with Maple-Horseradish Glaze

NEW MEXICAN RUBBED PORK TENDERLOIN with Bourbon-Ancho Sauce

PAN-ROASTED PORK TENDERLOIN FILLED with Sun-Dried Cranberries

PAN-ROASTED PORK CHOPS with Yellow Pepper Mole Sauce

BRAISED LAMB TIWA TACOS with Ancho Chile Jam

GRILLED LAMB PORTERHOUSE with Cascabel-Fig Sauce and Red Chile–Fig Marmalade

LAMB AND GOAT CHEESE ENCHILADAS with Almond Mole Sauce

LAMB SHANKS with Serrano-Vinegar Sauce and Sweet Potato Risotto with Roasted Chanterelles

CHILE-RUBBED RABBIT with Green Pea Risotto

PAN-ROASTED VENISON with Tangerine–Roasted Jalapeño Sauce

VENISON AND BLACK BEAN CHILI with Toasted Cumin Crema

SPICE-CRUSTED NEW YORK STRIP STEAKS WITH MESA GRILL STEAK SAUCE

SERVES 4 TO 6

THIS STEAK DISH HAS BEEN A MESA GRILL CLASSIC FOR MORE THAN TEN YEARS NOW AND I DON'T SEE IT COMING OFF THE MENU ANY TIME SOON. THE SPICE RUB IS A GOOD ONE TO HAVE ON HAND AND DEFINITELY ONE THAT YOU CAN MAKE IN ADVANCE. AS FOR THE STEAK SAUCE, WELL, IT'S SPICY, SWEET, AND TART ALL AT THE SAME TIME. TALK ABOUT WANTING TO LICK THE PLATE CLEAN—YOU'LL HAVE A HARD TIME HOLDING YOURSELF BACK WITH THIS ONE! SERVE WITH HORSERADISH TWICE-BAKED POTATOES *(page 193)*.

2 tablespoons ancho chile powder

1 tablespoon Spanish paprika

1 tablespoon ground coriander

1 tablespoon dry mustard

1½ teaspoons dried oregano

1½ teaspoons ground cumin

1½ teaspoons chile de árbol

Kosher salt

Freshly ground black pepper

4 (12-ounce) New York strip steaks

2 tablespoons canola oil

Mesa Grill Steak Sauce *(page 226)*

1. To make the spice rub, combine the ancho powder, paprika, coriander, dry mustard, oregano, cumin, chile de árbol, 1 tablespoon salt, and 1 tablespoon pepper in a small bowl.

2. Preheat a grill to medium-high or preheat a grill pan over medium-high heat. Brush both sides of the steaks with the oil and season with salt and pepper. Rub one side of each steak with about 2 tablespoons of the spice mixture.

3. Grill the steaks, rub side down, until lightly charred and a crust has formed, 3 to 4 minutes. Flip over the steaks and continue grilling for 5 to 6 minutes more for medium-rare; the steaks will be bright pink in the middle.

4. Spoon some of the Mesa Grill steak sauce into the center of each of 4 plates and top with the steaks.

GRILLED RIB-EYE STEAKS WITH CHIPOTLE-HONEY GLAZE AND GARLIC CHIPS

SERVES 4 TO 6

THIS VERY-SIMPLE-TO-PREPARE GLAZE NOT ONLY GIVES THE RIB EYE A GREAT SWEET AND SMOKY FLAVOR, BUT ALSO MAKES THE MEAT LOOK BEAUTIFUL.

½ cup honey

1 tablespoon chipotle chile puree (see page 18)

1 tablespoon Dijon mustard

¼ cup canola oil

Kosher salt

Four (12-ounce) rib-eye steaks

Freshly ground black pepper

Roasted Pepper Relish (page 220)

Garlic Chips (recipe follows) (optional)

Cilantro sprigs, for garnish)

1. To make the glaze, whisk together the honey, chipotle puree, mustard, 2 tablespoons of the oil, and 1 teaspoon salt.

2. Preheat a grill to high or preheat your broiler.

3. Brush the steaks with the remaining 2 tablespoons oil and season liberally with salt and pepper on both sides. If using your broiler, place the steaks on a broiler pan. Cook the steaks until golden brown on the first side, 4 to 5 minutes if grilling, 5 to 6 minutes if broiling. Turn the steaks over and continue cooking to medium-rare, 6 to 7 minutes on the grill, 7 to 8 minutes underneath the broiler, liberally brushing with some of the chipotle-honey glaze during the last minute of cooking. Remove from the heat and brush with more of the glaze. Let rest for 5 minutes before serving.

4. Top each steak with a large dollop of the roasted pepper relish and sprinkle with the garlic chips. Garnish with cilantro sprigs.

Garlic Chips
MAKES ABOUT ¼ CUP

½ cup canola oil

8 cloves garlic, sliced crosswise into paper-thin slices

Kosher salt

Heat the oil in a small sauté pan or medium saucepan over medium heat until it begins to shimmer. Add the garlic slices in batches and fry until lightly golden brown, 3 to 5 minutes. Remove with a slotted spoon to a plate lined with paper towels and season with salt. This can be made up to 1 day ahead and stored in a container with a tight-fitting lid.

BLACK PEPPER–CRUSTED FILETS MIGNONS WITH ANCHO–RED PEPPER SAUCE AND TOASTED GOAT CHEESE

SERVES 4

THIS IS THE WAY WE DO STEAK AU POIVRE AT MESA GRILL. I THINK THAT FILET MIGNON IS THE PERFECT CUT TO USE WITH STRONGLY FLAVORED CRUSTS AND SAUCES SUCH AS THIS ONE, FOR WHILE THE MEAT IS TENDER, ITS FLAVOR COULD USE A LITTLE BOOST. AND LIKE STEAK AU POIVRE, WHICH GETS ITS RICHNESS FROM THE CREAM SAUCE THAT CLASSICALLY ACCOMPANIES IT, THIS DISH GETS ITS LUSCIOUS HIT FROM TOASTED GOAT CHEESE. SERVE WITH MESA GRILL SPINACH (*page 210*). *See photograph on page 150.*

- 5 tablespoons canola oil
- 1 large red onion, coarsely chopped
- 3 cloves garlic, coarsely chopped
- 2 (14.5-ounce) cans plum tomatoes and their juice
- 3 red bell peppers, roasted, peeled, seeded (*see page 18*), and coarsely chopped
- 3 ancho chiles, soaked, seeded (*see page 18*), and coarsely chopped
- 1 tablespoon red wine vinegar
- 1 tablespoon honey
- ¼ cup chopped fresh cilantro
  Kosher salt and freshly ground black pepper
  Four (8-ounce) filets mignons
- 3 teaspoons cracked black pepper
- 8 ounces fresh goat cheese, sliced into 4 pieces
- ¼ cup pine nuts, toasted (*see page 19*)
  Thinly sliced green onion, white and green parts, for garnish (optional)

1. Heat 2 tablespoons of the oil in a medium saucepan over high heat. Add the onion and cook until soft, 3 to 4 minutes. Add the garlic and cook for 1 minute. Add the tomatoes, red peppers, and anchos and cook until the tomatoes soften and break down and the liquid thickens, 20 to 30 minutes.

2. Carefully transfer the mixture to a food processor and process until smooth. Add the vinegar, honey, and chopped cilantro, season with salt and freshly ground black pepper, and pulse a few times just to combine.

3. Preheat the broiler.

4. Heat the remaining 3 tablespoons oil in a seasoned cast-iron pan or a large nonstick pan over high heat. Season the steaks on both sides with salt. Season one side of each filet with the cracked black pepper, pressing it in to adhere to the steak. Place the filets in the pan, pepper side down, and cook until lightly golden brown and a crust has formed, 2 to 3 minutes. Turn the steaks over and continue cooking to medium-rare, 3 to 4 minutes more.

5. Remove to a baking sheet.

6. Top each filet with a slice of goat cheese and place under the broiler. Broil until the cheese becomes bubbly and turns golden brown, about 2 minutes.

7. Ladle some of the sauce onto large dinner plates, top with the steaks, and scatter some of the pine nuts around the plates. Garnish with green onion.

COFFEE-RUBBED FILETS MIGNONS WITH ANCHO-MUSHROOM SAUCE

SERVES 4

AS GOOD-LOOKING AS IT IS GOOD TASTING, THIS DISH HAS BEEN FEATURED IN THE PAGES OF MORE THAN ONE MAGAZINE. MESA GRILL LAS VEGAS PATRONS ARE ESPECIALLY FOND OF THE STEAK WITH ITS EARTHY, MOCHALIKE SPICE RUB. SERVE WITH CILANTRO OIL *(page 222)* AND SMOKED RED PEPPER SAUCE *(page 230)*, IF DESIRED.

- 1 tablespoon ancho chile powder
- 1 tablespoon finely ground espresso beans
- 2 teaspoons Spanish paprika
- 2 teaspoons dark brown sugar
- 1 teaspoon dry mustard
- ¾ teaspoon ground coriander
- ¾ teaspoon dried oregano
  Kosher salt
- ¾ teaspoon freshly ground black pepper
- ½ teaspoon ground ginger
- ½ teaspoon chile de árbol powder
- 2 tablespoons canola oil
  Four (8-ounce) filets mignons
  Ancho-Mushroom Sauce *(recipe follows)*

1. Combine the ancho powder, espresso, paprika, brown sugar, mustard, coriander, oregano, ¾ teaspoon salt, the pepper, ginger, and chile de árbol powder in a small bowl.

2. Heat the oil in a large sauté pan over high heat until smoking. Season one side of each filet with a heaping tablespoon of the rub. Place the filets in the pan, rub side down, and cook until a crust has formed, about 2 minutes. Turn the steaks over, reduce the heat to medium, and continue cooking to medium-rare, 6 to 7 minutes. The meat will be bright pink in the center. Remove from the pan and let rest for 5 minutes before serving.

3. Ladle the sauce onto large plates and top with the steaks.

Ancho-Mushroom Sauce
MAKES ABOUT 2½ CUPS

- 4 cups Enriched Chicken Stock *(page 38)* or low-sodium chicken broth
- 3 tablespoons olive oil
- 1½ pounds assorted mushrooms, such as shiitake, cremini, portobello, and oyster, thinly sliced
- 4 shallots, chopped
- 4 cloves garlic, finely chopped
- 2 ancho chiles, soaked, seeded, and pureed *(see page 18)*
- 2 tablespoons honey
- ¼ cup chopped fresh cilantro
  Kosher salt and freshly ground black pepper

1. Pour the chicken stock into a medium saucepan. Bring to a boil over high heat and cook until reduced to 2 cups.

2. Heat the oil in a large sauté pan over high heat. Add the mushrooms, shallots, and garlic and cook until the mushrooms are golden brown and their liquid has evaporated, 8 to 10 minutes.

3. Whisk the ancho puree into the reduced chicken stock and then pour the mixture into the pan with the mushrooms. Bring to a boil and cook, stirring occasionally, until the sauce is reduced by half, 10 to 15 minutes. Stir in the honey and cilantro and season with salt and pepper.

CHILE-RUBBED SHORT RIBS WITH CREAMY POLENTA AND COTIJA CHEESE
SERVES 4

MY LONGTIME CHEF NEIL MANACLE CAME UP WITH THIS DISH AS A SPECIAL A FEW YEARS BACK. NEEDLESS TO SAY, THAT SPECIAL WENT OVER VERY WELL, SO MUCH SO, IN FACT, THAT THIS HAS BECOME A MESA STAPLE IN THE COLDER MONTHS OF LATE FALL AND WINTER. IT'S INCREDIBLY SATISFYING AND COMFORTING: THE SHORT RIBS ARE CUT-WITH-THE-SIDE-OF-A-FORK TENDER AND THE BRAISING LIQUID BECOMES A RICH SAUCE. ACCENT WITH CILANTRO OIL *(page 222)* AND RED CHILE OIL *(page 228)* IF DESIRED.

- 3 tablespoons New Mexico red chile powder
- Kosher salt
- 2 teaspoons ground cinnamon, preferably Mexican cinnamon (canela)
- 2 teaspoons coarsely ground black pepper
- 3 pounds bone-in short ribs
- ¼ cup canola oil, plus extra as needed
- 4 cloves garlic, peeled
- 1 medium Spanish onion, coarsely chopped
- 2 medium carrots, peeled and coarsely chopped
- 1 stalk celery, coarsely chopped
- 1 cup dry red wine
- 4 cups Enriched Chicken Stock *(page 38)* or low-sodium chicken broth
- 6 sprigs fresh thyme
- Freshly ground black pepper
- Creamy Polenta with Cotija *(page 198)*

1. Preheat the oven to 325 degrees F.

2. Mix together the chile powder, 2 teaspoons salt, the cinnamon, and the coarsely ground black pepper in a small bowl. Lay the ribs on a baking sheet and season one side with the spice mixture, rubbing the mixture in so that it adheres to the meat.

3. Heat the oil in a large ovenproof Dutch oven over high heat until it shimmers. Working in batches, place the ribs in a single layer, rub side down, in the oil and cook until a crust has formed and the ribs are golden brown. Turn the ribs over and cook until the second side is golden brown. Remove to a plate and repeat with the remaining ribs, adding more oil if needed.

4. Remove all but 2 tablespoons of the fat in the pan and add the garlic, onion, carrots, and celery and cook until golden brown and caramelized, 6 to 7 minutes. Add the wine and boil until nearly reduced, 2 to 3 minutes. Add the stock and bring to a simmer.

5. Return the ribs to the pan along with the thyme and bring to a simmer. Place the lid on the pan and place in the oven. Cook until the meat is tender and is falling off the bone, 2 to 2½ hours.

6. Carefully remove the ribs to a large plate and let cool slightly. When cool enough to handle, remove the meat from the bones and discard the bones.

7. Strain the sauce into a medium saucepan and return it to the stove over high heat. Bring the sauce to a boil and continue cooking, stirring occasionally, until reduced to a sauce consistency, 10 to 15 minutes. Season with salt and freshly ground black pepper and discard the thyme sprigs. Return the ribs to the pan to reheat.

8. Serve over creamy polenta with cotija in large shallow bowls.

THE MESA GRILL BURGER WITH DOUBLE CHEDDAR CHEESE, GRILLED VIDALIA ONION, AND HORSERADISH MUSTARD

SERVES 4

EVERYONE LOVES A CLASSIC CHEESE-BURGER. I'VE JUST AMPED IT UP A LITTLE WITH SWEET AND CRUNCHY (DON'T OVERCOOK IT) GRILLED VIDALIA ONION, EXTRA CHEESE, AND A SIMPLE BUT BRACING MUSTARD. ONE IMPORTANT TIP: USE GROUND CHUCK NO LEANER THAN 80 PERCENT. YOU REALLY WANT TO MAKE SURE IT HAS A FAT CONTENT OF AT LEAST 20 PERCENT; OTHERWISE YOUR BURGER JUST WON'T BE AS MOIST AND FLAVORFUL.

¼ cup Dijon mustard

1 tablespoon prepared horseradish, drained

1 large Vidalia onion, sliced crosswise into ½-inch-thick slices

2 tablespoons canola oil

Kosher salt and freshly ground black pepper

2 pounds ground chuck

8 slices Cheddar cheese (each ¼ inch thick), preferably a mix of white and yellow

4 sesame seed hamburger buns

4 slices beefsteak tomato

4 lettuce leaves

1. Whisk together the mustard and horse-radish in a small bowl; set aside.

2. Preheat a grill to high or a grill pan over high heat.

3. Brush the onion slices with the oil on both sides and season with salt and pepper. Grill the onion slices for 3 to 4 minutes on each side, until lightly golden brown.

4. While the onion is grilling, form the meat into 4 burgers. Season the burgers on both sides with salt and pepper. Grill for 3 to 4 minutes on each side for medium. Add 2 slices of the cheese to the top of each burger, cover the grill, and let melt, about 1 minute.

5. Place the burgers on the buns sandwiched with onion, tomato, lettuce, and a dollop of horseradish mustard.

FIRE-ROASTED VEAL CHOPS WITH MAPLE-HORSERADISH GLAZE

SERVES 4

ANCHO CHILE POWDER AND THE BITE OF HORSERADISH PROVIDE A GREAT BALANCE TO SWEET MAPLE SYRUP IN THIS DELICIOUS GLAZE. WHILE I USE IT IN THE RESTAURANT WITH THE VEAL CHOPS CALLED FOR HERE, SERVED WITH MESA GRILL SPINACH *(page 210)* AND WILD RICE TAMALES WITH SAGE BUTTER *(page 207)*, IT WOULD ALSO BE JUST AS GOOD WITH PORK CHOPS. BE SURE TO SAVE SOME OF THE ADDITIONAL GLAZE TO SERVE ON THE SIDE; IT MAKES A GREAT DIPPING SAUCE FOR THE CHOPS, AS DOES SMOKED RED PEPPER SAUCE *(page 230)*.

- ½ cup pure maple syrup
- 2 tablespoons Dijon mustard
- 2 tablespoons prepared horseradish, drained
- 1 tablespoon ancho chile powder
- 4 (14-ounce) bone-in veal chops
- 2 tablespoons canola oil
- Kosher salt and freshly ground black pepper

1. Whisk together the maple syrup, mustard, horseradish, and ancho powder in a medium bowl and let sit for at least 15 minutes. This can be made up to 2 days ahead and stored in the refrigerator. Bring to room temperature before using.

2. Preheat a grill to high or a grill pan over high heat.

3. Brush the chops on both sides with the oil and season with salt and pepper. Place the chops on the grill and cook until golden brown and slightly caramelized, 4 to 5 minutes. Reduce the heat to medium, turn the chops over, close the lid of the grill, or tent with aluminum foil, and continue cooking to medium, 7 to 9 minutes more, brushing with the glaze during the last couple of minutes of cooking.

4. Remove the chops from the heat and let rest for 5 minutes before serving with the remaining glaze on the side.

NEW MEXICAN RUBBED PORK TENDERLOIN WITH BOURBON-ANCHO SAUCE

SERVES 4

THE BOURBON-ANCHO SAUCE OF THIS POPULAR MESA GRILL ENTRÉE IS LUSCIOUS, ALMOST BUTTERSCOTCH-Y, WITH JUST ENOUGH SPICE FROM THE CHILES TO CUT THROUGH THE SWEETNESS OF THE BOURBON AND BROWN SUGAR. THE RUB COATS THE PORK IN FLAVOR AND GIVES THE TENDER CUT A MUCH-NEEDED CRUST. AT THE RESTAURANT WE GO ALL OUT, SERVING THIS WITH SWEET POTATO TAMALES WITH PECAN BUTTER (page 207), SMOKED RED PEPPER SAUCE (page 230), AND CILANTRO OIL (page 222).

- 3 tablespoons ancho chile powder
- 2 tablespoons light brown sugar
- 1 tablespoon pasilla chile powder
- 2 teaspoons chile de árbol powder
- 2 teaspoons ground cinnamon
- 2 teaspoons ground allspice
  Kosher salt
- 2 tablespoons olive oil
- 2 pounds pork tenderloin
  Bourbon-Ancho Sauce (recipe follows)
  Chopped fresh chives, for garnish (optional)

1. Preheat the oven to 400 degrees F.

2. Stir together the ancho powder, brown sugar, pasilla powder, chile de árbol powder, cinnamon, allspice, and 1 teaspoon salt in a small bowl.

3. Heat the oil in a medium ovenproof sauté pan over high heat. Season the pork with salt on both sides, then dredge in the spice rub

and tap off any excess. Place the pork in the pan and sear on all sides until golden brown, 8 to 10 minutes.

4. Transfer the pan to the oven and roast the pork to medium, 8 to 10 minutes.

5. Remove the pork from the oven and let rest for 5 minutes. Slice into 1-inch-thick pieces. Ladle some of the bourbon-ancho sauce into the center of each of 4 large plates and top with 3 slices of the pork. Spoon more sauce on top and garnish with chives.

Bourbon-Ancho Sauce
MAKES 1½ CUPS

- 2 tablespoons olive oil
- 1 medium red onion, finely chopped
- 2 cups plus 2 tablespoons bourbon
- 3 ancho chiles, soaked, seeded, and pureed (see page 18)
- 5 cups Enriched Chicken Stock (page 38) or low-sodium chicken broth
- 1 cup thawed apple juice concentrate
- 8 black peppercorns
- ¼ cup packed light brown sugar
  Kosher salt

1. Heat the olive oil in a medium saucepan over high heat. Add the onion and cook until soft, 3 to 4 minutes. Add the 2 cups bourbon, bring to a boil, and cook until reduced to a few tablespoons, 5 to 6 minutes.

2. Add the ancho puree, stock, apple juice concentrate, peppercorns, and brown sugar and cook, stirring occasionally, until reduced by half, 15 to 20 minutes.

3. Strain through a fine-mesh strainer, return the mixture to the pan, and reduce over high heat to sauce consistency, 10 to 15 minutes. Add the 2 tablespoons bourbon, cook for 2 minutes, and season with salt. This can be made up to 1 day ahead and refrigerated. Reheat before serving.

PAN-ROASTED PORK TENDERLOIN FILLED WITH SUN-DRIED CRANBERRIES

SERVES 4 TO 6

THIS IS AN EXCELLENT RECIPE TO PULL OUT IN AUTUMN. THE FILLING IS SWEET AND TART AND SPICY, AND WHAT I LIKE MOST ABOUT IT IS HOW THE RED CHILES KICK THE FALL-FAVORITES CINNAMON AND CLOVES INTO ACTION. *See photograph on page 153.*

1 cup sun-dried cranberries

¼ cup chopped fresh cilantro or flat-leaf parsley

2 tablespoons pine nuts, toasted *(see page 19)*

2 tablespoons light brown sugar

2 teaspoons cascabel chile powder

¼ teaspoon chile de árbol powder

1 teaspoon ground cinnamon

½ teaspoon ground cloves

Kosher salt

2 pounds pork tenderloin

2 tablespoons olive oil

Freshly ground black pepper

Cranberry Sauce *(recipe follows)*

Thinly sliced green onion, white and green parts, for garnish (optional)

Red Chile Oil *(page 228)* (optional)

1. To make the filling, place the cranberries in a medium bowl and cover with boiling water. Let sit for 30 minutes to rehydrate. Drain the cranberries and reserve the soaking liquid.

2. Combine the cranberries, cilantro, pine nuts, brown sugar, cascabel powder, chile de árbol powder, cinnamon, and cloves in a food processor with ¼ cup of the soaking liquid. Process until smooth and season with salt. This can be made up to 2 days in advance and stored in a container with a tight-fitting lid in the refrigerator.

3. Preheat the oven to 425 degrees F.

4. To butterfly the pork, cut it almost in half lengthwise, keeping the blade of your knife parallel to the cutting board. Do not cut all the way through to the other side. Open up the halves like a book so that the tenderloin lies flat. Spread the cranberry filling evenly over the pork. Starting at one of the short ends, roll the tenderloin up like a jelly roll and tie with butcher's twine.

5. Heat the oil in a large ovenproof sauté pan over high heat until almost smoking. Season the tenderloin on both sides with salt and pepper. Place the tenderloin in the pan, seam side up, and cook until golden brown on all sides. Flip over and put in the oven. Roast to medium, 8 to 10 minutes.

6. Remove from the pan and let rest for 5 minutes before slicing. Slice into 1-inch-thick slices. Ladle some of the cranberry sauce onto each of 4 large plates and top with 3 slices of the pork. Garnish with green onion and red chile oil.

Cranberry Sauce
MAKES ABOUT 1½ CUPS

- 6 cups Enriched Chicken Stock *(page 38)* or low-sodium chicken broth
- ¼ cup dry white wine
- ¼ cup dry red wine
- ¼ cup thawed cranberry juice concentrate
- 3 tablespoons light brown sugar
- 1 teaspoon black peppercorns
- 1 teaspoon chipotle chile puree *(see page 18)*
- Kosher salt

1. Pour the chicken stock into a nonreactive medium saucepan. Bring to a boil over high heat and cook until reduced by half, 20 to 25 minutes.

2. Add the white and red wines, cranberry juice concentrate, brown sugar, peppercorns, and chipotle puree and continue cooking, stirring occasionally, until reduced to a sauce consistency, 15 to 20 minutes. Strain into a bowl and season with salt. This can be made up to 1 day in advance and refrigerated. Reheat before serving.

FALL MENU

Pumpkin Soup with Cinnamon Crema and Roasted Pumpkin Seeds *(page 47)*

Blue Corn–Crusted Red Snapper with Warm Tomato Relish *(page 119)*

Pan-Roasted Pork Tenderloin Filled with Sun-Dried Cranberries *(opposite)*

Potato, Sweet Onion, and Sage Gratin *(page 191)*

Caramel Apple Shortcakes with Apple Cider Reduction *(page 244)*

PAN-ROASTED PORK CHOPS WITH YELLOW PEPPER MOLE SAUCE
SERVES 4

THE YELLOW PEPPER MOLE MAY HAVE LOTS OF INGREDIENTS, BUT THE RESULT IS A DELIGHTFULLY COMPLEX SAUCE. GOLDEN RAISINS AND WHITE CHOCOLATE PRESERVE THE GOLDEN COLOR OF THE ROASTED PEPPERS, AND WHILE THOSE MAY SOUND SWEET, ONION, GARLIC, AND TOMATILLOS KEEP THE SAUCE SAVORY, FRESH, AND NEVER CLOYING. AT THE RESTAURANT WE GIVE THIS A HINT OF SMOKED RED PEPPER SAUCE *(page 230)* AND CILANTRO OIL *(page 222)*, TOO.

- ¼ cup plus 2 tablespoons canola oil
- Two (6-inch) yellow corn tortillas, coarsely chopped
- ¼ cup raw pumpkin seeds
- 1 medium red onion, chopped
- 4 cloves garlic, chopped
- 4 cups Enriched Chicken Stock *(page 38)* or low-sodium chicken broth
- 3 yellow bell peppers, roasted, peeled, seeded *(see page 18)*, and chopped
- 1 ripe mango, peeled, pitted, and chopped
- 2 tomatillos, husked, scrubbed, and chopped
- 3 tablespoons golden raisins
- 4 (10- to 12-ounce) center-cut bone-in pork chops
- Kosher salt and freshly ground white pepper
- ½ ounce white chocolate, chopped
- 1 tablespoon honey
- ¼ teaspoon ground cloves
- ½ teaspoon ground cinnamon

1. Heat the ¼ cup oil in a medium saucepan over high heat until smoking. Add the tortillas and fry until crisp, about 1 minute. Remove to a plate.

2. Add the pumpkin seeds to the pan and cook until golden, 2 to 3 minutes. Transfer to a plate.

3. Add the onion to the pan and cook until soft, 3 to 4 minutes. Add the garlic and cook for 1 minute. Add the stock, yellow peppers, mango, tomatillos, and raisins and boil, stirring occasionally, until reduced by half, 25 to 30 minutes.

4. Transfer the yellow pepper mixture, the fried tortillas, and the pumpkin seeds to a food processor and process until smooth. Strain the sauce into a clean medium saucepan and simmer over medium heat until it reaches a sauce consistency, 15 to 20 minutes. Keep warm over low heat.

5. Preheat the oven to 425 degrees F.

6. Heat the 2 tablespoons oil in a large oven-proof sauté pan over high heat until almost smoking. Season the chops on both sides with salt and pepper. Place the chops in the pan and cook until golden brown, 4 to 5 minutes; flip the chops over and place the pan in the oven. Roast until medium, 8 to 10 minutes.

7. Remove the chops from the pan and let rest for 5 minutes before serving. While the chops are resting, add the chocolate, honey, cloves, and cinnamon to the sauce and season with salt and pepper. Cook for 5 minutes. The mole sauce can be made up to 1 day in advance and refrigerated. Reheat before serving.

8. Ladle some of the sauce onto each of 4 large dinner plates and top with a pork chop. Garnish with cilantro.

BRAISED LAMB TIWA TACOS WITH ANCHO CHILE JAM

SERVES 8

I LEARNED TO MAKE THE FRY BREAD FOR THESE TACOS WHILE VISITING A NATIVE AMERICAN PUEBLO IN NEW MEXICO. TIWA TACOS ARE AN INTEGRAL PART OF SOUTHWESTERN NATIVE AMERICAN CUISINE; TIWA REFERS TO BOTH THE LANGUAGE AND THE PEOPLE OF THAT REGION. MY ADDITION TO THIS TRADITIONAL RECIPE IS THE ANCHO CHILE JAM; ITS RICH AND FRUITY FLAVOR GOES REALLY WELL WITH LAMB.

- 3 tablespoons canola oil
- 1 (3-pound) boneless leg of lamb, trimmed of fat
- 3 tablespoons ancho chile powder
  Kosher salt and freshly ground black pepper
- 1 large carrot, peeled and diced
- 1 stalk celery, diced
- 1 large Spanish onion, diced
- 4 cups Enriched Chicken Stock (*page 38*) or low-sodium chicken broth
  Fry Bread Tacquitos (*page 142*)
- 4 ounces watercress
  Ancho Chile Jam (*opposite*)
- 1 cup crema, crème fraîche, or sour cream
- ½ cup grated cotija cheese (2 ounces)
- ½ cup thinly sliced green onions (about 6), white and green parts

1. Preheat the oven to 350 degrees F.

2. Heat the oil over high heat in a large roasting pan set over 2 burners on the stove. Season the lamb with the ancho powder and salt and pepper. Put the lamb in the pan and cook until golden brown on all sides, 10 to 12 minutes.

3. Add the carrot, celery, onion, and chicken stock, cover with aluminum foil, and cook in the oven for 1½ to 2 hours, or until the lamb is fork-tender.

4. Remove the lamb to a platter and shred the meat with a fork. Strain the cooking liquid into a medium saucepan and boil over high heat until reduced to a sauce consistency, 15 to 20 minutes. Add the lamb to the sauce to heat through. The lamb can be made up to 1 day in advance, stored in the sauce in the refrigerator, and reheated before serving.

5. Place the tacos on 8 large dinner plates. Put watercress on each taco and then top with the lamb, ancho chile jam, crema, cotija cheese, and green onions.

Ancho Chile Jam
MAKES ABOUT ¾ CUP

6 ancho chiles, soaked *(see page 18)*

2 tablespoons canola oil

½ small red onion, finely chopped

1 clove garlic, finely chopped

2 tablespoons dark brown sugar

1 tablespoon molasses

Kosher salt

1. Remove 2 of the ancho chiles from their soaking liquid; stem and seed them and place in a blender with a little of the soaking liquid and blend until smooth. Scrape the mixture into a medium bowl. Stem, seed, and finely chop the remaining chiles and set aside.

2. Heat the oil in a small saucepan over high heat, add the onion, and cook until soft, 3 to 4 minutes. Add the garlic and cook for 1 minute. Add the ancho chile puree, ¼ cup of water, the brown sugar, and molasses; bring to a boil and cook for 5 minutes. Remove from the heat and fold in the chopped ancho chiles and season with salt. Transfer to a bowl and let cool to room temperature. This can be made up to 1 day in advance and refrigerated. Bring to room temperature before serving.

GRILLED LAMB PORTERHOUSE WITH CASCABEL-FIG SAUCE AND RED CHILE–FIG MARMALADE

SERVES 4

LAMB PORTERHOUSE CHOPS ARE MUCH MORE INTERESTING THAN A STANDARD RACK OF LAMB (THOUGH, OF COURSE, YOU COULD SUBSTITUTE THAT SHOULD YOU NOT BE ABLE TO FIND THESE). IT'S THE SAME CUT AS THAT OF A T-BONE STEAK, SO YOU GET BOTH THE TENDER FILLET AND THE FLAVORFUL STRIP IN EACH SERVING. I THINK THE EARTHY FLAVOR OF CASCABEL CHILES COMPLE-MENTS BOTH THE FIGS AND THE LAMB WONDERFULLY, AS DO ROASTED GARLIC TAMALES WITH THYME BUTTER (page 206). WE SERVE THE CHOPS WITH THE SAUCE AND THE MARMALADE AT MESA GRILL, BUT IF YOU ARE RUNNING SHORT ON TIME, FEEL FREE TO USE ONE OR THE OTHER.

8 dried figs

1½ cups red wine vinegar

½ cup rice wine vinegar

½ cup distilled white vinegar

½ cup ruby port

1½ cups sugar

6 cups Enriched Chicken Stock (page 38) or low-sodium chicken broth

8 cascabel chiles, toasted, seeded (see page 18), and crushed

Kosher salt and freshly ground black pepper

8 (4- to 5-ounce) lamb porterhouse chops

2 tablespoons olive oil

Red Chile–Fig Marmalade (recipe follows)

Fresh mint leaves, for garnish

1. Put the figs in a bowl, cover with boiling water, and let sit until softened, about 15 minutes. Drain the figs, reserving the soaking liquid. Combine the figs with ½ cup of the soaking liquid in a food processor and process until smooth.

2. While the figs are soaking, combine the red and rice wine vinegars, white vinegar, and port in a medium nonreactive saucepan and bring to a boil over high heat. Cook until reduced by half, about 10 minutes. Add the sugar and the fig puree and reduce by half again, stirring occasionally, 5 to 7 minutes.

3. Combine the chicken stock and crushed cascabels in a medium saucepan, bring to a boil over high heat, and reduce by half, 20 to 25 minutes. Add the reduced vinegar-fig mixture to the chicken stock–cascabel mixture and reduce by half again, stirring occasionally, 15 to 20 minutes. Strain the mixture into a clean medium saucepan and reduce to a sauce consistency, 10 to 15 minutes; season with salt and pepper.

4. Preheat a grill to high or a grill pan over high heat.

5. Brush the chops on both sides with the oil and season with salt and pepper. Place the chops on the grill and cook until golden brown and slightly charred, 3 to 4 minutes. Turn over the chops and continue grilling to medium, 2 to 3 minutes more. Remove from the grill and let rest for 5 minutes.

6. Ladle some of the sauce into the center of each of 4 dinner plates. Place 2 chops per plate in the center of the sauce and drizzle the edges of the meat with some more of the sauce. Top each chop with fig marmalade and garnish with mint leaves.

Red Chile–Fig Marmalade
MAKES ABOUT 1 CUP

2 tablespoons canola oil

1 small Spanish onion, finely diced

12 ounces dried figs, diced

1 tablespoon grated orange zest

½ cup ruby port

1 cup fresh orange juice (not from concentrate)

8 cascabel or 2 ancho chiles, soaked, seeded, and pureed *(see page 18)*

½ cup sugar

Kosher salt and freshly ground black pepper

3 tablespoons finely chopped fresh cilantro

Heat the oil in a medium saucepan over high heat. Add the onion and cook until soft. Add the figs, orange zest, port, orange juice, cascabel puree, and sugar and cook, stirring occasionally, until the figs have softened and the mixture is thick, 25 to 30 minutes. Season with salt and pepper, let cool to room temperature, and stir in the cilantro. Serve at room temperature.

LAMB AND GOAT CHEESE ENCHILADAS WITH ALMOND MOLE SAUCE

SERVES 4 TO 6

THESE ENCHILADAS CAN BE SERVED INDIVIDUALLY OR LAYERED IN A CASSEROLE, BAKED, AND SERVED FAMILY-STYLE—ALMOST LIKE A LASAGNA. HERE I USE LAMB AND GOAT CHEESE INSTEAD OF THE EXPECTED CHICKEN OR BEEF AND MILD CHEESE. THE RESULT IS WARM, RICHLY FLAVORED, PERFECTLY CHEESY—AND HARD NOT TO LIKE.

12 (6-inch) flour tortillas

1 pound lamb loins (4 to 6 loins), cold-smoked (*see page 17*)

2 tablespoons olive oil

Kosher salt and freshly ground black pepper

4 plum tomatoes, cold-smoked (*see page 17*), seeded, and cut into ½-inch dice

4 green onions, white and green parts, thinly sliced

2 cups finely grated Monterey Jack cheese (8 ounces)

12 ounces fresh goat cheese, crumbled

½ cup coarsely chopped fresh cilantro

Almond Mole Sauce (*recipe follows*)

1. Preheat the oven to 350 degrees F. Wrap the tortillas in aluminum foil and put in the oven to warm.

2. Slice the lamb loins in half lengthwise and then cut crosswise into ½-inch pieces. Heat the olive oil in a large sauté pan until almost smoking. Season the lamb with salt and pepper. Add the lamb to the pan and cook until browned, 2 to 3 minutes. Add the tomatoes and cook for 3 to 4 minutes. Remove from the heat and stir in the green onions

3. Remove the tortillas from the oven and lay them on a flat surface. Sprinkle 2 tablespoons of the Monterey Jack down the center of each tortilla and top with some of the lamb mixture. Sprinkle with the goat cheese and some of the cilantro. Fold the short ends in and roll tightly lengthwise. Either serve on individual plates topped with mole sauce and sprinkled with the remaining ½ cup Monterey Jack cheese and the remaining cilantro, or place the filled and rolled tortillas in a baking dish and top with the mole sauce and remaining Monterey Jack cheese, and heat in a 350 degree F oven for 10 minutes, until bubby. Garnish with the remaining cilantro.

Almond Mole Sauce
MAKES ABOUT 2 CUPS

¼ cup olive oil

4 (6-inch) blue or yellow corn tortillas

2 ancho chiles, seeded

2 New Mexico chiles, seeded

1 pasilla chile, seeded

½ medium red onion, coarsely chopped

½ head roasted garlic, cloves separated and peeled (*see page 19*)

½ cup slivered raw almonds

4 cups Enriched Chicken Stock (*page 38*) or low-sodium chicken broth

4 plum tomatoes, peeled, seeded, and chopped

½ teaspoon ground cinnamon

⅛ teaspoon ground cloves

¼ cup golden raisins

½ ounce Ibarra Mexican chocolate or bittersweet chocolate, coarsely chopped

2 tablespoons pure maple syrup

1 tablespoon honey

Juice of 1 lime

Kosher salt and freshly ground black pepper

1. In a large frying pan over high heat, heat the oil until almost smoking. Fry the tortillas, one at a time, until crisp, 20 to 30 seconds per side. Remove to a plate lined with paper towels. Add the three kinds of chiles to the pan and cook until crisp, 10 to 20 seconds per side. Remove with tongs and place in a food processor or blender.

2. Add the onion and garlic to the pan and cook until golden brown, about 2 minutes; add to the processor. Pour out all but 2 tablespoons of the oil from the pan, add the almonds, and toast until golden brown, 2 to 3 minutes; add to the processor.

3. Add 1 cup of the stock to the processor and puree the tortillas, chiles, onion, garlic, and almonds.

4. Pour the puree into a medium saucepan and add the remaining 3 cups stock, the tomatoes, cinnamon, cloves, and raisins. Bring to a boil over high heat. Reduce the heat to medium and simmer, stirring occasionally, until thickened to a sauce consistency, 15 to 20 minutes.

5. Add the chocolate, maple syrup, honey, and lime juice; season with salt and pepper and simmer for another 10 minutes. Remove from the heat. This can be made up to 1 day in advance and refrigerated. Reheat before serving.

LAMB SHANKS WITH SERRANO-VINEGAR SAUCE AND SWEET POTATO RISOTTO WITH ROASTED CHANTERELLES

SERVES 4

THIS SLOW-COOKED DISH WILL MAKE EVERY ROOM OF YOUR HOUSE SMELL AMAZING. THE SPICY SERRANOS AND ACIDIC VINEGAR CUT THROUGH THE RICHNESS OF THE LAMB, SO THIS DISH IS HEARTY BUT NOT HEAVY. SINCE THE ACTIVE TIME ON THE LAMB IS PRETTY LOW, I LIKE TO MAKE A SWEET POTATO AND CHANTERELLE RISOTTO TO SERVE ALONGSIDE.

3 tablespoons olive oil

4 (1-pound) lamb shanks

Kosher salt and freshly ground black pepper

1 large Spanish onion, coarsely chopped

2 medium carrots, coarsely chopped

2 celery stalks, coarsely chopped

2 cups dry red wine

6 sprigs fresh thyme

4 cups Enriched Chicken Stock (page 38) or low-sodium chicken broth

3 serrano chiles, finely diced

½ cup packed dark brown sugar

½ cup red wine vinegar

Sweet Potato Risotto with Roasted Chanterelles (recipe follows)

Chopped fresh chives, for garnish (optional)

1. Preheat the oven to 350 degrees F.

2. Heat the oil in a large ovenproof roasting pan or Dutch oven until almost smoking. Season the shanks on both sides with salt and pepper. Add the shanks to the pan and sear on all sides until golden brown, 8 to 10 minutes. Remove the shanks to a plate.

3. Add the onion, carrots, and celery to the pan, season with salt and pepper, and cook until the vegetables are lightly golden brown, 4 to 5 minutes. Add the wine and cook until reduced by half, 2 to 3 minutes. Add the thyme, stock, and lamb shanks and bring to a boil. Cover, place in the oven, and braise until the meat is very tender, 2 to 2½ hours.

4. Remove the shanks to a plate and tent loosely with aluminum foil. Strain the sauce through a fine-mesh strainer into a medium saucepan and place on the stove over high heat. Add the serranos and sugar and cook, stirring occasionally, until reduced to a sauce consistency, 15 to 20 minutes. Add the vinegar and cook for 1 minute; season with salt and pepper.

5. Spoon the risotto into 4 large shallow bowls. Top with the lamb shanks and spoon the sauce on top. Garnish with chives.

Sweet Potato Risotto with Roasted Chanterelles
SERVES 4

- 1 large sweet potato, scrubbed
- 8 ounces chanterelle mushrooms
- 3 tablespoons olive oil
- Kosher salt and freshly ground black pepper
- 4 tablespoons cold unsalted butter
- 1 large Spanish onion, finely chopped
- 1½ cups arborio rice
- 1 cup dry white wine
- ½ cup grated Parmesan cheese (2 ounces)
- 2 tablespoons pine nuts, lightly toasted *(see page 19)*

1. Preheat the oven to 425 degrees F.

2. Roast the sweet potato on a rack in the oven until tender when pierced with a knife, 35 to 45 minutes. When cool enough to handle, peel the sweet potato and puree the flesh in a food processor or pass it through a ricer. Set aside.

3. While the sweet potato is roasting, toss the mushrooms in a medium baking dish with 2 tablespoons of the oil and season with salt and pepper. Roast until golden brown, 15 to 20 minutes. Set aside.

4. Bring 6 cups of water to a boil in a medium saucepan.

5. Heat the remaining 1 tablespoon oil and 2 tablespoons of the butter in a medium pot over medium-high heat. Add the onion, season with salt and pepper, and cook until soft, 3 to 4 minutes. Add the rice and toss to coat in the mixture and cook for 2 minutes. Add the wine and boil until completely reduced, 2 to 3 minutes.

6. Add 2 cups of the boiling water and cook, stirring, until absorbed. Continue adding 1 cup of water at a time and cook, stirring often, until nearly all of the liquid has been absorbed and the rice is al dente, 25 to 30 minutes.

7. Stir in the sweet potato puree and mix until combined. Add the remaining 2 tablespoons butter and the Parmesan; season with salt and pepper. Fold in the pine nuts and the roasted chanterelles.

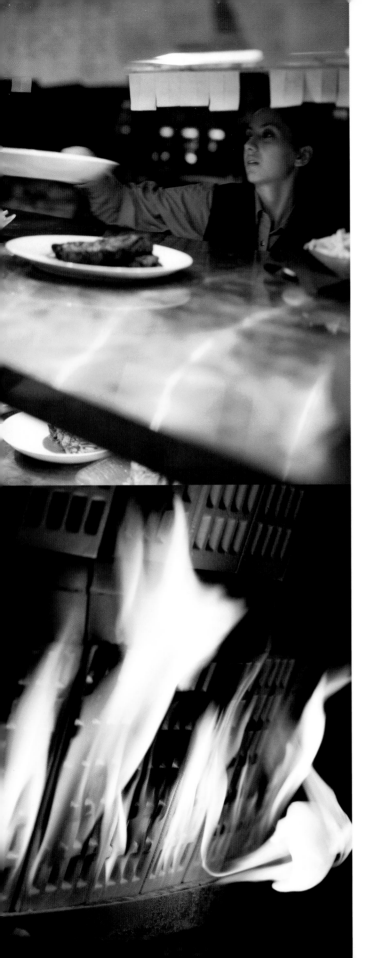

CHILE-RUBBED RABBIT WITH GREEN PEA RISOTTO
SERVES 4

THIS IS A BEAUTIFUL SPRING DISH. RABBIT HAS A NICE, TENDER TEXTURE AND A MILD FLAVOR THAT HOLDS UP WELL TO THE ANCHO CHILE RUB, WHICH WORKS IN TWO WAYS, LENDING A GREAT CRUST AND FANTASTIC FLAVOR TO THE MEAT. I USE THE RABBIT LOIN AND LEGS FOR THIS DISH AND EACH REQUIRES A DIFFERENT COOKING METHOD, BOTH OF WHICH ARE RELATIVELY EASY.

¼ cup ancho chile powder

1½ tablespoons cumin seeds, toasted (*see page 19*) and ground

   Kosher salt

   Freshly ground black pepper

4 (4- to 5-ounce) rabbit legs

6 tablespoons canola oil

1 small Spanish onion, coarsely chopped

1 stalk celery, coarsely chopped

1 medium carrot, peeled and coarsely chopped

1 cup dry red wine

4 cups Enriched Chicken Stock (*page 38*) or low-sodium chicken broth

1 tablespoon honey

4 (4-ounce) rabbit loins

   Green Pea Risotto (*page 203*)

1. Preheat the oven to 400 degrees F.

2. Combine the ancho powder, cumin, 2 teaspoons salt, and ½ teaspoon pepper in a small bowl. Season the rabbit legs on both sides with salt and pepper and then season on the skin side with the spice mixture.

3. Heat 3 tablespoons of the oil in a medium high-sided ovenproof sauté pan over medium-high heat. Place the legs in the pan, skin side down, and cook until golden brown and a crust has formed, 2 to 3 minutes. Turn the legs over and cook until golden brown. Remove to a plate.

4. Remove all but 2 tablespoons of the fat from the pan. Add the onion, celery, and carrot and cook until soft, 3 to 4 minutes. Add the wine and cook until reduced by half, 2 to 3 minutes. Add 3 cups of the stock and bring to a simmer. Return the legs to the pan, cover, and braise in the oven until the meat is tender and almost falling off the bone, 55 to 60 minutes.

5. Remove the legs to a plate and cover with aluminum foil to keep warm. Strain the cooking liquid into a small saucepan and add the remaining 1 cup stock. Cook over high heat, stirring occasionally, until thickened and reduced to a sauce consistency, 20 to 25 minutes. Stir in the honey and season with salt and pepper. Return the legs to the pan for a minute or two to heat through before serving.

6. While the braising liquid is reducing, heat the remaining 3 tablespoons oil in a large ovenproof sauté pan over high heat until almost smoking. Season each loin on both sides with salt and pepper. Rub the top side of the loins with the remaining rub. Place the loins in the pan, rub side down, and cook until golden brown and a crust forms, 2 to 3 minutes. Turn over the loins, transfer the pan to the oven, and roast to medium, 6 to 8 minutes. Remove from the pan and let rest for 5 minutes. Cut each loin into 1-inch pieces.

7. Spoon some of the risotto into 4 large shallow bowls and top each with 1 braised rabbit leg and some of the rabbit loin. Drizzle with the pan sauce.

PAN-ROASTED VENISON WITH TANGERINE–ROASTED JALAPENO SAUCE
SERVES 4

THE VENISON THAT WE SERVE AT MESA GRILL IS FARM-RAISED AND NEVER GAMY. IT'S ALSO INCREDIBLY LEAN, SO WE SERVE IT MEDIUM-RARE AND THE MEAT IS NEVER DRY. I LOVE TO PAIR IT WITH A SWEET AND SPICY SAUCE SUCH AS THIS ONE. TANGERINE JUICE IS A GREAT CHOICE HERE BECAUSE OF ITS BRIGHT AND SLIGHTLY TART FLAVOR. SERVE THIS DISH WITH POTATO, SWEET ONION, AND SAGE GRATIN *(page 191)*.

- 1 cup red wine vinegar
- 1 cup distilled white vinegar
- 2 cups sugar
- 1 cup thawed tangerine juice concentrate
- ¼ cup olive oil
- 1 small red onion, finely diced
- 4 jalapeño chiles, roasted, peeled, seeded *(see page 18)*, and chopped
- 1 cup dry red wine
- 6 cups Enriched Chicken Stock *(page 38)* or low-sodium chicken broth
- 4 (8-ounce) venison steaks
  Kosher salt and freshly ground black pepper

1. Combine the red and white vinegars and the sugar in a medium saucepan over high heat and bring to a boil, stirring to melt the sugar. Whisk in the tangerine juice and boil, stirring occasionally, until the mixture has thickened and is reduced by half, 10 to 15 minutes.

2. Heat 2 tablespoons of the oil in a large saucepan over medium heat. Add the onion and jalapeños and cook until soft, 3 to 4 minutes. Raise the heat to high, add the wine, and cook until reduced to ¼ cup. Add the chicken stock, bring to a boil, and cook, stirring occasionally, until reduced to 2 cups, 20 to 25 minutes.

3. Whisk the tangerine mixture into the onion mixture and reduce to a sauce consistency, stirring occasionally, 15 to 20 minutes.

4. Preheat the oven to 400 degrees F.

5. While the sauce is reducing, heat the remaining 2 tablespoons oil in a large oven-proof sauté pan over high heat. Season the venison on both sides with salt and pepper. Add the venison to the pan and cook until golden brown and a crust has formed, 3 to 4 minutes. Turn over, place the pan in the oven, and continue cooking for 3 to 4 minutes for medium-rare. The meat will be red in the center.

6. Strain the sauce into a small saucepan and season with salt and pepper. Drizzle the venison steaks with the sauce.

VENISON AND BLACK BEAN CHILI WITH TOASTED CUMIN CREMA

SERVES 4 TO 6

YOU COULD CERTAINLY USE BEEF IN PLACE OF THE VENISON HERE, BUT I LIKE HOW THE VENISON TAKES THIS OFF THE BEATEN CHILI PATH. THIS IS A WARMING, FILLING CHILI AND I THINK YOU'LL FIND IT RIGHT AT HOME AMONG YOUR SUPER BOWL PARTY SPREAD OR OUT TAILGATING.

¼ cup canola oil

2 pounds boneless venison shoulder, cut into ½-inch cubes

Kosher salt and freshly ground black pepper

1 large red onion, finely diced

4 cloves garlic, finely chopped

3 tablespoons ancho chile powder

1 tablespoon pasilla chile powder

1 tablespoon ground cumin

1 (12-ounce) bottle dark beer

4 cups Enriched Chicken Stock (*page 38*) or low-sodium chicken broth or water

1 (15.5-ounce) can plum tomatoes, drained and pureed

1 tablespoon chipotle chile puree (*see page 18*)

2 tablespoons honey

1 (15.5-ounce) can black beans, rinsed and drained

2 tablespoons fresh lime juice

Toasted Cumin Crema (*page 41*)

Thinly sliced green onion, white and green parts, for garnish (optional)

1. Heat 2 tablespoons of the oil in a large Dutch oven over high heat. Season the venison with salt and pepper. Add half of the meat to the pan in an even layer and cook until browned on all sides, 6 to 8 minutes. Remove the meat to a plate and repeat with the remaining 2 tablespoons oil and venison.

2. Add the onion to the pan and cook until soft, 3 to 4 minutes. Add the garlic and cook for 1 minute. Add the ancho powder, pasilla powder, and cumin and cook for 2 minutes. Add the beer, bring to a boil, and cook until reduced by half, 3 to 4 minutes.

3. Return the venison to the pan, and add the chicken stock, tomatoes, chipotle puree, and honey. Bring to a boil, then reduce the heat to medium, cover the pan, and simmer for 1 hour.

4. Add the beans and continue cooking for 15 minutes. Remove from the heat, add the lime juice, and season with salt and pepper.

5. Ladle the chili into bowls and serve with a dollop of toasted cumin crema. Garnish with sliced green onion. This can be made up to 1 day in advance and refrigerated. Reheat before serving.

You know, just by labeling the following dishes "Sides," I'm relegating them to the edge of the plate. And while it's true that you don't often see potatoes being given star billing ahead of a steak, that's no reason a side can't be every bit as much of a knockout as the main dish. Every component of your plate should be as fabulous as you can make it—and that's what makes for a memorable meal.

Take those potatoes, for instance. I see no reason why perfectly creamy, pesto-swirled whipped potatoes or crispy, pungent twice-baked potatoes with horseradish couldn't be every bit as noteworthy as the meat, fish, or poultry with which they're paired. Even the basics like spinach and succotash can edge their way toward outstanding. You'll see. And then there's the side dish I would call Mesa Grill's signature—the tamale. Ours is lighter than a traditional tamale, with sweet kernels of corn mixed in with the cornmeal masa. Top it with a luscious flavored butter, and you may find yourself asking who would need anything else.

SIDES

SIDES

WHIPPED POTATOES with Cilantro Pesto

GREEN ONION SMASHED POTATOES

POTATO, SWEET ONION, AND SAGE GRATIN

HORSERADISH TWICE-BAKED POTATOES

SOUTHWESTERN FRIES

    Adobo-Seasoned French Fries

SOUTHWESTERN POTATO SALAD

SWEET POTATO GRATIN

SWEET POTATO AND PLANTAIN PUREE with Maple Syrup and Cinnamon

CREAMY POLENTA with Cotija

GREEN CHILE–TOASTED PINE NUT COUSCOUS

CREAMY GREEN CHILE RICE

BLACK RICE

SPICY YELLOW RICE with Red Beans

GREEN PEA RISOTTO

CHAYOTE SUCCOTASH

ROASTED GARLIC TAMALES with Thyme Butter

    Sweet Potato Tamales with Pecan Butter

    Wild Rice Tamales with Sage Butter

CORN with Roasted Chiles, Crème Fraîche, and Cotija Cheese

BRUSSELS SPROUTS with Pomegranate and Walnuts

MESA GRILL SPINACH

MESA GRILL BLUE AND YELLOW CORN MUFFINS

WHIPPED POTATOES WITH CILANTRO PESTO

SERVES 4

FOLD, DON'T MIX, THE PESTO INTO THESE CREAMY POTATOES. YOU WANT TO MARBLE THE POTATOES WITH RIBBONS OF THE VIBRANT GREEN PESTO.

3 pounds Idaho potatoes, peeled and cut into quarters

Kosher salt

1 cup packed fresh cilantro leaves

¼ cup packed fresh flat-leaf parsley leaves

1 clove garlic, coarsely chopped

2 tablespoons pine nuts

½ cup olive oil

¼ cup grated Parmesan cheese (1 ounce)

Freshly ground black pepper

8 tablespoons (1 stick) unsalted butter, at room temperature

1 cup heavy cream

1 cup milk

1. Put the potatoes in a large pot and add enough cold water to cover them by 1 inch. Add 1 tablespoon salt and bring to a boil over high heat. Cook until the potatoes are very tender when pierced with a knife, 25 to 30 minutes.

2. While the potatoes are cooking, combine the cilantro, parsley, garlic, and pine nuts in a food processor and process until smooth. With the motor running, slowly add the oil and process until emulsified. Add the cheese, season with salt and pepper, and pulse a few times until combined. The pesto can be made up to 1 day ahead and stored in the refrigerator. Bring to room temperature before adding to the potatoes.

3. Combine the butter, cream, and milk in a small saucepan and bring to a simmer over low heat.

4. Drain the potatoes well and return them to the pot on the stove over low heat. Add the hot milk mixture to the potatoes and mash using a masher or whip with a handheld mixer until smooth. Fold the cilantro pesto into the mashed potatoes and season with salt and pepper. Transfer to a serving bowl.

GREEN ONION SMASHED POTATOES

SERVES 4

EVERYONE LOVES MASHED POTATOES, AND THIS VARIATION WILL BE NO EXCEPTION. THE ADDITION OF CRÈME FRAÎCHE GIVES THE POTATOES AN APPEALING TANGY-NESS.

- 3 pounds small new potatoes, scrubbed
  Kosher salt
- 8 tablespoons (1 stick) unsalted butter, at room temperature
- ¾ cup crème fraîche or sour cream
  Freshly ground black pepper
- 6 green onions, green and white parts, thinly sliced

1. Put the potatoes in a large pot and cover by 1 inch with cold water. Add 1 tablespoon salt and bring to a simmer over high heat. Cook until the potatoes are tender when pierced with a knife, 12 to 15 minutes. Drain and return to the pot.

2. Mix together the butter and crème fraîche in a bowl and season liberally with salt and pepper. Using a wooden spoon, gently smash the potatoes while folding in the crème fraîche mixture. Fold in the green onions and season with more salt and pepper if needed. Transfer to a serving bowl.

POTATO, SWEET ONION, AND SAGE GRATIN

SERVES 4

THIS GRATIN HAS AN INCREDIBLE WARMING QUALITY, MAKING IT A PERFECT AUTUMN AND WINTER SIDE DISH FOR ANY ROASTED MEAT.

- 2 tablespoons unsalted butter, plus extra for the pan
- 2 tablespoons olive oil
- 4 large sweet onions, such as Vidalia or Walla Walla, halved and thinly sliced
  Kosher salt and freshly ground black pepper
- 3 tablespoons finely chopped fresh sage
- 4 large Idaho potatoes, peeled and sliced ⅛ inch thick
- 2 cups heavy cream

1. Preheat the oven to 375 degrees F. Butter a 9-inch baking dish and set aside.

2. Heat the oil and butter in a large sauté pan over medium heat. Add the onions and cook, stirring occasionally, until soft and caramelized, 30 to 35 minutes. Season with salt and pepper and stir in the sage.

3. Place a layer of potatoes on the bottom of the baking dish, top with a seventh of the onion mixture and about 3 tablespoons of the cream, and season with salt and pepper. Repeat to make 7 or 8 layers. Press on the gratin to submerge the potatoes in the cream mixture. Place the dish on a baking sheet and cover with aluminum foil.

4. Bake for 30 minutes, remove the foil, and continue baking for 30 to 45 minutes, until the potatoes are tender when pierced with a knife and the top is golden brown. Let rest for 10 minutes before slicing. This can be made up to 1 day in advance and refrigerated. Reheat in the oven before serving.

HORSERADISH TWICE-BAKED POTATOES

SERVES 4

I'M NOT SURE THAT I CAN THINK OF A BETTER ACCOMPANIMENT TO STEAK. THE HORSERADISH, WHICH IS SUCH A CLASSIC FLAVORING WITH STEAK, CUTS RIGHT THROUGH THE RICHNESS OF THE POTATOES SO THEY'RE SATISFYING, NOT HEAVY.

6 medium Idaho potatoes, scrubbed

8 tablespoons (1 stick) unsalted butter, cut into pieces

1½ to 2 cups whole milk or heavy cream, heated

¼ cup prepared horseradish, drained

Kosher salt and freshly ground black pepper

½ cup sour cream or crème fraîche

¼ cup chopped fresh chives

1. Preheat the oven to 375 degrees F.

2. Place the potatoes on a baking sheet and bake until soft when pierced with a knife, 55 to 65 minutes. Remove from the oven and let cool for 5 minutes.

3. Preheat the broiler.

4. Slice the potatoes in half lengthwise and carefully remove the flesh, leaving a thin layer of potato near the skin. Put the flesh in a bowl. Reserve 8 of the best skins and discard the others. Add the butter, 1½ cups hot milk, and the horseradish to the flesh and mash until smooth, or run the potatoes through a food mill and then add the butter, milk, and horseradish and stir until combined. Season with salt and pepper, and add up to ½ cup additional hot milk if needed. The potatoes should not be dry.

5. Fill each potato skin with the mashed potato mixture and return to the baking sheet. Broil until golden brown, 3 to 4 minutes. Top each potato half with a dollop of sour cream and some chopped chives. Serve immediately.

SOUTHWESTERN FRIES
SERVES 4

THE SECRET TO GREAT FRENCH FRIES IS IN THE DOUBLE COOKING. ONCE TO MAKE THEM TENDER ON THE INSIDE AND THE OTHER TO MAKE THEM GOLDEN BROWN AND CRISP ON THE OUTSIDE. I LIKE MINE SHOWERED IN CRUNCHY SALT, CHILE POWDER, AND FRESH CILANTRO.

See photograph on page 186.

- 2 tablespoons ancho chile powder
- 1 tablespoon kosher salt
- 5 large Idaho potatoes, peeled
- 4 cups vegetable oil
- ¼ cup chopped fresh cilantro

1. Combine the ancho powder and salt in a small bowl.

2. Cut the potatoes into ¼-inch-thick slices, then cut each slice into ¼-inch-thick fries. Place the fries in a large bowl of cold water.

3. Heat the oil in a large saucepan to 325 degrees F as measured on a deep-frying thermometer. Drain the fries in batches on paper towels. Fry each batch for 3 to 4 minutes, until a pale blond color. Remove to a sheet pan lined with paper towels.

4. Raise the heat of the oil to 375 degrees F. Working in batches, fry the potatoes again, until golden brown, 2 to 3 minutes. Remove to a sheet pan lined with paper towels and season with the chile mixture and cilantro.

ADOBO-SEASONED FRENCH FRIES

ADOBO SEASONING IS A TRADITIONAL CUBAN BLEND OF SPICES. THESE ADDICTIVE FRIES ARE THE PERFECT ACCOMPANIMENT TO ANY STEAK DISH AND, OF COURSE, THE MESA GRILL BURGER *(page 162)*.

Prepare Southwestern Fries substituting 1 teaspoon granulated garlic powder, 1 teaspoon granulated onion powder, 1 teaspoon freshly ground black pepper, and 1 teaspoon ground turmeric for the ancho chile powder and salt. Substitute 2 teaspoons finely chopped fresh oregano for the cilantro.

SOUTHWESTERN POTATO SALAD

SERVES 4

THIS STAPLE IS MADE NEW AGAIN WITH A FULL-FLAVORED MAYONNAISE. THE SPICY AND SAVORY DRESSING SHOULD BE MIXED WITH THE POTATOES WHILE THEY'RE STILL WARM SO THAT THEY ABSORB ALL OF THAT INCREDIBLE FLAVOR.

- 2 pounds small new potatoes
  Kosher salt
- 1 cup prepared mayonnaise
- 2 tablespoons Dijon mustard
- 2 tablespoons fresh lime juice
- 2 tablespoons ancho chile powder
- ½ teaspoon cayenne pepper
- 1 large ripe beefsteak tomato, seeded and chopped
- ¼ cup chopped fresh cilantro
- 1 jalapeño chile, finely diced
- 3 green onions, white and green parts, thinly sliced
- 1 medium red onion, halved and thinly sliced
- 4 cloves garlic, finely chopped
  Freshly ground black pepper

1. Put the potatoes in a large pot and add enough cold water to cover . Add 1 tablespoon salt and bring to a boil over high heat. Cook until the potatoes are tender when pierced with a knife, 12 to 15 minutes.

2. Drain well, let cool slightly, and slice ¼ inch thick. Put in a large bowl and cover with aluminum foil to keep warm while you prepare the dressing.

3. Stir together the mayonnaise, mustard, lime juice, ancho powder, cayenne, tomato, cilantro, jalapeño, green onions, red onion, and garlic in a medium bowl. Pour the mixture over the potatoes and mix gently until combined. Season with salt and pepper to taste. Serve cold or at room temperature. This can be made up to 1 day ahead and stored in the refrigerator.

SWEET POTATO GRATIN

SERVES 4 TO 6

THIS DECADENT GRATIN COULD BECOME YOUR NEXT HOLIDAY CLASSIC. THE SLIGHTLY SPICY AND SMOKY CHIPOTLE PUREE PROVIDES A GREAT BALANCE TO THE SWEET POTATOES AND CREAM AND TAKES THIS DISH TO ANOTHER LEVEL OF FLAVOR. IT'S AMAZING HOW GOOD THREE INGREDIENTS CAN BE.

2 cups heavy cream

1 tablespoon chipotle chile puree
(see page 18)

4 medium sweet potatoes, peeled and sliced ⅛ inch thick

Kosher salt and freshly ground black pepper

Thinly sliced green onion, white and green parts, for garnish (optional)

1. Preheat the oven to 375 degrees F.

2. Whisk together the cream and chipotle puree.

3. In a 10-inch square baking dish with 2-inch-high sides, arrange an even layer of potatoes on the bottom of the dish, drizzle with 3 tablespoons of the cream mixture, and season with salt and pepper. Repeat with the remaining potatoes, cream, and salt and pepper to form 9 to 10 layers. Press down on the gratin to totally submerge the potatoes in the cream mixture.

4. Cover with aluminum foil and bake for 30 minutes. Uncover and continue baking for 30 to 45 minutes, until the cream has been absorbed, the potatoes are cooked through, and the top is browned.

5. Remove from the oven and let rest for 10 minutes before slicing. Top with green onion. This can be made up to 1 day ahead and refrigerated. Reheat before serving.

SWEET POTATO AND PLANTAIN PUREE WITH MAPLE SYRUP AND CINNAMON

SERVES 6 TO 8

THIS PUREE UPSTAGES STANDARD THANKSGIVING DISHES. THE PLANTAINS ADD A COMPLEMENTARY SWEET FLAVOR, BUT THE RESULT IS ANYTHING BUT CLOYING.

5 large sweet potatoes, scrubbed

2 very ripe plantains

8 tablespoons (1 stick) unsalted butter, quartered, at room temperature

Pinch of salt

2 teaspoons ground cinnamon

¼ cup plus 2 tablespoons pure maple syrup

1 to 1½ cups heavy cream

1. Preheat the oven to 375 degrees F.

2. Put the potatoes on a large baking sheet and roast until the potatoes are soft, 55 to 65 minutes. During the last 15 minutes of roasting, add the plantains to the baking sheet with the potatoes and roast until completely black and soft. Keep the oven on.

3. Slice each potato in half lengthwise, scoop out the flesh, and place it in the bowl of a large food processor. Peel the plantains (see page 11) and add the flesh to the sweet potatoes. Add the butter, salt, cinnamon, and the ¼ cup maple syrup and process until smooth. Add 1 cup cream and pulse until combined; if the mixture seems too dry, add up to ½ cup additional cream until the mixture is creamy.

4. Spoon the puree into a medium baking dish and place in the oven for 10 to 15 minutes to heat through and brown slightly on top. Remove and drizzle the top with the 2 tablespoons maple syrup.

CREAMY POLENTA WITH COTIJA

SERVES 4

THIS IS A GREAT INDULGENT, RICH, CREAMY SIDE DISH. THE COTIJA CHEESE GIVES A WONDERFUL NATURAL SALTINESS TO THE POLENTA.

5 cups Enriched Chicken Stock (page 38) or low-sodium chicken broth

Kosher salt

1 cup medium-grind white cornmeal

8 tablespoons (1 stick) unsalted butter, cut into pieces

¼ cup heavy cream

⅓ cup grated cotija cheese

Freshly ground black pepper

1. Combine the stock and 2 teaspoons salt in a large saucepan and bring to a boil over high heat. Add the cornmeal in a fine stream, whisking constantly with a wire whisk. Once all the cornmeal has been added, reduce the heat to low and cover the pan. Stir the mixture, using a wooden spoon, every 5 minutes and continue cooking until all the liquid has been absorbed and the mixture is very creamy, 25 to 30 minutes.

2. Remove from the heat and stir in the butter, heavy cream, and cotija cheese until combined; season with salt and pepper.

GREEN CHILE–TOASTED PINE NUT COUSCOUS

SERVES 4

THIS DISH JUST LOOKS, TASTES, AND FEELS HEALTHY. IT'S NUTTY AND SLIGHTLY SWEET FROM THE DRIED FRUIT—ALMOST LIKE A SAVORY GRANOLA. SOUNDS A LITTLE WEIRD, BUT IT TASTES GREAT.

- 3 tablespoons unsalted butter
- 1½ cups couscous
- 2¼ cups Enriched Chicken Stock (*page 38*) or low-sodium chicken broth or vegetable broth
- ½ teaspoon kosher salt
- ¼ teaspoon freshly ground black pepper
- 1 Anaheim chile, roasted, peeled, seeded (*see page 18*), and finely diced
- 3 tablespoons dried cherries
- 6 dried apricots, finely diced
- 3 tablespoons pine nuts, toasted (*see page 19*)
- 2 green onions, white and green parts, thinly sliced
- 2 tablespoons finely chopped fresh cilantro

1. Melt 2 tablespoons of the butter in a medium saucepan over medium heat. Add the couscous and stir until it is coated with the butter and slightly toasted, about 2 minutes. Add the stock and salt and pepper and bring to a boil.

2. Stir in the Anaheim chile, cherries, and apricots, cover, and reduce the heat to low. Cook for 5 to 6 minutes, until all of the liquid has been absorbed. Add the remaining 1 tablespoon butter, the pine nuts, green onions, and cilantro and fluff with a fork. Transfer to a serving bowl.

CREAMY GREEN CHILE RICE
SERVES 4

I HAVE TO THANK MY FRIEND ZARELA MARTINEZ OF HER EPONYMOUS RESTAURANT FOR THIS DISH. THE POBLANOS GIVE A NICE PEPPER BACKGROUND TO THE RICE, AND THE GREEN ONIONS AND CILANTRO REINFORCE THE GREEN FACTOR.

1½ cups heavy cream

2 cups long-grain white rice

Kosher salt

Freshly ground black pepper

2 poblano chiles, roasted, peeled, seeded (*see page 18*), and finely diced

3 green onions, white and green parts, thinly sliced

¼ cup finely chopped fresh cilantro

1. Pour the heavy cream into a small saucepan and bring to a boil over high heat. Lower the heat to medium and simmer until the cream has reduced by half, 5 to 7 minutes.

2. While the cream is reducing, bring 3¾ cups cold water to a boil in a medium saucepan over high heat. Stir in the rice and season with salt. Bring to a boil again, stir, cover the pan, reduce the heat to medium, and cook until all of the liquid is absorbed, 15 to 18 minutes.

3. Remove the rice from the heat and let sit for 5 minutes with the lid on. Remove the lid and fluff the rice with a fork. Return the rice to the stove over medium heat, add the reduced cream, and season with salt and pepper. Stir in the poblanos, green onions, and cilantro and transfer to a serving bowl.

BLACK RICE
SERVES 4

THIS IS A TASTY AND ECONOMICAL DISH. INSTEAD OF THROWING OUT THE WATER YOU'VE USED TO COOK BLACK BEANS, USE IT TO MAKE RICE. NOT ONLY WILL IT MAKE YOUR RICE BLACK, IT ALSO GIVES IT FABULOUS FLAVOR. YOU CAN SERVE THIS DISH WITH THE COOKED BLACK BEANS OR SAVE THEM TO MAKE BLACK BEAN–MANGO SALSA (*page 217*) OR BLACK BEAN SOUP WITH TOASTED CUMIN CREMA AND THREE RELISHES (*page 40*).

1 cup dried black beans, picked over

1 teaspoon chipotle chile puree (*page 18*)

2 cloves garlic, peeled

1 teaspoon ground cumin

2 cups long-grain white rice

Kosher salt and freshly ground black pepper

4 green onions, white and green parts, thinly sliced

1. Combine the beans, chipotle puree, garlic, and cumin in a medium saucepan and cover with 6 cups of cold water. Bring to a boil, reduce the heat to medium, and simmer until the beans are soft, 1¼ to 1½ hours. Drain the cooking liquid into a bowl and set aside. Discard the garlic and save the beans for another use.

2. Measure out 3¾ cups of the cooking liquid, pour into a medium saucepan, and bring to a boil over high heat. Stir in the rice and season with salt and pepper. Bring back to a boil, reduce the heat to medium, cover the pot, and cook until the rice is tender and the liquid has been absorbed, 15 to 18 minutes. Remove from the heat and let sit, covered, for 5 minutes. Remove the lid, fluff with a fork, and fold in the green onions. Transfer to a serving bowl.

SPICY YELLOW RICE WITH RED BEANS
SERVES 4

TRADITIONALLY, YELLOW RICE GETS ITS COLOR FROM TURMERIC. HERE, SAFFRON PROVIDES THE YELLOW HUE AND A SUBTLE FLAVOR THAT'S GREAT WITH MEAT, FISH, OR POULTRY, OR SIMPLY AS A MEAL ON ITS OWN.

Large pinch of saffron threads

2 tablespoons canola oil

1 medium red onion, finely chopped

3 cloves garlic, finely chopped

2 tablespoons ancho chile powder

2 teaspoons ground cumin

¼ teaspoon cayenne pepper

2 cups long-grain white rice

1 teaspoon kosher salt

One (15.5-ounce) can red beans, rinsed and drained

¼ cup thinly sliced green onions, white and green parts

1. Bring 3¾ cups of cold water to a simmer in a medium saucepan, stir in the saffron, cover, and remove from the heat. Let steep while you prepare the rice.

2. Heat the oil in a medium saucepan over medium-high heat. Add the onion and cook until soft, 3 to 4 minutes. Add the garlic and cook for 30 seconds. Stir in the ancho powder, cumin, and cayenne and cook for 30 seconds.

3. Add the rice and stir to coat the grains. Add the saffron water and salt, raise the heat to high, and bring to a simmer. Cover the pot, lower the heat to medium, and cook for 15 to 18 minutes, until the liquid has been absorbed and the rice is tender.

4. Remove the pan from the heat, add the beans, cover, and let sit for 5 minutes. Fluff with a fork and fold in the green onions. Transfer to a serving bowl.

GREEN PEA RISOTTO
SERVES 4

THE PUREED PEAS LEND THEIR VIBRANT COLOR AND SWEETNESS TO EVERY BITE. AND DEFINITELY USE FROZEN PEAS— THEY REALLY ARE THE BEST AND MOST CONSISTENT IN QUALITY, AS THEY'RE FROZEN AT THEIR PEAK.

- 6 to 7 cups Enriched Chicken Stock (*page 38*) or low-sodium chicken broth
- 1½ cups frozen peas, thawed
- 2 tablespoons olive oil
- 1 large Spanish onion, finely diced
- 1½ cups arborio rice
- 1 cup dry white wine
- Kosher salt and freshly ground black pepper
- 2 tablespoons cold unsalted butter, cut into pieces
- ½ cup grated cotija cheese (2 ounces)
- 8 ounces arugula, thinly sliced

1. Pour the stock into a medium saucepan and bring to a simmer over low heat.

2. Combine 1 cup of the peas and ¼ cup of the stock in a blender or food processor and process until smooth. Set aside.

3. Heat the oil in a medium saucepan over medium heat. Add the onion and cook until soft, 3 to 4 minutes. Add the rice and toss to coat with the onion mixture. Raise the heat to high, add the wine, and cook until completely reduced, 2 to 3 minutes.

4. Add 2 cups of the hot stock and cook, stirring often, until all of the liquid has been absorbed. Continue adding 1 cup of stock at a time and cook, stirring often, until all of the liquid has been absorbed and the rice is al dente, 25 to 30 minutes.

5. Stir in the pea puree, season with salt and pepper, and cook for 2 minutes. Add the butter, the remaining ½ cup peas, ¼ cup of the cheese, and the arugula. Add a little more stock and cook for 2 minutes more.

6. Pour into bowls and sprinkle the top with the remaining ¼ cup cheese.

CHAYOTE SUCCOTASH
SERVES 4

SUCCOTASH IS A QUINTESSENTIALLY AMERICAN DISH, AND THE ADDITION OF CHAYOTE GROUNDS IT IN THE SOUTHWEST. SERVING THE SUCCOTASH IN THE HOLLOWED-OUT SHELLS OF THE CHAYOTES MAKES FOR AN EXTRA-SPECIAL PRESENTATION.

2 chayotes (about 1 pound)

3 tablespoons olive oil

Kosher salt and freshly ground black pepper

1 small red onion, finely chopped

2 cloves garlic, finely chopped

1 red bell pepper, seeded and finely diced

1 medium zucchini, finely diced

1 cup frozen lima beans, thawed

1 cup fresh corn kernels (*see page 9*) or frozen corn kernels, thawed

3 tablespoons unsalted butter

2 tablespoons fresh lime juice

2 tablespoons chopped fresh cilantro

1. Preheat the oven to 400 degrees F.

2. Rub the chayotes with 1 tablespoon of the oil and season with salt and pepper. Place on a baking sheet and roast until just tender when pierced with a knife, 30 to 40 minutes. Remove from the oven, let cool slightly, and slice in half lengthwise. Scoop out the flesh of the chayotes, coarsely chop, and remove to a plate. Reserve the shells.

3. Heat the remaining 2 tablespoons oil in a large sauté pan over medium-high heat. Add the onion and cook until soft, 3 to 4 minutes. Add the garlic and cook for 30 seconds. Add the red pepper and zucchini and cook for 5 minutes. Add the lima beans and corn and cook for an additional 5 minutes.

4. Stir in the reserved chayote flesh. Add the butter, lime juice, and cilantro and season with salt and pepper. Scoop the mixture into the roasted chayote shells. Serve ½ chayote per person.

ROASTED GARLIC TAMALES WITH THYME BUTTER
SERVES 8 TO 10

THIS TAMALE MAKES A WONDERFUL SIDE DISH FOR JUST ABOUT ANYTHING. ROASTING THE GARLIC MAKES IT MELLOW AND SWEET AND THE HONEY IN THE FILLING AND THE THYME BUTTER REINFORCES THAT NATURAL SWEETNESS.

24 dried corn husks

4 cups fresh corn kernels *(see page 9)*

1 small red onion, chopped

1 head roasted garlic, peeled *(see page 19)*

9 tablespoons (1 stick plus 1 tablespoon) unsalted butter, melted

⅔ cup fine yellow cornmeal

2 tablespoons honey

Kosher salt and freshly ground black pepper

Thyme Butter *(recipe follows)*

1. Two hours before you form the tamales, clean the husks under running water. Soak them in warm water for about 2 hours, or until softened.

2. Puree the corn, onion, roasted garlic, and 1½ cups of water in a food processor or blender. Transfer the mixture to a medium bowl and stir in the butter. Add the cornmeal and honey, season with salt and pepper, and mix until there are no visible lumps; the mixture will be loose.

3. Remove the corn husks from the water and set aside the best 20 husks. Pat dry. Tear the remaining 4 husks into 1-inch-wide strips to be used for tying. Lay 2 husks flat on a work surface with the tapered ends facing left and right and the broad centers overlapping each other by about 3 inches. Place about ⅓ cup of the masa mixture in the center. Bring the long sides up over the masa, slightly overlap-ping, and pat down to close. Tie each end of the bundle with a strip of corn husk, pushing the filling toward the middle as you tie. Trim the ends to about ½ inch beyond the tie. The tamales can be assembled up to 4 hours ahead and refrigerated.

4. Bring a couple of inches of water to a boil in the bottom of a steamer. Arrange the tamales in a single layer on a steamer rack, cover tightly with aluminum foil, and steam for 45 to 75 minutes, until firm to the touch.

5. To serve, arrange 1 tamale on each of 8 serving plates. Using a paring knife, cut a slit lengthwise in the top of each tamale and push both ends of the tamale toward the middle to expose the masa. Top each serving with a heaping tablespoon of thyme butter. Do not eat the husks.

Thyme Butter
MAKES ABOUT ¾ CUP

12 tablespoons (1½ sticks) unsalted butter, at room temperature

2 tablespoons finely chopped fresh thyme

1 teaspoon honey

Kosher salt and freshly ground black pepper

Combine the butter, thyme, and honey in a bowl. Season with salt and pepper and mix well. Scrape onto a sheet of plastic wrap, form into a log, and wrap well. Refrigerate until solid, at least 2 hours and up to 24 hours. Remove from the refrigerator 10 minutes before using to soften slightly.

SWEET POTATO TAMALES WITH PECAN BUTTER

SWEET POTATOES ARE ONE OF MY MOST FAVORITE VEGETABLES. I USE THEM IN GRATINS, SOUPS, PUREED WITH PLANTAINS, DOUBLE-BAKED WITH CHIPOTLE—SO WHY NOT AS A FILLING FOR TAMALES? THESE TAMALES ARE JUST THE THING YOU WANT TO EAT IN THE FALL AND WINTER. THEY'RE WARM, SWEET, AND COMFORTING.

Prepare Roasted Garlic Corn Tamales, omitting the roasted garlic and adding 1 cup pureed roasted sweet potato (see page 198), 2 teaspoons ground cinnamon, 1 teaspoon ground allspice, ½ teaspoon ground cloves, and 2 tablespoons pure maple syrup. Decrease the honey to 1 tablespoon. Serve with Pecan Butter (recipe follows) instead of Thyme Butter.

Pecan Butter
MAKES ABOUT 1 CUP

- 12 tablespoons (1½ sticks) unsalted butter, at room temperature
- ¼ cup pecans, toasted (see page 19) and finely chopped
- 3 tablespoons pure maple syrup
- ¼ teaspoon ground cinnamon
  Kosher salt and freshly ground black pepper

Combine the butter, pecans, maple syrup, and cinnamon in a bowl. Season with salt and pepper and mix well. Scrape onto a sheet of plastic wrap, form into a log, and wrap well. Refrigerate until solid, at least 2 hours and up to 24 hours. Remove from the refrigerator 10 minutes before using to soften slightly.

WILD RICE TAMALES WITH SAGE BUTTER

THESE TAMALES COMBINE NUTTY WILD RICE AND SWEET CORN WITH ONE OF MY FAVORITE TASTES OF FALL—SAGE. I ALWAYS FIND MYSELF USING SAGE IN MY THANKSGIVING MEALS, AND THIS SIDE WOULD BE A WELCOME ADDITION TO THAT CELEBRATION.

Prepare Roasted Garlic Tamales, decreasing the roasted garlic to 4 cloves and adding 1 cup cooked wild rice. Serve with Sage Butter (recipe follows) instead of Thyme Butter.

Sage Butter
MAKES ABOUT 1 CUP

- 12 tablespoons (1½ sticks) unsalted butter, at room temperature
- 3 tablespoons finely chopped fresh sage
- 2 teaspoons honey
  Kosher salt and freshly ground black pepper

Combine the butter, sage, and honey in a bowl. Season with salt and pepper and mix well. Scrape onto a sheet of plastic wrap, form into a log, and wrap well. Refrigerate until solid, at least 2 hours and up to 24 hours. Remove from the refrigerator 10 minutes before using to soften slightly.

CORN WITH ROASTED CHILES, CREME FRAICHE, AND COTIJA CHEESE

SERVES 4

I THINK OF THIS AS A SPICY AND RICH VERSION OF CREAMED CORN. THE LIME JUICE AND CILANTRO ARE KEY, KEEPING THE FLAVORS OF THE DISH FRESH.

- 3 tablespoons canola oil
- 1 medium red onion, finely chopped
- 2 cloves garlic, finely chopped
- 1 serrano chile, roasted, peeled, seeded (*see page 18*), and finely diced
- 1 small poblano chile, roasted, peeled, seeded (*see page 18*), and finely diced
- 1 red bell pepper, roasted, peeled, seeded (*see page 18*), and finely diced
- 2 cups fresh corn kernels (*see page 9*)
- 2 tablespoons cold unsalted butter
- 2 tablespoons crème fraîche

  Juice of 1 lime
- 2 tablespoons finely chopped fresh cilantro

  Kosher salt and freshly ground black pepper
- ¼ cup grated cotija cheese (1 ounce)

1. Heat the oil in a large sauté pan over medium-high heat. Add the onion and cook until soft, 3 to 4 minutes. Add the garlic and serrano chile and cook for 1 minute. Stir in the poblano, red pepper, and corn and cook until the corn is tender, 8 to 10 minutes.

2. Stir in the butter, crème fraîche, lime juice, and cilantro and season with salt and pepper. Transfer to a serving bowl and sprinkle with the cotija cheese.

BRUSSELS SPROUTS WITH POMEGRANATE AND WALNUTS

SERVES 4

IF YOU'RE LOOKING FOR A WAY TO TURN YOUR FRIENDS AND FAMILY WHO CLAIM NOT TO LIKE BRUSSELS SPROUTS ON TO THEM, THIS IS THE DISH TO TRY. THE POMEGRANATE SEEDS AND WALNUTS PROVIDE CRUNCHY AND SWEET ELEMENTS THAT MAKE IT HARD TO SAY NO TO.

- 1 pound Brussels sprouts, trimmed
- 2 tablespoons canola oil
  Kosher salt and freshly ground black pepper
- 2 fresh pomegranates
- 4 tablespoons cold unsalted butter, cut into pieces
- ¼ cup walnuts, toasted (see page 19) and coarsely chopped

1. Preheat the oven to 375 degrees F.

2. Place the Brussels sprouts on a large baking sheet, toss with the oil, and season with salt and pepper. Roast in the oven until just tender when pierced with a knife, 25 to 30 minutes.

3. While the Brussels sprouts are roasting, seed the pomegranates. Cut them in half crosswise, then cut each half in half again. Working over a bowl, use a small spoon or your fingers to gently pull the seeds away from the pulp. (The juice may stain your fingers temporarily, but it washes off easily.)

4. Transfer the sprouts to a large bowl, add the butter, and stir until melted. Stir in the pomegranate seeds and walnuts.

MESA GRILL SPINACH

SERVES 4

BELIEVE IT OR NOT, WE GET ASKED FOR THIS INCREDIBLY SIMPLE RECIPE. THE SECRET TO WHAT MAKES IT SO GOOD (OKAY, BEYOND THE BUTTER) IS USING FLAT-LEAF SPINACH. IT HAS A GREAT, SILKY TEXTURE WHEN COOKED.

- 12 tablespoons (1½ sticks) unsalted butter
- 2 pounds fresh flat-leaf spinach, left slightly damp after washing
  Kosher salt and freshly ground black pepper

Heat the butter in a large skillet over medium heat. Add the spinach, season with salt and pepper, and cook until the spinach is just wilted, 2 to 3 minutes.

MESA GRILL BLUE AND YELLOW CORN MUFFINS

MAKES 12 MUFFINS

THIS IS PROBABLY THE MOST CONSUMED ITEM IN MESA'S LONG HISTORY, AS THESE MUFFINS GRACE EVERY BREAD-BASKET THAT LEAVES THE KITCHEN. THEY HAVE A SURPRISING SPICINESS TO THEM AND ARE WONDERFUL TOPPED WITH BUTTER AND JALAPEÑO-CRANBERRY JELLY *(page 231)*. IT'S A LITTLE EXTRA WORK TO MAKE TWO BATTERS TO ACHIEVE THE BLUE AND GOLD COLOR, SO FEEL FREE TO TAKE A SHORTCUT AND USE JUST BLUE OR YELLOW CORNMEAL. THE MUFFINS WILL BE JUST AS GOOD. *See photograph on page 189.*

Nonstick cooking spray

6 tablespoons unsalted butter

½ cup finely diced red onion

4 cloves garlic, finely chopped

1⅓ cups whole milk

4 large eggs

2 tablespoons honey

½ cup finely diced red bell pepper

2 jalapeño chiles, finely diced

½ cup fresh corn kernels *(see page 9)* or frozen corn kernels, thawed

2 tablespoons finely chopped fresh cilantro

1 cup blue cornmeal

1 cup yellow cornmeal

1⅓ cups all-purpose flour

1 tablespoon baking powder

½ teaspoon baking soda

4 teaspoons kosher salt

1. Set a rack in the middle of the oven and preheat the oven to 400 degrees F. Grease a 12-muffin pan with nonstick cooking spray.

2. In a small saucepan, melt the butter over medium heat. Add the onion and cook until soft, 3 to 4 minutes. Add the garlic and cook for 30 seconds. Remove from the heat and let cool slightly. Divide the mixture evenly between 2 large bowls.

3. In another large bowl, whisk together the milk, eggs, honey, red pepper, jalapeños, corn, and cilantro. Pour the mixture into a measuring cup and add half of the mixture to each of the large bowls containing the onion mixture.

4. Put the blue cornmeal and yellow corn-meal in 2 separate bowls. To each bowl, add ⅔ cup flour, 1½ teaspoons baking powder, ¼ teaspoon baking soda, and 2 teaspoons salt. Mix each cornmeal mixture into a bowl with the liquid mixture.

5. Pour an equal amount of each batter side by side into each muffin cup and bake for about 16 minutes, or until a toothpick inserted into the center of a muffin comes out with a few moist crumbs on it. Let the muffins cool in the pan for 5 minutes and then remove to a cooling rack. The batters can be made up to 1 day in advance and refrigerated.

It's rare that a plate leaves my kitchen without a finishing touch of some kind. Sometimes it's as small as a swirl of Red Chile Oil or a sprinkling of cilantro. More often than not, though, each dish is completed and complemented by a relish, sauce, or vinaigrette created especially for it. We are not a bunch of minimalists at Mesa Grill; we believe in explosive flavor, exciting color, and tantalizing textures. I push all of my food to the limit by relying heavily on my repertoire of sauces, relishes (a word that is nearly interchangeable with *salsa* in my culinary dictionary), and vinaigrettes. Spicy Salmon Tartare on Crisp Hominy Cakes wouldn't be the hit it is without creamy Avocado Relish and Mesa Hot Sauce to provide some balance of color, spice, and texture. It simply wouldn't be a finished dish.

The wonderful thing about the following recipes is their versatility and simplicity. Many were created with specific dishes in mind, but that does not limit their usefulness. Mix and match. I'm sure you'll find that what you thought was boring (maybe a simply grilled chicken breast?) can become extraordinary with a little help from one of these. Grace your table with a burst of color, texture, and flavor.

RELISHES

SAUCES, AND VINAIGRETTES

RELISHES, SAUCES, AND VINAIGRETTES

AVOCADO RELISH

AVOCADO-TOMATILLO RELISH

BLACK BEAN–MANGO SALSA

CRANBERRY-MANGO RELISH

MIXED TOMATO SALSA

GRILLED PINEAPPLE AND PICKLED GREEN CHILE SALSA

PINEAPPLE-TOMATILLO SALSA

ROASTED PEPPER RELISH

TOMATILLO-JALAPENO SALSA

BLISTERED SERRANO HOT SAUCE

CILANTRO OIL

CILANTRO VINAIGRETTE

CITRUS VINAIGRETTE

GREEN CHILE VINAIGRETTE

MANGO-HABANERO HOT SAUCE

MESA GRILL BBQ SAUCE

MESA GRILL HOT SAUCE

MESA GRILL STEAK SAUCE

RED CHILE GRAVY

RED CHILE OIL

RED TOMATILLO SAUCE

SMOKED CHILE DRESSING

SMOKED RED PEPPER SAUCE

SWEET AND HOT YELLOW PEPPER SAUCE

JALAPEÑO-CRANBERRY JELLY

Clockwise from left: Mixed Tomato Salsa (page 218), Grilled Pineapple and Pickled Green Chile Salsa (page 219), and Cranberry-Mango Relish (page 217)

AVOCADO RELISH

MAKES ABOUT 3 CUPS

THIS TASTY RELISH MAKES A SIMPLY
GRILLED PIECE OF FISH OR CHICKEN
EXPONENTIALLY MORE APPETIZING.
AND, OF COURSE, IT'S JUST AS FABULOUS
AS A DIP FOR TORTILLA CHIPS.

- 3 ripe Hass avocados, peeled, pitted, and diced
- ½ small red onion, finely diced
- 1 serrano chile, finely diced (optional)

  Juice of 2 limes
- 2 tablespoons canola oil
- 2 teaspoons honey

  Kosher salt and freshly ground black pepper
- 3 tablespoons finely chopped fresh cilantro

Combine the avocados, onion, serrano, lime
juice, oil, honey, and salt and pepper to taste
in a medium bowl. Fold in the cilantro until
combined. This can be made up to 30 minutes in advance and refrigerated.

AVOCADO-TOMATILLO RELISH

MAKES ABOUT 4 CUPS

THIS BRIGHT RELISH MELDS COOL,
CREAMY AVOCADOS WITH TART, ACIDIC
TOMATILLOS FOR AN ALTOGETHER
FRESH, GREEN TOPPING OR DIP.

- 3 ripe Hass avocados, peeled, pitted, and diced
- 3 tomatillos, husked, scrubbed, and diced

  Juice of 2 limes
- 3 tablespoons canola oil
- 1 tablespoon honey

  Kosher salt and freshly ground black pepper
- 3 green onions, white and green parts, thinly sliced
- 3 tablespoons chopped fresh cilantro

Stir together the avocados, tomatillos, lime
juice, oil, honey, and salt and pepper to taste
in a medium bowl. Fold in the green onions
and cilantro until combined. This can be
made up to 30 minutes in advance and
refrigerated.

BLACK BEAN–MANGO SALSA

MAKES ABOUT 2½ CUPS

I FIRST DEVELOPED THIS SALSA AS A CRUCIAL PART OF MESA'S SEARED TUNA TOSTADA (page 124). BUT IT'S TOO DELICIOUS TO BE SAVED JUST FOR ONE DISH. SERVE IT WITH SIMPLY GRILLED CHICKEN OR SHRIMP OR ANY SEAFOOD.

- 1 cup canned black beans, rinsed and drained
- 1 ripe mango, peeled, pitted, and finely diced
- ½ small red onion, finely diced
- 1 jalapeño chile or serrano chile, seeded and finely diced
- ¼ cup fresh lime juice (2 to 3 limes)
- 1 to 2 tablespoons honey, depending on the sweetness of the mango
- ¼ cup olive oil
- ¼ cup coarsely chopped fresh cilantro

  Kosher salt and freshly ground black pepper

Combine the beans, mango, onion, chile, lime juice, honey, oil, and cilantro in a large bowl and season with salt and pepper. This can be prepared and refrigerated, covered, up to 1 day ahead. Bring to room temperature 1 hour before serving.

CRANBERRY-MANGO RELISH

MAKES ABOUT 6 CUPS

I KNOW THAT THERE ARE SOME PEOPLE OUT THERE WHO STILL EAT THEIR CRANBERRY SAUCE OUT OF A CAN, BUT FOR ME, THERE'S NO SUBSTITUTE FOR THE REAL THING. TRY THIS ONE WITH YOUR BIRD AT THANKSGIVING.

- 3 tablespoons unsalted butter
- 1 small red onion, finely diced
- 2 tablespoons grated fresh ginger
- 2 cups orange juice (not from concentrate)
- 1 tablespoon grated orange zest
- ¼ cup packed light brown sugar
- 1 pound fresh or frozen cranberries
- 2 ripe mangoes, peeled, pitted, and diced

1. Melt the butter in a medium saucepan over medium-high heat. Add the onion and ginger and cook until the onion is soft, 3 to 4 minutes. Add the orange juice, zest, and brown sugar and cook until the sugar is completely melted and the mixture thickens slightly, 5 to 7 minutes.

2. Add half of the cranberries and cook until they pop, 5 to 7 minutes. Add the remaining cranberries and cook for 5 minutes. Remove from the heat and add the mangoes. Serve at room temperature. This can be prepared and refrigerated, covered, up to 1 day ahead. Bring to room temperature 1 hour before serving.

MIXED TOMATO SALSA

MAKES ABOUT 2½ CUPS

THIS IS EXCELLENT USED AS A TOPPING FOR FISH OR CHICKEN OR EATEN WITH A BIG BOWL OF TORTILLA CHIPS. IF HEIRLOOM TOMATOES AREN'T AVAILABLE, JUST USE RED AND YELLOW CHERRY AND PEAR TOMATOES. IT WILL STILL BE GREAT.

1 pound heirloom tomatoes, diced, or cherry and pear tomatoes, quartered

1 jalapeño chile, finely diced

2 cloves garlic, finely chopped

3 tablespoons balsamic vinegar

1 teaspoon honey

3 tablespoons olive oil

1 tablespoon finely chopped fresh Mexican oregano or 1 teaspoon dried

3 tablespoons finely chopped fresh cilantro

Kosher salt and freshly ground black pepper

Combine the tomatoes, jalapeño, garlic, balsamic vinegar, honey, oil, oregano, and cilantro in a medium bowl and season with salt and pepper. Let sit at room temperature for at least 15 minutes before serving and up to 1 day in the refrigerator. Serve at room temperature.

GRILLED PINEAPPLE AND PICKLED GREEN CHILE SALSA

MAKES ABOUT 3 CUPS

THE SWEET PINEAPPLE AND PICKLED CHILES WORK PERFECTLY TOGETHER AND THE COLOR IS OFF THE CHARTS. THIS IS AN IDEAL ACCOMPANIMENT TO GRILLED SHRIMP OR SWORDFISH.

- 1 small ripe pineapple, peeled, cored, and sliced ½ inch thick
- ¼ cup olive oil
- 4 green onions, white and green parts, thinly sliced
- 2 pickled serrano chiles (recipe follows), thinly sliced
- 2 pickled jalapeño chiles (recipe follows), thinly sliced
- 2 tablespoons fresh lime juice
- 2 tablespoons rice wine vinegar
- 1 tablespoon honey

  Kosher salt and freshly ground black pepper

1. Preheat a grill to high or a grill pan over high heat.

2. Brush the pineapple slices on both sides with 2 tablespoons of the olive oil and grill until golden brown, 2 to 3 minutes per side.

3. Remove from the grill and cut into ¼-inch dice. Combine in a bowl with the green onions, serranos, jalapeños, lime juice, vinegar, the remaining 2 tablespoons oil, and the honey and season with salt and pepper to taste. This can be made up to 1 day in advance and refrigerated.

Pickled Green Chiles
MAKES 20

- 4 cups white wine vinegar
- 2 cups red wine vinegar
- ¼ cup sugar
- 2 tablespoons kosher salt
- 1 teaspoon coriander seeds
- 1 teaspoon black peppercorns
- 1 teaspoon fennel seeds
- 1 teaspoon mustard seeds
- 10 serrano chiles
- 10 jalapeño chiles

1. Combine the vinegars, sugar, salt, coriander seeds, peppercorns, fennel seeds, and mustard seeds in a medium saucepan and bring to a boil. Continue boiling until the sugar and salt have completely dissolved; remove from the heat and let cool to room temperature.

2. Place the chiles in a glass jar or nonreactive bowl and pour the vinegar mixture over. Cover and refrigerate for at least 24 hours. The chiles are best if stored at least 3 days before eating and will keep up to 3 weeks.

PINEAPPLE-TOMATILLO SALSA

MAKES ABOUT 2 CUPS

I LOVE THE REFRESHING TASTE OF THIS SALSA. SWEET PINEAPPLE PAIRED WITH THE TART HERBAL FLAVOR OF THE TOMATILLOS JUST WORKS PERFECTLY.

- 1 cup finely diced fresh pineapple (about ¼ small pineapple)
- ½ cup finely diced tomatillos (about 3 tomatillos)
- ¼ cup finely chopped red onion
- 1 jalapeño chile, seeded and finely chopped
- 2 tablespoons coarsely chopped fresh cilantro
- 3 tablespoons fresh lime juice
- 1 tablespoon honey
- 2 tablespoons olive oil

  Kosher salt and freshly ground black pepper

Combine the pineapple, tomatillos, onion, jalapeño, cilantro, lime juice, honey, and oil in a medium bowl and season with salt and pepper. This can be made up to 1 day in advance and refrigerated. Bring to room temperature before serving.

ROASTED PEPPER RELISH

MAKE ABOUT 2 CUPS

THIS RELISH HAS GREAT, TRUE PEPPER FLAVOR WITH A LITTLE HEAT. THE ROASTED RED BELL PEPPERS ADD A SOFT SWEETNESS TO THE POBLANOS, AS DOES THE ROASTED GARLIC. CILANTRO AND PARSLEY KEEP IT FRESH.

- 2 red bell peppers, roasted, peeled, seeded (*see page 18*), and cut into strips
- 2 poblano chiles, roasted, peeled, seeded (*see page 18*), and cut into strips
- 3 cloves roasted garlic, peeled (*see page 19*) and coarsely chopped
- 3 tablespoons olive oil
- 2 tablespoons finely chopped fresh flat-leaf parsley
- 2 tablespoons finely chopped fresh cilantro

  Kosher salt and freshly ground black pepper

Combine the roasted red peppers, poblanos, and garlic, the oil, parsley, and cilantro in a medium bowl and season with salt and pepper to taste. Let sit at room temperature for 30 minutes before serving. This can be made up to 1 day in advance and refrigerated. Bring to room temperature before serving.

TOMATILLO-JALAPENO SALSA

MAKES ABOUT 2 CUPS

THIS IS MY VERSION OF SALSA VERDE, OR GREEN SALSA. ROASTING THE TOMATILLOS, ONION, AND GARLIC GIVES THIS A SLIGHTLY SWEET TASTE, WHICH HELPS BALANCE THE HEAT OF THE JALAPEÑOS.

- 6 tomatillos, husked and scrubbed
- 1 small red onion, coarsely chopped
- 6 cloves garlic, peeled
- 3 jalapeño chiles, stemmed
- ¼ cup canola oil

    Kosher salt and freshly ground black pepper
- ¼ cup fresh lime juice (2 to 3 limes)
- 2 tablespoons honey
- ¼ cup chopped fresh cilantro

1. Preheat the oven to 375 degrees F.

2. Toss the tomatillos, onion, garlic, and jalapeños with the oil and season with salt and pepper to taste. Roast in a pan in the oven for 30 to 40 minutes, until all of the vegetables are soft.

3. Transfer the mixture to the bowl of a food processor or blender and process until smooth. Add the lime juice, honey, and cilantro and pulse until just combined. Serve at room temperature. This can be made up to 8 hours in advance and refrigerated. Bring to room temperature before serving.

BLISTERED SERRANO HOT SAUCE

MAKES ABOUT 1 CUP

THIS BRIGHT GREEN, SPICY SAUCE IS GOOD ON ANYTHING FROM EGGS TO FISH. IT GOES PARTICULARLY WELL DRIZZLED OVER SALMON TARTARE.

- 1 small red onion, coarsely chopped
- 10 serrano chiles, cut in half
- ¼ cup plus 2 tablespoons canola oil

    Kosher salt
- ½ cup rice wine vinegar
- ¼ cup chopped fresh cilantro
- 2 tablespoons honey

1. Preheat the oven to 400 degrees F.

2. Combine the onion and serranos in a small baking dish, toss with the 2 tablespoons canola oil, and season with salt. Roast in the oven until the onion is soft and the serranos are golden brown and blistered, 15 to 20 minutes.

3. Transfer the mixture to a blender, add the vinegar, cilantro, honey, and salt to taste, and blend until smooth. With the motor running, slowly add the ¼ cup oil and blend until emulsified. This can be made up to 2 days ahead and refrigerated. Bring to room temperature before serving.

CILANTRO OIL
MAKES ABOUT ¾ CUP

CILANTRO OIL GARNISHES JUST ABOUT
EVERY ONE OF MY DISHES AT MESA
GRILL. IT ADDS NOT ONLY A DASH OF
COLOR, BUT THE FABULOUS FRESH TASTE
OF CILANTRO, TOO.

1½ cups canola oil

1 cup packed fresh cilantro leaves
(stems included)

10 fresh spinach leaves

½ teaspoon kosher salt

Combine the oil, cilantro, spinach, and salt
in a blender and blend for 5 minutes. Strain
through a fine-mesh strainer (don't press on
the solids, or the oil will get cloudy) into a
bowl. This can be made up to 2 days in
advance and refrigerated. Bring to room
temperature before serving.

CILANTRO VINAIGRETTE
MAKES ABOUT 1 CUP

THIS VINAIGRETTE MAKES A PERFECT
DRESSING TOSSED WITH MIXED GREENS
OR DRIZZLED OVER MEAT, FISH, POULTRY,
OR GRILLED VEGETABLES.

2 tablespoons rice wine vinegar

1½ teaspoons Dijon mustard

2 teaspoons honey

Kosher salt and freshly ground black
pepper

1 cup chopped fresh cilantro

¼ cup plus 2 tablespoons canola oil

Combine the vinegar, mustard, honey, and
2 tablespoons of cold water in a blender,
season with salt and pepper, and blend until
smooth. Add the cilantro and blend until
incorporated. With the motor running, slowly
add the oil and blend until emulsified. This
can be made up to 8 hours in advance and
refrigerated. Bring to room temperature
before serving.

CITRUS VINAIGRETTE

MAKES ABOUT 2 CUPS

I LOVE THE FRESH TASTE OF THIS
VINAIGRETTE AND USE IT TO DRESS
DELICATE GREENS OR TO POUR DIRECTLY
ONTO GRILLED FISH JUST AS IT COMES
OFF THE GRILL.

- ¾ cup orange juice (not from concentrate)
- ¼ cup fresh lime juice (2 to 3 limes)
- 1 cup chopped fresh basil
- 1 cup packed fresh cilantro leaves
- 1 teaspoon kosher salt
- ¼ teaspoon freshly ground black pepper
- 1 heaping tablespoon honey
- ½ cup canola oil

Combine the orange and lime juices, basil,
cilantro, salt, pepper, honey, and oil in a
blender and blend for 1 minute. This can be
made up to 8 hours in advance and refrigerated. Bring to room temperature before
serving.

GREEN CHILE VINAIGRETTE

MAKES ABOUT 1 CUP

THIS THICK VINAIGRETTE CAN ALSO
DOUBLE AS A DIPPING SAUCE FOR
GRILLED SHRIMP OR BLUE CORN SQUID
(*page 94*).

- 2 poblano chiles, roasted, peeled, seeded (*see page 18*), and chopped
- 4 cloves roasted garlic, peeled (*see page 19*)
- 3 tablespoons red wine vinegar
- 3 tablespoons fresh lime juice
- 1 tablespoon honey

  Kosher salt and freshly ground black pepper
- ¾ cup canola oil
- ¼ cup chopped fresh cilantro

Combine the poblanos, garlic, vinegar, lime
juice, ¼ cup of water, and honey in a blender,
season with salt and pepper, and blend until
smooth. With the motor running, slowly add
the oil and blend until emulsified. Add the
cilantro and blend for 5 seconds more. There
should be flecks of the cilantro in the vinaigrette. This can be made up to 8 hours in
advance and refrigerated.

MANGO-HABANERO HOT SAUCE
MAKES ABOUT 1 CUP

HABANERO CHILES ARE SOME OF THE HOTTEST OUT THERE, BUT BENEATH THEIR INTENSE HEAT IS A REALLY NICE FRUITINESS. ADDING MANGO TO THE HOT SAUCE ENHANCES THE FLAVOR OF THE HABANERO AS WELL AS BALANCES ITS HEAT.

- 2 tablespoons canola oil
- 1 small Spanish onion, finely chopped
- 2 cloves garlic, finely chopped
- 3 ripe mangoes, peeled, pitted, and coarsely chopped
- 1 habanero chile, chopped
- 2 to 4 tablespoons honey, depending on the sweetness of the mangoes
- 1 cup white wine vinegar

  Kosher salt

1. Heat the oil in a medium saucepan over medium-high heat. Add the onion and cook until soft, 3 to 4 minutes. Add the garlic and cook for 30 seconds. Add the mangoes, habanero, and 1 cup of water and cook, stirring often, until the mangoes get very soft and the water evaporates, 8 to 10 minutes. Add the honey and vinegar and cook over low heat until the mixture thickens slightly, 5 to 7 minutes.

2. Transfer the mixture to a blender and blend until smooth. If the mixture is too thick to pour, add a few more tablespoons of water. Strain the mixture through a fine-mesh strainer set over a small bowl; season with salt. This sauce can be made 2 days in advance and refrigerated.

MESA GRILL BBQ SAUCE

MAKES ABOUT 3 CUPS

I LOVE TO SLATHER THIS BARBECUE SAUCE ON PORK, BEEF, CHICKEN, AND EVEN FISH. IT'S A COMPLEX SAUCE THAT IS SLIGHTLY SWEET FROM THE MOLASSES AND HONEY AND SLIGHTLY SMOKY FROM THE CHIPOTLE CHILES. IT'S EVERYTHING THAT YOU'D WANT FROM A BARBECUE SAUCE, AND IT'S SO MUCH BETTER THAN ANYTHING IN A BOTTLE.

- 2 tablespoons canola oil
- 1 large Spanish onion, coarsely chopped
- 5 cloves garlic, coarsely chopped
- 2 (15.5-ounce) cans plum tomatoes and their juice, pureed
- ¼ cup ketchup
- ¼ cup red wine vinegar
- ¼ cup Worcestershire sauce
- ¼ cup molasses
- 3 tablespoons Dijon mustard
- 3 tablespoons dark brown sugar
- 2 tablespoons honey
- 3 tablespoons ancho chile powder
- 3 tablespoons pasilla chile powder
- 1 tablespoon chipotle chile puree
  (*see page 18*)

  Kosher salt and freshly ground black pepper

1. Heat the oil over medium-high heat in a heavy-bottomed medium saucepan. Add the onion and cook until soft, 3 to 4 minutes. Add the garlic and cook for 1 minute. Add the tomatoes and 1 cup of water, bring to a boil, and cook, stirring occasionally, for 10 minutes.

2. Add the ketchup, vinegar, Worcestershire, molasses, mustard, brown sugar, honey, ancho powder, pasilla powder, and chipotle puree, lower the heat to medium, and simmer, stirring occasionally, until thickened, 25 to 30 minutes.

3. Transfer the mixture to a food processor and puree until smooth. Season with salt and pepper to taste. Pour into a bowl and allow to cool to room temperature. The sauce will keep for up to 1 week in the refrigerator stored in a tightly sealed container.

MESA GRILL HOT SAUCE

MAKES ABOUT 1 CUP

THIS HOT SAUCE IS JUST THAT—HOT—
BUT IT'S MORE ABOUT CAPTURING THE
FLAVOR OF THE SMOKY CHIPOTLES THAN
ANY KIND OF BURN-YOUR-MOUTH-OUT
HEAT. I LOVE IT WITH SALMON TARTARE
(page 90), SPRINKLED ON SPICY YELLOW
RICE WITH RED BEANS (page 202), YOU
NAME IT.

- 1 cup red wine vinegar
- 3 tablespoons chipotle chile puree
  (see page 18)
- 1½ tablespoons Dijon mustard
- 2 tablespoons honey
- 1 teaspoon salt

Whisk together the vinegar, chipotle puree,
mustard, honey, and salt in a small bowl. Let
sit for at least 30 minutes before serving to
allow the flavors to meld. The sauce will keep
for up to 2 weeks in the refrigerator stored in
a tightly sealed container.

MESA GRILL STEAK SAUCE

MAKES ABOUT 1¾ CUPS

THERE ARE PURISTS OUT THERE WHO
THINK A GOOD STEAK NEEDS LITTLE
MORE THAN A DUSTING OF SALT AND
PEPPER. I'D AGREE WITH THEM—UP TO A
POINT. BECAUSE A GREAT STEAK SAUCE
CAN ELEVATE ANY CUT TO PERFECTION.
OURS COMBINES SWEET MAPLE SYRUP,
SHARP DIJON MUSTARD, AND THE
CLASSIC STEAK ACCOMPANIMENT—
HORSERADISH—TO CREATE AN
ADDICTIVELY TASTY STEAK SAUCE.

- 1 cup ketchup
- ½ cup prepared horseradish, drained
- 3 tablespoons honey
- 2 tablespoons Dijon mustard
- 2 tablespoons pure maple syrup
- 2 teaspoons Worcestershire sauce
- 2 tablespoons ancho chile powder

  Kosher salt and freshly ground black
  pepper

Whisk together the ketchup, horseradish,
honey, mustard, maple syrup, Worcestershire, and ancho powder in a small bowl until
combined, and season with salt and pepper.
Cover and refrigerate for at least 1 hour to
allow the flavors to meld. Bring to room
temperature before serving. The sauce will
keep for up to 2 days in the refrigerator
stored in a tightly sealed container.

RED CHILE GRAVY

MAKES ABOUT 2 CUPS

IF THE PURPOSE OF GRAVY IS TO ADD
MOISTURE AND FLAVOR TO POULTRY
AND MEATS, WHY NOT ACTUALLY MAKE
IT FLAVORFUL? THIS GRAVY MAKES THE
MOST OF YOUR BIRD. I SERVE IT WITH
CORNISH GAME HENS WITH WILD RICE–
GOAT CHEESE STUFFING *(page 145)*. NEW
MEXICO CHILES, GARLIC, AND THYME
TAKE THE GRAVY AND YOUR MEAL TO
THE NEXT LEVEL.

- 2 tablespoons olive oil

- 1 medium red onion, coarsely chopped

- 2 cloves garlic, coarsely chopped

- 2 tablespoons ancho chile powder

- 5 cups Enriched Chicken Stock *(page 38)* or low-sodium chicken broth

- 3 New Mexico red chiles, toasted and seeded *(see page 18)*

- 1 tablespoon unsalted butter

- 1 tablespoon all-purpose flour

- 1 teaspoon finely chopped fresh thyme

- 2 teaspoons honey

  Kosher salt and freshly ground black pepper

1. Heat the oil in a medium saucepan over high heat. Add the onion and cook until soft, 3 to 4 minutes. Add the garlic and cook for 30 seconds. Add the ancho powder and cook for 30 seconds more. Add the stock and chiles, bring to a boil, and cook until reduced by half and the chiles are softened, 15 to 20 minutes.

2. Transfer the mixture to a food processor and process until smooth. Strain the mixture into a bowl.

3. Melt the butter in a small saucepan over medium heat. Whisk in the flour and cook for 1 minute. Whisk in the sauce mixture and thyme, bring to a boil, and cook, stirring occasionally, until thickened to a sauce consistency, 5 to 7 minutes. Stir in the honey and season with salt and pepper. This can be made up to 1 day in advance and refrigerated. Reheat before serving.

RED CHILE OIL

MAKES ABOUT 1 CUP

A SWIRL OF THIS VIBRANT RED OIL FINISHES MOST PLATES LEAVING MESA'S KITCHENS. IT TASTES GOOD, TO BE SURE, BUT IT'S ALSO A CRUCIAL PART OF CREATING A BEAUTIFULLY PRESENTED PLATE.

- 5 guajillo chiles, toasted and seeded (*see page 18*)
- 1 cup canola oil
- ½ teaspoon kosher salt

Combine the guajillos, oil, and salt in a blender and blend for 5 minutes. Strain into a bowl. This can be made up to 1 day in advance and refrigerated.

RED TOMATILLO SAUCE

MAKES ABOUT 2 CUPS

CONDIMENTS FEATURING TOMATILLOS ARE COMMONLY GREEN (THE COLOR OF THE TOMATILLO ITSELF), WHILE HERE SPICY NEW MEXICO RED CHILE POWDER STAINS THE SAUCE RED. I MOST COMMONLY PAIR THIS SAUCE WITH GRILLED TUNA, BUT IT'S ADAPTABLE TO A VARIETY OF MEATS AND POULTRY. IT'S AN ASSERTIVE SAUCE, HOWEVER, AND I WOULDN'T SERVE IT ALONGSIDE A MORE DELICATE TYPE OF SEAFOOD.

- 8 tomatillos, husked and scrubbed
- 1 medium red onion, coarsely chopped
- 3 cloves garlic
- 1 serrano chile, coarsely chopped
- ¼ cup olive oil
  Kosher salt and freshly ground black pepper
- 3 tablespoons New Mexico red chile powder
- ¼ cup red wine vinegar
- 2 tablespoons honey
- ¼ cup chopped fresh cilantro

1. Preheat the oven to 375 degrees F.

2. Put the tomatillos, onion, garlic, and serrano in a small baking dish, toss with the oil, and season with salt and pepper. Roast until the vegetables are soft, 20 to 25 minutes.

3. Transfer the mixture to a food processor or blender, add the chile powder, vinegar, ½ cup of water, the honey, and cilantro, and process until smooth. Season with salt and pepper and scrape into a bowl. This can be made up to 1 day in advance and refrigerated. Reheat before serving.

SMOKED CHILE DRESSING
MAKES ABOUT 1 CUP

THIS DRESSING IS WHAT BINDS TOGETHER ALL OF THE ELEMENTS OF MY POACHED SALMON SALAD *(page 56)*. MAKING IT IN THE BLENDER IS AN IMPORTANT STEP IN CREATING A SMOOTH AND COHESIVE DRESSING.

¼ cup red wine vinegar

1 clove garlic, coarsely chopped

2 tablespoons chopped red onion

1 tablespoon chipotle chile puree
   (see page 18)

1 tablespoon honey

1 teaspoon kosher salt

¾ cup canola oil

Combine the vinegar, garlic, onion, chipotle puree, honey, and salt in a blender and blend until smooth. With the motor running, slowly add the oil and blend until emulsified. This can be made up to 1 day in advance and refrigerated.

SMOKED RED PEPPER SAUCE
MAKES ABOUT 2½ CUPS

THIS IS ONE OF THE WORKHORSES OF THE MESA GRILL KITCHEN. ROASTED RED PEPPERS AND CHIPOTLE PUREE GIVE THE SAUCE A DEEP COLOR AND FLAVOR THAT COMPLEMENTS SO MANY DISHES.

4 red bell peppers, roasted, peeled, seeded *(see page 18)*, and chopped

½ small red onion, coarsely chopped

4 cloves roasted garlic, peeled
   (see page 19)

¼ cup red wine vinegar

1 tablespoon honey

1 tablespoon Dijon mustard

1 tablespoon chipotle chile puree
   (see page 18)

Kosher salt and freshly ground black pepper

½ cup canola oil

Combine the red peppers, onion, garlic, vinegar, honey, mustard, and chipotle puree in a blender, season with salt and pepper, and blend until smooth. With the motor running, slowly add the oil and blend until emulsified. Strain the sauce into a bowl. This sauce can be made 1 day in advance and refrigerated.

SWEET AND HOT YELLOW PEPPER SAUCE

MAKES ABOUT 1 CUP

YELLOW BELL PEPPERS AND HABANERO CHILES ARE AT COMPLETELY DIFFERENT ENDS OF THE PEPPER HEAT SPECTRUM—MAYBE THAT'S WHY COMBINING THE TWO WORKS SO WELL. I SERVE THIS SAUCE ALONGSIDE THE FRIED SQUASH BLOSSOMS WITH RICOTTA AND ROASTED CORN *(page 72)* AND FIND THAT IT REALLY COMPLEMENTS THE DELICATE AND SWEET RICOTTA FILLING.

- 2 cups sugar
- 1½ cups rice wine vinegar
- 1 habanero chile
- 2 large yellow bell peppers, seeded and chopped

  Kosher salt

1. Combine the sugar, vinegar, and habanero in a medium nonreactive saucepan over high heat, bring to a boil, and cook until the mixture is reduced by half. Reduce the heat to medium, add the yellow peppers, and cook, stirring occasionally, until the peppers are soft, 8 to 10 minutes. Remove the habanero and discard.

2. Carefully transfer the mixture to a blender and blend until smooth. If the mixture is too thick to pour, thin with a few tablespoons of water. Season with salt. Pour into a bowl and let cool to room temperature. This can be made up to 2 days in advance and refrigerated.

JALAPENO-CRANBERRY JELLY

MAKES ABOUT 2 CUPS

THIS JELLY IS GREAT TO HAVE ON HAND, AS IT GOES BEAUTIFULLY WITH GRILLED LAMB, TURKEY, VENISON—ALL SORTS OF MEAT DISHES. NOT ONLY THAT, I THINK IT'S GREAT WITH MESA GRILL BLUE AND YELLOW CORN MUFFINS *(page 211)*, TOO! POWDERED FRUIT PECTIN, SUCH AS SURE-JELL, IS AVAILABLE IN MOST GROCERY STORES.

- 2 cups red wine vinegar
- 2 cups sugar
- 2 star anise
- 2 cups fresh or frozen cranberries
- 5 jalapeño chiles, finely diced

  Grated zest of 3 oranges
- ½ cup fresh orange juice (about 2 oranges)
- 1 tablespoon fruit pectin powder, preferably fast-acting

1. Bring the vinegar and sugar to a boil in a heavy-bottomed nonreactive saucepan over high heat and stir until the sugar has melted. Add the star anise, cranberries, jalapeños, orange zest, and orange juice. Reduce the heat to medium and simmer for 20 minutes, stirring occasionally.

2. Remove the mixture from the heat, discard the star anise, and add the pectin, mixing well. Return the pan to the stove, raise the heat to high, and cook until the mixture comes back to a boil. Pour into a sterilized glass pint jar and seal according to the manufacturer's directions, or store, covered, in a nonreactive bowl or jar for up to 1 week in the refrigerator.

I will now freely admit two things to you: (1) I have an insatiable sweet tooth and (2) I am no pastry chef. As I see it, no meal is complete without a sinful dessert, or at the very least a scoop of ice cream. I've been lucky enough to have had two very talented and dedicated pastry chefs fulfilling that need. Wayne Harley Brachman was my first pastry chef and Vicki Wells picked up the ball and then some with her elegant, Southwestern-inspired takes on French and American classics.

Always satisfying, Mesa Grill's desserts run the gamut from homey and comforting, like Wayne's divine Chocolate Custard Corn Pone, to stylish and refined—though no less decadent—choices such as Vicki's individually sized Warm Chocolate Cakes with Dulce de Leche. Should you happen to be one of those rampant crème brûlée devotees, you'll go crazy for the two versions we have here, a dreamy Lime-Vanilla and a to-die-for Milk Chocolate–Peanut Butter. Whatever dessert piques your interest, I know you can't be disappointed with what we have to offer. I know I haven't been yet.

DESSERTS

WARM CHOCOLATE CAKES with Dulce de Leche

CHOCOLATE-COCONUT BREAD PUDDING with Passion Fruit Sauce

CHOCOLATE CUSTARD CORN PONE with Freshly Whipped Cream

MILK CHOCOLATE–PEANUT BUTTER CREME BRULEE

LIME-VANILLA CREME BRULEE

CARAMEL APPLE SHORTCAKES with Apple Cider Reduction

SPICY COCONUT TAPIOCA with Mango and Blackberries

TROPICAL FRUIT SALAD with Pineapple-Tequila Sherbet

TWISTED SOUR CREAM–COCONUT STICKS

BLUE CORN BISCOTTI

WARM CHOCOLATE CAKES WITH DULCE DE LECHE

SERVES 6

THIS IS MESA GRILL'S BEST-SELLING DESSERT—IN LAS VEGAS AND NEW YORK. REALLY, WHAT'S NOT TO LIKE ABOUT A CHOCOLATE CAKE WITH A MOLTEN INTERIOR OF RICH DULCE DE LECHE? MAKE SURE YOU HAVE THE DULCE DE LECHE—EITHER HOMEMADE OR STORE-BOUGHT—ON HAND BEFORE YOU START MAKING THE CAKE BATTER.

- 8 tablespoons (1 stick) unsalted butter, plus extra for the molds
- 1 tablespoon all-purpose flour, plus extra for the molds
- 4 ounces bittersweet chocolate, chopped
- 2 large eggs
- 2 large egg yolks
- ¼ cup sugar
- 2 large egg whites
- 6 tablespoons Dulce de Leche (recipe follows)

  Vanilla or pecan ice cream, for serving

  Hot fudge sauce, for serving (optional)

1. Preheat the oven to 425 degrees F. Butter and lightly flour six 4-ounce ramekins or custard cups. Tap out the excess flour and refrigerate the molds for 15 minutes to set the butter.

2. Melt the butter and chocolate in the top of a double boiler over simmering water. Remove from the heat and let cool slightly.

3. In the bowl of an electric stand mixer fitted with the paddle attachment, beat together the whole eggs, yolks, and the sugar on medium-high speed until light and thick. Add the melted chocolate mixture and beat to combine. Mix in the 1 tablespoon flour until just combined. Transfer to a large bowl.

4. Wash and dry the mixing bowl, add the egg whites, and whip on medium speed until soft peaks form. Fold the whites into the chocolate mixture. Fill each ramekin halfway with the batter. Place 1 heaping tablespoon of the dulce de leche in the center and then top with the remaining batter.

5. Place the ramekins on a baking sheet, and bake until the sides have set but the centers remain soft, 6 to 7 minutes.

6. Run a small knife around the perimeter of each cake to loosen slightly and then invert each mold onto a plate to unmold. Serve with ice cream and hot fudge sauce.

Dulce de Leche
MAKES ABOUT 1 CUP

- 2 cups whole milk
- 1 cup canned unsweetened coconut milk
- 2½ tablespoons dark corn syrup
- ¼ cup sugar
- 2 cinnamon sticks, preferably Mexican cinnamon (canela)
- 1 vanilla bean, split lengthwise and seeds scraped
- ¼ teaspoon baking soda

1. Combine the milk, coconut milk, corn syrup, sugar, cinnamon sticks, and vanilla bean and seeds in a medium saucepan and bring to a boil over medium-high heat. Dissolve the baking soda in a small bowl with a few tablespoons of water and whisk into the milk mixture. Cook the mixture, stirring occasionally, until reduced by half and caramelized, 8 to 10 minutes.

2. Remove the vanilla bean, transfer the mixture to a bowl, and refrigerate until firm, about 2 hours. This will keep, tightly covered, in the refrigerator for up to 1 week.

CHOCOLATE-COCONUT BREAD PUDDING WITH PASSION FRUIT SAUCE

SERVES 4

THIS DECADENT BREAD PUDDING COMBINES TWO OF MY ALL-TIME FAVORITE THINGS—CHOCOLATE AND COCONUT. THE ACIDITY OF THE PASSION FRUIT SAUCE ADDS ANOTHER LAYER OF FABULOUS FLAVOR.

½ loaf brioche or challah, cut into 2-inch cubes

2 tablespoons unsalted butter, melted

One 14-ounce can unsweetened coconut milk

1 cup heavy cream

¼ cup sugar

4 large egg yolks

1 tablespoon dark rum

1 teaspoon pure coconut extract or pure vanilla extract

4 ounces bittersweet chocolate, coarsely chopped

¼ cup finely shredded dried unsweetened coconut

Passion Fruit Sauce *(recipe follows)*

1. Preheat the oven to 325 degrees F.

2. Put the bread cubes on a baking sheet, toss with the butter, and bake until lightly golden brown, 12 to 15 minutes, turning once.

3. Combine the coconut milk and ½ cup of the heavy cream in a small saucepan and bring to a simmer over medium heat. Remove from the heat and let cool slightly. Whisk together the sugar and egg yolks in a large bowl until pale. Whisk in the warm coconut mixture, dark rum, and coconut extract until combined. Add the bread cubes to the cream mixture and toss to coat. Let sit for 5 minutes.

4. Bring the remaining ½ cup heavy cream to a simmer in a small saucepan. Remove from the heat, add the chocolate, let sit for 1 minute, and then whisk until the chocolate ganache is smooth.

5. Transfer the bread mixture to a 9-inch square baking dish and drizzle the top with the chocolate ganache and the coconut. Bake for 25 to 30 minutes, until set around the sides but still slightly loose in the center. Remove from the oven and let sit at room temperature for 30 minutes. Serve warm or at room temperature drizzled with the passion fruit sauce. This can be made up to 1 day in advance and refrigerated. Reheat before serving.

Passion Fruit Sauce

MAKES ABOUT ½ CUP

- 6 passion fruit
- ¼ cup sugar
- ¼ cup orange juice (not from concentrate)
- 2 tablespoons white rum

Cut the passion fruit in half and scoop out the flesh and seeds into a small saucepan. Add the sugar, orange juice, and rum and cook, stirring occasionally, over high heat until the sugar has melted and the sauce has thickened, 5 to 7 minutes. Transfer to a bowl and chill in the refrigerator until cold, at least 2 hours. This can be made up to 1 day in advance.

HOLIDAY MENU

Cranberry Margarita *(page 27)*

Roasted Cauliflower and Green Chile Soup with Blue Corn–Goat Cheese Taquitos *(page 39)*

Caramelized Apple Salad with Blue Cheese, Black Walnuts, and Spicy Orange Vinaigrette *(page 61)*

Cornish Game Hens with Wild Rice–Goat Cheese Stuffing *(page 145)*

Sweet Potato Gratin *(page 196)*

Chocolate-Coconut Bread Pudding with Passion Fruit Sauce *(opposite)*

CHOCOLATE CUSTARD CORN PONE WITH FRESHLY WHIPPED CREAM

SERVES 6 TO 8

THIS IS A FANTASTIC VERSION OF A CHOCOLATE BREAD PUDDING. THE ALMOST GRAINY TEXTURE OF THE CORN BREAD IS WHAT MAKES THIS ONE SPECIAL—WELL, THAT AND THE INCREDIBLY RICH CHOCOLATE CUSTARD. TOP WITH HOT FUDGE SAUCE AND CHOCOLATE SHAVINGS, IF DESIRED.

- 1 tablespoon unsalted butter, plus extra for the pan
- 7 ounces semisweet chocolate, coarsely chopped
- ½ cup all-purpose flour
- ½ cup white cornmeal
- ¾ cup sugar
- 1 tablespoon ancho chile powder
- 1 teaspoon baking powder
- ¼ teaspoon kosher salt
- 2 large eggs
- ½ cup buttermilk
- 2 cups whole milk
- 1 cup heavy cream
- 6 large egg yolks

  Freshly Whipped Cream (*recipe follows*)

1. To make the corn bread, set a rack in the middle of the oven and preheat the oven to 375 degrees F. Lightly butter a 9-inch square cake pan. Line the bottom with parchment paper.

2. Melt 3 ounces of the chocolate and the 1 tablespoon butter in the top of a double boiler over barely simmering water, or in a microwave. Remove from the heat and let cool.

3. Whisk together the flour, cornmeal, ¼ cup of the sugar, the ancho powder, baking powder, and salt in a large bowl. Whisk together the whole eggs, buttermilk, and cooled chocolate mixture in a small bowl, add to the flour mixture, and whisk until just combined. Spread the batter evenly in the prepared pan.

4. Bake for about 20 minutes, or until set and a tester comes out clean. Let cool in the pan on a wire rack. Break the corn bread into 1-inch chunks. Spread in a shallow 2-quart baking dish.

5. Reduce the oven temperature to 325 degrees F.

6. To make the custard, melt the remaining 4 ounces chocolate in the top of a double boiler over barely simmering water, or in a microwave. Remove from the heat and let cool.

7. In a medium heavy-bottomed saucepan, combine the milk, cream, and 1 tablespoon of the sugar and bring to a simmer over medium heat. Meanwhile, put the remaining ¼ cup plus 3 tablespoons sugar and the egg yolks in a large bowl and whisk until pale. While gently whisking the yolks, drizzle the hot cream mixture over them so that they are gradually warmed up. Whisk in the melted chocolate.

8. Using a fine-mesh strainer, strain the custard over the corn bread chunks. Wiggle the chunks around so they are well soaked. Place the baking dish in a roasting pan and add enough hot water to come halfway up the sides of the dish.

9. Bake for about 40 minutes, or until set around the sides but still loose in the center. Remove from the oven and let cool slightly. Serve warm with freshly whipped cream.

Freshly Whipped Cream
MAKES 2 CUPS

- 1 cup heavy cream
- 2 tablespoons sugar
- 1 teaspoon pure vanilla extract

Whip the heavy cream, sugar, and vanilla in a large bowl with an electric mixer on medium-high speed until soft peaks form.

MILK CHOCOLATE–PEANUT BUTTER CREME BRULEE

SERVES 4

I CAN'T THINK OF TOO MANY PEOPLE WHO DON'T LOVE THE CLASSIC COMBINATION OF CHOCOLATE AND PEANUT BUTTER. THIS DESSERT TAKES THAT CANDY-COUNTER FAVORITE AND MAKES IT ELEGANT.

- 3 cups heavy cream
- ½ cup whole milk
- ½ cup peanuts, toasted *(see page 19)*
- ½ cup granulated sugar
- 3½ ounces milk chocolate, finely chopped
- ¼ cup smooth peanut butter, such as Jif
- 7 large egg yolks
- ¼ teaspoon kosher salt
- ½ cup turbinado sugar or other raw sugar

1. Bring the heavy cream and milk to a simmer in a medium saucepan over medium heat, remove from the stove, and stir in the peanuts. Let sit, covered, for at least 1 hour in the refrigerator and up to 24 hours. Strain the mixture, wipe out the pan, and return the mixture to the pan.

2. Preheat the oven to 350 degrees F.

3. Place the mixture back on the stove, add ¼ cup of the granulated sugar, and bring to a simmer, stirring until the sugar has dissolved. Remove from the heat and whisk in the chocolate and peanut butter. Whisk together the yolks, the remaining ¼ cup granulated sugar, and the salt in a large bowl until pale in color. Slowly whisk in the hot chocolate mixture and continue whisking until combined. Strain the mixture through a fine-mesh strainer into a bowl.

4. Place four 8-ounce ramekins inside a large baking dish and using a ladle, divide the mixture evenly among the ramekins. Pour hot water into the dish until it reaches halfway up the sides of the ramekins. Bake until the custard is set around the edges but still jiggles in the center, 40 to 45 minutes. The custard will continue to cook as it cools. Let cool to room temperature, then cover each ramekin with plastic wrap and refrigerate until cold, at least 4 hours and up to 24 hours.

5. Preheat the broiler until very hot.

6. Sprinkle an even coat of the turbinado sugar over each custard, place the ramekins on a baking sheet, and broil until the sugar is melted and dark golden brown, about 2 minutes. Remove from the oven and serve immediately.

LIME-VANILLA CREME BRULEE

SERVES 4

IT MAY SEEM LIKE AN OXYMORON, BUT THIS CRÈME BRÛLÉE TASTES BOTH RICH AND LIGHT; THE FRESH, TART TASTE OF LIME ZEST CUTS THROUGH THE RICHNESS OF THE EGG CUSTARD. AS NICE AS THIS DESSERT IS, IT WOULD BE MADE EVEN NICER ACCOMPANIED BY A TROPICAL FRUIT SALAD LIGHTLY DRESSED IN LIME JUICE.

3½ cups heavy cream

½ cup whole milk

Grated zest of 3 limes

1 vanilla bean, split lengthwise and seeds scraped

7 large egg yolks

1 large egg

½ cup granulated sugar

½ teaspoon kosher salt

½ cup turbinado sugar or other raw sugar

1. Combine the cream, milk, zest, and vanilla bean and seeds in a medium saucepan and bring to a simmer, stirring occasionally, over medium heat. Remove from the heat and let sit for at least 30 minutes. Return the pan to the stove and bring the mixture to a simmer.

2. Preheat the oven to 300 degrees F.

3. Whisk together the egg yolks, whole egg, granulated sugar, and salt until pale. Slowly whisk in the hot cream mixture until combined and strain into a bowl.

4. Place four 8-ounce ramekins in a large baking pan and ladle the mixture into the ramekins. Pour hot water about halfway up the sides of the molds and bake until the custard is set around the edges but still jiggles in the center, 40 to 45 minutes. The custard will continue to cook as it cools. Let cool to room temperature, then cover each ramekin with plastic wrap and refrigerate until cold, at least 4 hours and up to 24 hours.

5. Preheat the broiler.

6. Sprinkle an even coat of the turbinado sugar over each custard, place the ramekins on a baking sheet, and broil until the sugar is melted and dark golden brown, about 2 minutes. Remove from the oven and serve immediately.

CARAMEL APPLE SHORTCAKES WITH APPLE CIDER REDUCTION

SERVES 6

PERHAPS BEST KNOWN WITH A FILLING OF SUMMER STRAWBERRIES, SHORT-CAKES ARE GOOD TO MAKE YEAR-ROUND WITH IN-SEASON FRUITS. IN THIS FALL RENDITION, APPLES ARE CARAMELIZED TO AN ALMOST CANDIED SWEETNESS AND PAIRED WITH FLAKY BISCUITLIKE SHORTBREAD AND REFRESHING SOUR CREAM WHIPPED CREAM. *See photograph on page 232.*

SHORTCAKES

1½ cups all-purpose flour, plus extra for forming the biscuits

¼ cup plus 3 tablespoons sugar

1 tablespoon plus ¼ teaspoon baking powder

¼ teaspoon baking soda

¼ teaspoon kosher salt

6 tablespoons cold unsalted butter, cut into small cubes

About 1 cup buttermilk

2 tablespoons whole milk or heavy cream

Apple Cider Reduction *(recipe follows)*

APPLES AND CREAM

3 tablespoons unsalted butter

½ vanilla bean, split lengthwise and seeds scraped

5 Granny Smith apples, peeled, cored, and cut into eighths

½ cup sugar

¼ cup apple brandy, such as applejack

¾ cup very cold heavy cream

¾ cup very cold sour cream

1. Preheat the oven to 375 degrees F. Line a baking sheet with parchment paper.

2. To make the shortcakes, whisk together the flour, the 3 tablespoons sugar, the baking powder, baking soda, and salt in a large bowl.

3. Cut the butter into the mixture with a pastry cutter or your fingertips until the mixture turns a light yellow and the butter is still visible but in much smaller pieces. Gently stir in ½ cup of the buttermilk. Keep stirring in more buttermilk until a soft dough is formed; you may not need all of the buttermilk.

4. Pat the dough out on a floured surface to a 1½-inch thickness. Cut out six 2-inch rounds with a metal cutter or the top of a glass; dip the cutter into flour before cutting each time to prevent sticking. Place the biscuits on the prepared baking sheet and brush the tops with the milk and sprinkle with the ¼ cup sugar.

5. Bake the biscuits until golden brown, 12 to 15 minutes. Remove to a baking rack and let cool.

6. To caramelize the apples, melt the butter over medium-high heat in a large sauté pan. Add the vanilla bean and seeds and apple slices and cook until the apples begin to brown, 5 to 7 minutes. Stir in the sugar and continue to cook, stirring occasionally, until the apples are soft and caramelized.

7. Remove the pan from the heat and stir in the apple brandy. Carefully return to the heat and cook, stirring occasionally, for 5 minutes. Remove from the heat and let cool slightly. Remove the vanilla bean.

8. Whip the heavy cream in a medium bowl with an electric mixer on medium speed until slightly thickened. Add the sour cream and continue whipping until soft peaks form.

9. To serve, drizzle a few tablespoons of the apple cider reduction onto each of 6 plates. Split the shortcakes in half and place the bottoms on the plates. Spoon several heaping tablespoons of the caramelized apples over each shortcake bottom and top with a few dollops of the whipped cream and another drizzle of the apple cider reduction. Replace the tops.

Apple Cider Reduction
MAKES ABOUT I CUP

- 1 quart apple cider
- 2 tablespoons apple cider vinegar
- 2 tablespoons apple brandy, such as applejack
- ½ vanilla bean, split lengthwise and seeds scraped
- 1 cinnamon stick

Combine the apple cider, apple cider vinegar, apple brandy, vanilla bean and seeds, and cinnamon stick in a large saucepan and bring to a boil over high heat. Cook, stirring occasionally, until reduced to a thick syrup, 25 to 30 minutes. Remove from the heat and let cool to room temperature. Remove the vanilla bean and cinnamon stick before serving. This can be made up to 1 day in advance and refrigerated. Bring to room temperature before serving.

SPICY COCONUT TAPIOCA WITH MANGO AND BLACKBERRIES

SERVES 4

THIS COULDN'T BE FURTHER AWAY FROM THE TAPIOCA PUDDING CUPS YOU PICK UP AT THE SUPERMARKET. IT'S SUBTLY SPICY, RICH, AND ABSOLUTELY DELICIOUS. THE CREAMINESS OF COCONUT MILK AND CRÈME FRAÎCHE IS OFFSET BY THE SPICINESS OF CINNAMON AND NUTMEG AND THAT SURPRISING INGREDIENT, SERRANO CHILE. GINGER AND LIME ZEST ADD A CLEAN, LIGHT NOTE TO THE DISH. THIS IS ONE OF VICKI WELLS'S SIGNATURE DESSERTS.

½ cup tapioca

2 (14-ounce) cans unsweetened coconut milk

2 cinnamon sticks

1 (1-inch) piece fresh ginger, peeled

Grated zest of 1 lime

½ serrano chile (optional)

½ whole nutmeg, crushed

¼ cup sugar

⅓ cup simple syrup (see page 19)

⅓ cup crème fraîche

Mango and Blackberry Salad (recipe follows)

1. Put the tapioca in a bowl, pour 2 cups of cold water over it, and let sit for 1 hour.

2. Combine the coconut milk, cinnamon sticks, ginger, zest, serrano, nutmeg, and sugar in a large saucepan and cook, stirring occasionally, over medium heat until reduced to 3 cups, 25 to 30 minutes.

3. Set a medium bowl in a large bowl of ice water.

4. Strain the coconut milk mixture into a medium saucepan. Drain the tapioca and add it to the pan. Place the pan over medium heat, bring to a simmer, and cook for 2 minutes. Pour the mixture into the bowl set in the ice-water bath and stir until cool.

5. Whisk the simple syrup and crème fraîche into the coconut milk–tapioca mixture. Serve immediately, in bowls topped with mango and blackberry salad.

Mango and Blackberry Salad
MAKES ABOUT 2 CUPS

1 ripe mango, peeled, pitted, and diced

1 cup fresh blackberries

¼ cup sugar

½ vanilla bean, split lengthwise and seeds scraped

1 tablespoon finely grated fresh ginger

Fresh mint leaves, for garnish

Combine the mango, blackberries, sugar, vanilla bean and seeds, and ginger in a medium bowl and let sit at room temperature for 30 minutes. Remove the vanilla bean before garnishing with fresh mint leaves and serving. This can be made up to 1 day ahead and stored in the refrigerator.

TROPICAL FRUIT SALAD WITH PINEAPPLE-TEQUILA SHERBET

SERVES 4

THIS REFRESHING FRUIT SALAD AND SHERBET IS A PERFECT LIGHT ENDING TO A FULL-FLAVORED MESA MEAL. SERVE WITH TWISTED SOUR CREAM–COCONUT STICKS (*opposite*), IF DESIRED.

PINEAPPLE-TEQUILA SHERBET

- 1 ripe pineapple, peeled
- 1½ cups simple syrup (*see page 19*)
- ¼ cup silver tequila
- ½ cup heavy cream
- ½ teaspoon kosher salt

FRUIT SALAD

- 2 ripe Asian pears, seeded and diced
- 2 Granny Smith apples, cored and diced
- 2 ripe papayas, peeled, seeded, and diced
- 2 ripe mangoes, peeled, pitted, and diced
- 2 kiwis, peeled and diced
- 12 strawberries, diced
- 1 tablespoon good-quality white tequila
- 1 tablespoon fresh lime juice
- 2 tablespoons sugar
- ½ vanilla bean, split lengthwise and seeds scraped
- ¼ teaspoon kosher salt

1. To make the sherbet, chop the pineapple into large chunks, including the core. Place in a food processor with the simple syrup, process until smooth, and then strain through a fine-mesh strainer into a bowl.

2. Stir in the tequila, heavy cream, and salt and freeze in an ice cream maker according to the manufacturer's instructions.

3. Scrape into a clean bowl, cover the surface with plastic wrap, and freeze until firm, at least 4 hours. The sherbet can be made up to 1 day in advance.

4. To make the fruit salad, combine the Asian pears, apples, papayas, mangoes, kiwis, strawberries, tequila, lime juice, sugar, vanilla bean and seeds, and salt in a large bowl; cover and refrigerate for at least 1 hour and up to 8 hours. Remove the vanilla bean before serving.

5. To serve, place a scoop of the sherbet into each of 4 bowls and spoon the fruit salad around.

TWISTED SOUR CREAM–COCONUT STICKS

MAKES 8

THESE CRISPY COOKIES ARE PERFECT SERVED WITH TROPICAL FRUIT SALAD WITH PINEAPPLE-TEQUILA SHERBET *(opposite)* OR A CUP OF COFFEE.

- ⅔ cup sour cream
- 1 large egg yolk
- 1½ cups all-purpose flour, plus extra for rolling out the dough
- ½ teaspoon kosher salt
- ½ pound (2 sticks) cold unsalted butter, cut into small pieces
- 1 cup sugar
- ⅔ cup finely shredded dried unsweetened coconut

1. Whisk together the sour cream and egg yolk in a small bowl.

2. Combine the 1½ cups flour and the salt in the bowl of an electric stand mixer fitted with the paddle attachment and mix for 5 seconds. Add the butter and mix until the mixture looks like coarse sand. Add the sour cream mixture and mix until just combined.

3. Scrape the dough onto a piece of plastic wrap and form into a disk. Wrap and refrigerate until firm, at least 1 hour and up to 24 hours.

4. Preheat the oven to 350 degrees F. Line a baking sheet with parchment paper. Remove the dough from the refrigerator and let sit for 5 minutes.

5. Lightly dust a work surface with flour and roll out the dough to a ¼-inch thickness. Sprinkle the top of the dough with the sugar and roll again to make sure the sugar adheres to the dough and to make the dough slightly thinner.

6. Sprinkle the dough with the coconut and roll again as for the sugar. Using a sharp knife, cut the dough into a 12 x 12-inch square and cut into 8 equal strips. Hold each strip of dough by the ends, stretch it to the length of the baking sheet, twist it, and transfer to the prepared baking sheet; refrigerate for 15 minutes to chill.

7. Remove from the refrigerator and bake for 15 to 20 minutes, until golden brown. Let cool completely on a wire rack. These can be made up to 1 day ahead and stored in an airtight container.

BLUE CORN BISCOTTI
MAKES 24

THESE MIGHT BE SOME OF MY FAVORITE COOKIES. THEY WERE CREATED BY MESA GRILL'S ORIGINAL PASTRY CHEF, THE TALENTED WAYNE HARLEY BRACHMAN. THE NUTTY BLUE CORNMEAL IS A GREAT MATCH FOR PECANS AND PISTACHIOS.

2½ cups all-purpose flour, plus extra for shaping the dough

1¼ cups sugar

2 tablespoons yellow cornmeal

¼ cup plus 2 tablespoons blue cornmeal

1½ teaspoons baking powder

½ teaspoon kosher salt

¾ cup pecans or pistachios, or a combination, coarsely chopped

8 tablespoons (1 stick) unsalted butter, at room temperature

2 large eggs

2 tablespoons anisette or Sambuca

1. Set a rack in the middle of the oven and preheat the oven to 375 degrees F. Line a baking sheet with parchment paper.

2. Put the flour, sugar, yellow and blue cornmeals, baking powder, salt, and pecans in the bowl of an electric stand mixer and stir together with a fork. Fit the mixer with the paddle attachment at its slowest speed, and beat in the butter bit by bit until the mixture just comes together. Add the eggs and liqueur, and beat until the dough is thoroughly blended.

3. Transfer the dough to a floured work surface, and shape it into a log 3 inches wide, 12 inches long, and 1 inch high. Place the log on the prepared baking sheet and bake for about 30 minutes, or until lightly browned. Remove from the oven and let cool on the baking sheet for 20 minutes.

4. Reduce the oven temperature to 350 degrees F.

5. Transfer the dough log to a cutting board. With a serrated knife, slice the log into ½-inch slices, and lay them, cut side up, on the baking sheet. Bake for 10 to 12 minutes, until lightly browned around the edges. Let cool on the baking sheet on a wire rack. These can be made up to 2 days in advance and stored in an airtight container.

Sweet and savory Mango-Glazed Bacon, fluffy Scrambled Eggs Chilaquiles, heavenly Pumpkin French Toast . . . I think that brunch might be my favorite meal of the week. It's more than eggs; it's an event. It's a slow meal especially designed for lazy Sunday mornings. We New Yorkers take brunch seriously; just look at the lines snaking out of breakfast joints around the city on the weekend. It's the perfect time to catch up with friends, rehash the goings-on of the night before, prepare yourself for the week ahead . . . and it's all done over a morning cocktail.

My daughter often requests a "breakfast" dish for dinner and I have no issues complying. I'll bring a touch of Sunday to any day.

BRUNCH

CRISPY BACON AND HASH BROWN QUESADILLAS

SCRAMBLED EGGS CHILAQUILES with
Roasted Tomatillo Sauce

RANCH-STYLE EGGS with Chorizo and
Tomato–Red Chile Sauce

EGG AND AGED SIRLOIN TORTILLAS with
Three-Pepper Relish

SOUTHWESTERN HOME FRIES

MANGO-GLAZED BACON

MESA GRILL GRITS

BLUE CORN–BLUEBERRY PANCAKES with
Orange-Honey Butter and Cinnamon-Maple Syrup

PUMPKIN FRENCH TOAST with
Allspice Butter and Fig-Maple Syrup

CRISPY BACON AND HASH BROWN QUESADILLAS
SERVES 4

THIS BREAKFAST QUESADILLA IS A MESA GRILL, LAS VEGAS, INVENTION. PAIRED WITH A SPICY BLOODY MARY *(page 31)*, IT'S THE PERFECT WAY TO GET YOUR DAY STARTED AFTER A LONG NIGHT OUT ON THE TOWN.

HASH BROWNS

- 2 large Idaho potatoes, scrubbed
- ¼ cup canola oil
- 2 large Spanish onions, halved and thinly sliced

  Kosher salt and freshly ground black pepper
- 1 poblano chile, roasted, peeled, seeded *(see page 18)*, and finely diced
- 1 tablespoon ancho chile powder

QUESADILLAS

- 8 ounces thick-cut bacon, diced
- 12 (6-inch) flour tortillas
- 2½ cups grated Monterey Jack cheese (10 ounces)
- 2 tablespoons canola oil
- 2 teaspoons ancho chile powder
- 2 tablespoons unsalted butter
- 4 large eggs

  Kosher salt and freshly ground black pepper

  Mixed Tomato Salsa *(page 218)*

  Grated cotija cheese, for garnish (optional)

  Thinly sliced green onion, white and green parts, for garnish (optional)

1. To make the hash browns, put the potatoes in a medium pot of cold, salted water, bring to a boil, and cook until nearly tender but a knife inserted into the centers still meets a little resistance, 15 to 20 minutes. Drain, let cool slightly, and then peel. Grate the potatoes on a grater using the large holes.

2. Heat 2 tablespoons of the oil in a large, preferably nonstick, sauté pan over medium heat. Add the onions, season with salt and pepper, and cook, stirring occasionally, until golden brown and caramelized, 15 to 20 minutes. Scrape the onions out of the pan and onto a plate.

3. Return the pan to the stove over high heat and add the remaining 2 tablespoons oil. Add the potatoes and cook, stirring occasionally, until golden brown, 12 to 15 minutes. Stir in the onions, poblano, ancho powder, and salt and pepper to taste. Remove from the heat.

4. Preheat the oven to 425 degrees F.

5. Place the bacon in a large nonstick sauté pan over medium-high heat and cook, turning once, until crisp, 8 to 10 minutes. Using a slotted spoon, transfer the bacon to a plate lined with paper towels to drain. Discard the bacon fat and wipe out the pan with paper towels.

6. To assemble the quesadillas, place 8 of the tortillas on a work surface. Divide the cheese, hash browns, and bacon among the tortillas. Stack the tortillas to make four 2-layer quesadillas and cover each with one of the remaining 4 tortillas. Brush the tops with the oil and sprinkle with the ancho powder.

7. Transfer to a baking sheet (you may need 2). Bake until golden brown and the cheese has melted, 8 to 10 minutes.

8. While the quesadillas are baking, fry the eggs. Return the nonstick sauté pan that you cooked the bacon in to the stove over medium heat, add the butter, and heat until melted. Carefully crack the eggs into the pan, season with salt and pepper, and cook until the whites are completely firm but the yolks are still soft, about 2 minutes.

9. Transfer the quesadillas to plates and top each with a fried egg, add some of the mixed tomato salsa, and garnish with cotija cheese and green onion.

SCRAMBLED EGGS CHILAQUILES WITH ROASTED TOMATILLO SAUCE

SERVES 4

THIS DECADENT EGG DISH IS ALMOST LIKE A FREE-FORM LASAGNA, WITH LAYERS OF TORTILLAS, EGG, SOUR CREAM, CHEESE, AND ROASTED TOMATILLO SAUCE. THE SAUCE IS TART AND SPICY—PLAY THAT AGAINST THE CREAMY SCRAMBLED EGGS AND CRUNCHY TORTILLAS, AND YOU'VE GOT BRUNCH HEAVEN.

CHILAQUILES

2 cups canola oil

Twelve 6-inch blue corn tortillas

Kosher salt

½ cup plus 4 teaspoons sour cream or crème fraîche

1½ cups grated white Cheddar cheese (6 ounces)

Roasted Tomatillo Sauce (recipe follows)

¼ cup chopped fresh cilantro

SOFT SCRAMBLED EGGS

8 tablespoons (1 stick) unsalted butter

12 large eggs, lightly beaten

Kosher salt and freshly ground black pepper

1. Heat the oil in a medium saucepan over medium heat until it reaches 350 degrees F as measured on a deep-frying thermometer.

2. Fry the tortillas, one at a time, until just crispy, 20 to 30 seconds. Remove to a plate lined with paper towels and season lightly with salt.

3. To scramble the eggs, heat the butter over low heat in a large skillet. Add the eggs, season with salt and pepper to taste, and cook slowly, stirring constantly with a wooden spoon, until soft curds form, 3 to 4 minutes.

4. To serve the chilaquiles, place a teaspoon of the sour cream in 4 large shallow bowls to secure the tortillas. Place a fried tortilla on top of each dab of sour cream. Spread a tablespoon of the sour cream evenly over each tortilla and top with some of the eggs and then Cheddar cheese. Repeat to make 2 layers, then top the stacks with the remaining 4 tortillas. Ladle the warm roasted tomatillo sauce over the chilaquiles and garnish with chopped cilantro.

Roasted Tomatillo Sauce
MAKES ABOUT 1½ CUPS

8 tomatillos, husked and scrubbed

1 large red onion, quartered

4 cloves garlic, peeled

¾ cup plus 3 tablespoons canola oil

Kosher salt and freshly ground black pepper

1 cup packed fresh spinach leaves

2 teaspoons chipotle chile puree
(see page 18)

¼ cup fresh lime juice (2 to 3 limes)

3 tablespoons honey

1. Preheat the oven to 375 degrees F.

2. Combine the tomatillos, onion, and garlic on a rimmed baking sheet, toss with the 3 tablespoons oil, and season with salt and pepper. Roast in the oven until the vegetables are soft and golden brown, 20 to 25 minutes.

3. While the tomatillos are roasting, bring a medium saucepan of salted water to a boil. Add the spinach and boil until tender but still bright, about 2 minutes. Drain, rinse under cold water to cool, then drain again. Squeeze between your hands to remove the excess moisture.

4. Transfer the tomatillos, onion, and garlic to a food processor and add the chipotle puree, lime juice, and spinach and process until smooth. With the motor running, slowly add the ¾ cup oil and blend until emulsified. Add the honey and salt and pepper. Serve warm. This can be made up to 1 day ahead and refrigerated. Reheat before serving.

BRUNCH MENU

Spicy Bloody Mary *(page 31)*

Scrambled Eggs Chilaquiles with Roasted Tomatillo Sauce *(opposite)*

Blue Corn–Blueberry Pancakes with Orange-Honey Butter and Cinnamon-Maple Syrup *(page 266)*

Mango-Glazed Bacon *(page 265)*

Southwestern Home Fries *(page 263)*

RANCH-STYLE EGGS WITH CHORIZO AND TOMATO–RED CHILE SAUCE
SERVES 4

THIS IS OUR VERSION OF HUEVOS RANCHEROS. MAKE SURE THAT YOUR TORTILLAS ARE CRISPY AND YOUR SAUCE IS SPICY, AND YOU'LL HAVE A BREAKFAST THAT CAN'T BE BEAT, EVEN BY THE BELOVED TRADITIONAL RENDITION.

- 2 cups canola oil

  Four (6-inch) yellow or white corn tortillas

  Kosher salt

- 8 ounces Spanish chorizo sausage, diced
- 4 tablespoons (½ stick) unsalted butter, cut into 4 pieces
- 12 large eggs, lightly beaten

  Freshly ground black pepper

- ½ cup plus 4 teaspoons sour cream or crème fraîche

  Tomato–Red Chile Sauce (recipe follows)

- ¾ cup coarsely grated white Cheddar cheese (3 ounces)
- 1 Hass avocado, peeled, pitted, and coarsely chopped

  Fresh cilantro leaves, for garnish (optional)

1. Heat the oil in a medium saucepan over medium heat until it reaches 350 degrees F as measured on a deep-frying thermometer.

2. Fry the tortillas, one at a time, until just crispy, 20 to 30 seconds. Remove to a plate lined with paper towels and season lightly with salt.

3. Heat a large nonstick sauté pan over high heat. Add the chorizo and cook until golden brown on all sides, 6 to 8 minutes. Remove with a slotted spoon to a plate lined with paper towels.

4. Remove all but 1 tablespoon of the rendered fat from the pan. Add the butter to the pan, and once it melts, reduce the heat to medium-low. Add the eggs and the chorizo, season with salt and pepper, and cook, stirring constantly with a wooden spoon, until soft curds form, 3 to 4 minutes.

5. To serve, place a teaspoon of the sour cream in 4 large shallow bowls to secure the tortillas. Place a fried tortilla on top of each dab of sour cream. Spread 2 tablespoons of the sour cream over the top of each tortilla and top with some of the eggs. Ladle the warm tomato–red chile sauce over and sprinkle with the cheese. Top with some avocado and cilantro. Serve immediately.

Tomato–Red Chile Sauce
MAKES ABOUT 1 CUP

- 2 tablespoons olive oil
- 1 medium red onion, finely chopped
- 4 cloves garlic, finely chopped
- 2 tablespoons ancho chile powder
- 1 tablespoon pasilla chile powder
- 1 cup dry red wine

  One (15.5-ounce) can plum tomatoes and their juice, pureed

- 2 tablespoons honey

  Kosher salt

1. Heat the oil in a medium saucepan over high heat. Add the onion and cook until soft, 3 to 4 minutes. Add the garlic and ancho and pasilla powders and cook for 1 minute. Add the wine, bring to a boil, and cook until reduced by half, 3 to 4 minutes.

2. Add the tomatoes, ½ cup of water, and the honey and cook, stirring occasionally, over medium-high heat until the sauce has thickened, 10 to 15 minutes. Season with salt. This can be made up to 1 day in advance and refrigerated. Reheat before serving.

EGG AND AGED SIRLOIN TORTILLAS WITH THREE-PEPPER RELISH
SERVES 4

HERE IS MY HOMAGE TO THAT DINER CLASSIC, STEAK AND EGGS. THE TORTILLAS CAN BE USED TO SWEEP EVERYTHING UP IN A "MAKE YOUR OWN" STYLE TACO. I WOULDN'T SKIP THE RELISHES, AS THEY REALLY MAKE THIS DISH EXTRA-SPECIAL.

- 2 (8-ounce) dry-aged sirloin steaks
- 2 medium red onions, sliced ½ inch thick
- ¼ cup canola oil
  Kosher salt and freshly ground black pepper
- 8 (6-inch) flour tortillas
  Soft Scrambled Eggs (see page 258)
  Three-Pepper Relish (recipe follows)
  Avocado Relish (page 262) (optional)
  Chopped fresh cilantro, for garnish

1. Preheat a grill to high or a grill pan over high heat.

2. Brush the steaks and onion slices on both sides with the oil and season with salt and pepper. Grill for 3 to 4 minutes on each side, until the steaks are medium-rare and the onions are lightly charred and just cooked through.

3. Remove to a cutting board. Let the steaks rest for 5 minutes and then slice thinly on the bias. Finely chop the onions.

4. Grill the tortillas for 10 seconds on each side.

5. Place the scrambled eggs in the middle of each of 4 plates. Place a heaping tablespoon each of onions, three-pepper relish, and avocado relish to one side of the eggs. Place some sliced steak and 2 tortillas per person, folded in quarters, on the other side of the eggs and sprinkle with chopped cilantro.

Three-Pepper Relish
MAKES I CUP

- 1 poblano chile, roasted, peeled, seeded (see page 18), and thinly sliced
- 1 red bell pepper, roasted, peeled, seeded (see page 18), and thinly sliced
- 1 yellow bell pepper, roasted, peeled, seeded (see page 18), and thinly sliced
- 2 tablespoons canola oil
- 2 tablespoons finely chopped fresh cilantro
  Kosher salt and freshly ground black pepper

Combine the 3 peppers in a medium bowl, add the oil and cilantro, and season with salt and pepper.

SOUTHWESTERN HOME FRIES

SERVES 4

THESE SPICY HOME FRIES ARE AT HOME WITH ANY EGG DISH. PARBOILING THE POTATOES IS AN IMPORTANT STEP; YOU WANT YOUR POTATOES TO HAVE A TENDER INTERIOR WHILE GETTING GOLDEN AND CRISPY ON THE OUTSIDE. SPICY JALAPEÑO, GARLIC, AND ANCHO CHILE POWDER TELL YOU AT FIRST BITE THAT THIS IS NO STANDARD DINER FARE.

See photograph on page 252.

2½ Idaho potatoes, scrubbed and cut into 1½-inch dice

Kosher salt

8 tablespoons (1 stick) unsalted butter

1 small Spanish onion, finely chopped

1 jalapeño chile, finely diced

2 cloves garlic, finely chopped

2 tablespoons ancho chile powder

Freshly ground black pepper

2 tablespoons finely chopped fresh cilantro

1 tablespoon thinly sliced green onion, white and green parts

1. Put the potatoes in a large saucepan, add enough cold water to cover, and add 1 tablespoon salt. Bring to a boil over high heat and cook until the potatoes are tender when pierced with a knife, 20 to 25 minutes. Drain well.

2. Heat the butter over medium heat in a large sauté pan. Add the onion and jalapeño and cook until soft, 3 to 4 minutes. Add the garlic and cook for 30 seconds. Stir in the ancho powder and stir until combined. Add the potatoes, season with salt and pepper, and cook until golden brown on the bottom, 4 to 6 minutes. Turn over and cook until the bottom is golden brown, 4 to 6 minutes. Stir in the cilantro and green onion and transfer to a bowl.

MANGO-GLAZED BACON
SERVES 4 TO 6

AS A KID, I USED TO LOVE DIPPING SUPER-CRISP BACON INTO MAPLE SYRUP—A TOTALLY DECADENT BREAKFAST TREAT. THIS MANGO-GLAZED BACON ACCOMPLISHES THAT SAME SWEET AND SALTY TASTE SENSATION EVEN IF THERE ARE NO PANCAKES IN SIGHT. AND IT'S DEFINITELY CRISP, AS THE GLAZE PRACTICALLY CANDIES THE BACON AS IT COOKS. DELICIOUS.

- 1 cup sugar
- 1 cup red wine vinegar
- 1 ripe mango, peeled, pitted, and coarsely chopped
- 1 tablespoon honey

  Kosher salt and freshly ground black pepper
- 1 pound thick-cut bacon

1. Preheat the oven to 375 degrees F.

2. Combine the sugar and vinegar in a small saucepan and cook over high heat until the sugar is melted. Add the mango and cook, stirring occasionally, until the mixture is reduced by half and the mango is soft, 5 to 6 minutes.

3. Transfer the mixture to a food processor and process until smooth. Strain through a fine-mesh strainer into a bowl, stir in the honey, and season with salt and pepper. The glaze can be made up to 2 days in advance and refrigerated. Bring to room temperature before using.

4. Place the bacon on a baking sheet lined with parchment paper and brush the slices on both sides with some of the glaze. Bake, brushing the top of the bacon with more of the glaze every few minutes, until golden brown and just crisp, 10 to 12 minutes.

MESA GRILL GRITS
SERVES 4

AT MESA GRILL WE GRIND THE HOMINY FOR OUR GRITS OURSELVES. DOING THAT—EVEN WHEN STARTING WITH AND PROCESSING CANNED HOMINY INSTEAD—HELPS TO ENSURE FRESH-TASTING, FAR-FROM-GUMMY GRITS. AND WHILE IT MIGHT SEEM LIKE WE USE A LOT OF CREAM, THE END RESULT IS A LUXURIOUS AND SURPRISINGLY UPSCALE SIDE DISH FOR BRUNCH OR DINNER.

See photograph on page 255.

- 2 tablespoons unsalted butter
- 1 small Spanish onion, finely diced
- 2 cloves garlic, finely chopped

  Two (15.5-ounce) cans posole (hominy), rinsed and drained
- 2 cups heavy cream
- 2 tablespoons chopped fresh cilantro

  Kosher salt and freshly ground black pepper

1. Heat the butter in a medium saucepan over medium heat. Add the onion and garlic and cook until the onion is soft, 3 to 4 minutes. Add the posole and cook for 15 minutes. Transfer the mixture to a food processor and process until almost smooth (it should still have some texture).

2. Return the mixture to the pan and add the cream. Cook over low heat until the mixture thickens, 12 to 15 minutes. Stir in the cilantro and season with salt and pepper before serving.

BLUE CORN–BLUEBERRY PANCAKES WITH ORANGE-HONEY BUTTER AND CINNAMON-MAPLE SYRUP

SERVES 4

THIS IS A GREAT BRUNCH DISH THAT TAKES A FAMILIAR CONCEPT—BLUEBERRY PANCAKES—AND MAKES IT REALLY SPECIAL WITH A SWEET AND NUTTY BLUE CORNMEAL BATTER AND OUTRAGEOUSLY GOOD TOPPINGS. THE BLUE CORNMEAL, SO PERFECT WITH THE BUTTER AND SYRUP, ALSO LENDS A WONDERFUL TEXTURE TO THE PANCAKES, WHICH ARE HEARTY BUT NOT HEAVY.

Nonstick cooking spray

1½ cups all-purpose flour

½ cup blue cornmeal

2 teaspoons baking powder

2 teaspoons kosher salt

¼ cup sugar

2 large eggs

1½ cups whole milk

2 tablespoons unsalted butter, melted

1 cup fresh or frozen blueberries, thawed

Orange-Honey Butter *(recipe follows)*

Cinnamon-Maple Syrup *(recipe follows)*

1 cup mixed fresh berries (optional)

Confectioners' sugar, for serving

1. Preheat the oven to 200 degrees F. Preheat a nonstick griddle or large nonstick sauté pan over medium-high heat and spray with nonstick cooking spray.

2. Mix together the flour, cornmeal, baking powder, salt, and sugar in a medium bowl. Whisk the eggs in a separate bowl and add the milk and melted butter; whisk until combined. Add the wet ingredients to the dry ingredients and mix until just combined (there should be some lumps), then gently fold in the blueberries.

3. Ladle approximately ¼ cup of the batter onto the griddle for each pancake. Cook until the bottom is lightly golden brown, flip over, and continue cooking for about 30 seconds. Remove to an ovenproof plate and keep warm in the oven while you cook additional pancakes.

4. Serve 3 pancakes per serving topped with the orange-honey butter, cinnamon-maple syrup, and berries, if desired. Dust with confectioners' sugar.

Orange-Honey Butter
MAKES ABOUT 1½ CUPS

2 cups orange juice (not from concentrate)

12 tablespoons (1½ sticks) unsalted butter, at room temperature

2 tablespoons honey

Pinch of kosher salt

1. Pour the orange juice into a small saucepan over high heat and cook, stirring occasionally, until thickened and reduced to about 3 tablespoons. Remove from the heat and let cool to room temperature.

2. Put the butter in a bowl, add the reduced orange juice, the honey, and salt, and mix until combined. Cover with plastic wrap and refrigerate until firm, at least 2 hours and up to 2 days.

Cinnamon-Maple Syrup
MAKES ABOUT 1½ CUPS

1½ cups pure maple syrup

3 cinnamon sticks

Heat the syrup and cinnamon sticks in a saucepan over low heat for 10 minutes. Remove from the heat and let steep for 1 hour. Remove the cinnamon sticks and pour the syrup into a small pitcher. This can be made up to 1 week in advance and refrigerated. Reheat before serving.

PUMPKIN FRENCH TOAST WITH ALLSPICE BUTTER AND FIG-MAPLE SYRUP

SERVES 4

PUMPKIN IS ONE OF MY FAVORITE INGREDIENTS. THIS DISH SMELLS—AND TASTES—OF AUTUMN AT ITS BEST. FRENCH TOAST IS TRADITIONALLY A GREAT WAY TO MAKE USE OF STALE BREAD, BUT THIS FRENCH TOAST IS SO GOOD, I GO OUT AND BUY THE BREAD THE DAY BEFORE JUST FOR IT!

- 1 heaping cup canned pumpkin puree (not flavored pie filling)
- 6 large eggs
- 2 large egg yolks
- ¼ cup sugar
- 2 teaspoons ground cinnamon
- ½ teaspoon freshly grated nutmeg
- ½ teaspoon ground cloves
- 1 teaspoon pure vanilla extract
- 2 cups whole milk
- 1 cup heavy cream
- ¼ teaspoon kosher salt
- 8 (1-inch-thick) slices day-old brioche or challah
- 4 tablespoons unsalted butter, cut into 4 pieces
- ¼ cup canola oil

  Allspice Butter (*recipe follows*)

  Fig-Maple Syrup (*recipe follows*)

1. Preheat the oven to 375 degrees F.

2. Whisk together the pumpkin, whole eggs, egg yolks, sugar, cinnamon, nutmeg, cloves, vanilla, milk, cream, and salt in a large baking dish. Place the bread in the baking dish, and turn the bread to coat evenly; let sit for 5 minutes.

3. Heat 2 tablespoons of the butter and 2 tablespoons of the oil in a large nonstick sauté pan over medium-high heat until the butter is completely melted. Place 4 slices of the bread in the pan and cook until golden brown on the bottom, 2 to 3 minutes. Turn the slices over and cook until the bottom is golden brown, 2 to 3 minutes more. Transfer to a baking sheet. Wipe the pan out with paper towels and repeat with the remaining 2 tablespoons butter, 2 tablespoons oil, and 4 slices bread.

4. Transfer the baking sheet to the oven and bake for 5 minutes.

5. Serve 2 slices per serving topped with the allspice butter and some of the fig-maple syrup.

Allspice Butter
MAKES ABOUT ½ CUP

- 8 tablespoons (1 stick) unsalted butter, at room temperature
- 2 teaspoons ground allspice
- 2 tablespoons pure maple syrup
- ¼ teaspoon kosher salt

In a small bowl, combine the butter, allspice, maple syrup, and salt. Cover with plastic wrap and refrigerate for at least 30 minutes and up to 2 days.

Fig-Maple Syrup
MAKES ABOUT 2½ CUPS

- 8 fresh figs, quartered
- 1¼ cups pure maple syrup

Combine the figs and syrup in a small saucepan and simmer over low heat until the figs are soft, about 10 minutes. This can be made up to 4 hours in advance and refrigerated. Reheat before serving.

SOURCES

CACTUS PEAR SYRUP
www.cherisdesertharvest.com

CAST-IRON GRILL PAN/GRIDDLE
www.lodgemfg.com

CHEESES
www.dairysection.com
www.murraycheese.com

DUCK, GAME, CHORIZO
www.dartagnan.com;
800-327-8426

FRESH AND DRIED CHILES
www.kitchenmarket.com

FRESH SEAFOOD
www.gortonsfreshseafood.com

LOBSTER AND FISH STOCK
www.clubsauce.com

SPECIALTY INGREDIENTS (corn husks, chiles, pomegranates, molasses, tamarind paste, posole, blue corn products, raw pumpkin seeds)
www.melissas.com;
800-588-0151
www.mexgrocer.com

SPICES
www.kalustyans.com;
908-688-6111
www.penzeys.com

TEQUILA AND MEZCAL
www.beerliquors.com